Find The Right Word

W0402837

Hans Löffler · Leonard Goldman

Find
The Right Word

Englische Synonyme mit Übungen

LANGENSCHEIDT · VERLAG ENZYKLOPÄDIE
Leipzig · Berlin · München · Wien · Zürich · New York

6. Auflage 1999
© 1988 Verlag Enzyklopädie Leipzig
unter dem Titel
"English Synonyms in Action"
© 1994 Langenscheidt · Verlag Enzyklopädie Leipzig, Berlin, München
Druck: Druckhaus Langenscheidt, Berlin-Schöneberg
Printed in Germany
ISBN 3-324-00314-8

VORWORT

Haben Sie schon einmal das Gefühl gehabt, mißverstanden zu werden oder in der Unterhaltung mit anderen Menschen plötzlich auf eine unerwartete Schranke zu stoßen? Es gibt dabei Schwierigkeiten genug in der Muttersprache; um wieviel eher ist dies der Fall, wenn man sich einer Fremdsprache bedient. Es bleibt eine Binsenweisheit, daß – abgesehen von der Sprache des Körpers, den Gesten, der Mimik usw. – das gesprochene und geschriebene Wort das wichtigste Medium für die Übermittlung unserer Gedanken, Gefühle, Wünsche, Hoffnungen an unsere Mitmenschen darstellt.

Das vorliegende Buch möchte Ihnen nun in Ihrem Bemühen um die richtige Ausdrucksweise im Englischen eine zusätzliche Hilfe bieten. Die Autoren haben sich dabei auf die Anwendung bedeutungsverwandter Wörter, der Synonyme, konzentriert. Mit dieser Synonymik sollte ein praktisches Hilfsmittel für den Unterricht oder Selbstunterricht auf mittlerer bis fortgeschrittener Stufe geschaffen werden, nicht aber eine umfassende Darstellung der englischen Synonyme oder gar ein akademisches Nachschlagewerk. Bei der Auswahl der behandelten Synonyme haben sich die Verfasser eine weitgehende Beschränkung auferlegt, die sich an den Bedürfnissen langjähriger Unterrichtserfahrung orientiert. Da diese Synonymik vor allem dem **deutschsprachigen Benutzer** Nutzen bringen soll, werden englische Äquivalente für das deutsche Stichwort oder dessen Synonyme behandelt. Es kann mithin vorkommen, daß unter einem Stichwort Lexeme geboten werden, die vom Standpunkt der englischen Sprache aus sogar Antonyme darstellen. Das extremste Beispiel dieser Art ist die Zuordnung von *lend* und *borrow* zur gleichen Gruppe, nämlich ‚leihen', obgleich die beiden Verben im Sinne von *give* und *take* gebraucht werden.

Dieses Unterrichtswerk beschränkt sich jedoch nicht darauf, sozusagen eine Synonymik im „Westentaschenformat" zu bieten, sondern sieht seine ganz spezielle Aufgabe **in der praktischen Anleitung** zum richtigen Gebrauch bedeutungsverwandter Wörter des Englischen. Die Erfahrung zeigt, daß die umfangreicheren Werke zur englischen Synonymik zwar eine große Fülle von Informationen bieten, den weniger geübten Benutzer dennoch nicht selten im Zweifel über die zu treffende oder die getroffene Wortwahl lassen. Das liegt ebensosehr an der Schwierigkeit der Materie wie auch an der besonderen Aufgabenstellung der großen Nachschlagewerke. Das Anliegen der Autoren des vorliegenden Buches war es nun, abgesehen von der Einführung in eine Anzahl der wichtigsten Synonymgruppen, den Versuch einer praktischen Anleitung zum Gebrauch der Synonyme zu unternehmen, und dies nicht nur durch die Schaffung einer **Kontrollmöglichkeit** in Gestalt von **Übungssätzen** mit beigefügtem Schlüssel, sondern vor allem auch durch **zusätzliche Erläuterungen** innerhalb des Schlüssels, die dem besseren Verständnis der gebotenen Lösungen dienen. Diese Kurzkommentare, die aus Gründen der Raumersparnis nur dort den Lösungen beigegeben wurden, wo dies den Autoren besonders wünschenswert erschien, sollen dem Benutzer dieser Synonymik einen genaueren Einblick in das Für und Wider einer bestimmten Entscheidung gewähren und somit das Verständnis für die richtige Anwendung der Synonyme fördern.

Abgesehen von den einführenden Beispielsätzen werden die Synonyme zunächst in Kollokationen vorgeführt, d. h. in für den alltäglichen Gebrauch der Sprache typischen Wortfügungen. Diese Kollokationen erscheinen in den folgenden Übungs- bzw. Kontrollsätzen in geeigneten Zusammenhängen erneut. Wiederholung ist ein altbewährter pädagogischer Grundsatz.

Das Übungsmaterial wurde, wenn auch nicht durchgängig, in zwei Schwierigkeitsgrade eingeteilt. Die mit (A) gekennzeichneten Übungen bieten i. allg. etwas leichteres Material als die mit (B) markierten, wobei allerdings ein subjektiver Maßstab angelegt wurde. Sehr wahrscheinlich wird man auch nach sorgfältigem Studium der Einführungen und Kollokationen nicht selten zu Lösungen gelangen, die mit den im Schlüssel angegebenen nicht übereinstimmen. Man lasse sich hierdurch nicht irritieren, sondern **wiederhole die Übungen,** bis sich befriedigende Ergebnisse einstellen. Aus naheliegenden Gründen war es nicht möglich, in jedem einzelnen Falle die Wahl dieses oder jenes Synonyms zu erläutern. Die Autoren hoffen jedoch, daß die im Schlüssel gegebenen zusätzlichen Hinweise ausreichen, um in die über das Grundsätzliche hinausgehenden „Geheimnisse“ des richtigen Synonymgebrauchs einzuführen. Auf jeden Fall sehe man die vervollständigten Übungssätze als **zusätzliches Beispielmaterial** an, das man sich in Auswahl ebenfalls einprägen sollte.

Bei der Benutzung des Buches ist ferner zu beachten, daß die in deutscher und englischer Sprache gebotenen Einführungen nicht durchweg inhaltlich deckungsgleich sind und daher beide Versionen sorgfältig studiert werden müssen. Auf diese Weise soll das genauere Erfassen der Bedeutungsnuancen gefördert werden.

Da, wo es besonders wichtig erschien, sind den Erläuterungen auch Hinweise zur stilistischen Gebrauchsebene und zuweilen sogar Bemerkungen zum syntaktischen Gebrauch der Synonyme hinzugefügt worden. Was die vorgelegten Beispiels- und Übungssätze angeht, so gründen sie sich alle auf den tatsächlichen praktischen Sprachgebrauch. Natürlich ist es möglich, daß dieser oder jener Engländer in der gegebenen Situation ein anderes Synonym benutzt hätte – parallele Erscheinungen kennt jedermann aus dem Gebrauch der eigenen Muttersprache – der Benutzer dieses Buches kann aber sicher sein, daß das hier gebotene Material im vollen Einklang mit der Sprachpraxis des Englischen steht.

Obgleich diese Synonymik keineswegs Anspruch darauf erhebt, über ihren Gegenstand alle Weisheit zu bieten, sind die Verfasser doch überzeugt, daß sie die Grundlage für ein besseres Verständnis englischer Synonyme bildet und den Lernenden auf dem Wege zur richtigen Anwendung bedeutungsähnlicher Wörter im Englischen ein gutes Stück voranzubringen vermag.

Hans Löffler, Leipzig / Leonard Goldman, Brighton

FOREWORD

Have you ever felt that you were misunderstood, that communication with others encountered an insuperable barrier? It's difficult enough in your own language; how much more difficult in a foreign tongue. Leaving aside all other means of communication, "body language", gestures, meaning glances and so on, it remains a truism that speech und writing are the most obvious ways of conveying your feelings, desires, hopes and requests to your fellow man–and woman. So that you may learn how to acquire the ability to express yourself accurately in English, we have prepared this little offering as a guide. It is not intended as an academic reference work, nor will readers find the answer to all their questions, but they will find a fairly large number of synonym groups which will be valuable to the more advanced student of the language. The work may be used as a "Teach Yourself" textbook or as an aid to learning at school or university.

We have deliberately imposed limitations upon our choice of synonyms. We should like to make it plain, for example, that, despite our title, we often group words together that are by no means all synonyms in English. We do this because we want the **German reader** to extract the maximum benefit; and we therefore give possible English equivalents of the German key-word, or its German synonyms. The most extreme example of this is the inclusion of *borrow* and *lend* in the same group. These two are antonyms in English but are both translations of *leihen* and are thus included under that key-word. This guide to more exact usage is not, however, intended as a kind of pocket book of synonyms but sees its special task rather as **a practical guide** to the correct usage of English words of similar meaning. Experience shows that the more comprehensive books of synonyms, in spite of the abundance of information contained, often leave their readers – especially those who lack practice – in doubt as to whether the word they have chosen, or are about to choose, is the correct one. This problem arises from the difficulty of the material itself, as well as from the particular aims which such large reference works set themselves. So it is our purpose in this book not only to introduce the reader to a number of the most important synonym groups, but to try to put forward practical hints in the use of each synonym.

We do this in several ways: there are the **exercises** in practical usage, the key in which readers can **check their answers** and, additionally, **further explanations** in that key, which can help them to a better understanding of the solutions offered. Apart from the exercises, the synonyms are also presented in numerous collocations, i.e. typical usages. These collocations are then given again in the practice or exercise sentences, in suitable contexts. This is one more way in which the correct use of the synonym is induced. Repetition is a well tried pedagogic principle.

The practice material is usually (though not always) divided into two grades of difficulty, the A sentences containing somewhat less difficult material than the B sentences. The distinction, it must be said, is a subjective one. It is very probable that, after studying the introductions and collocations, the reader will sometimes arrive at conclusions different from those given in the key. Do not worry about this, but **repeat the exercises** until satisfactory results ensue. It is obviously not always possible to give a fully satisfactory explanation of the reasons for choosing a particular solution. We hope, however, that the additional comments in the key will be sufficient to reveal the "secret" of correct usage.

The completed exercises should be seen as **examples of additional material**, whose usage must be stamped on the memory. Herein lies the most effective way of complementing the theoretical introductory explanations.

A reading of the introductory comments on the synonym groups will show that the German and English versions are not always exact, literal translations, so it is valuable to study both carefully. This will lead to a more exact grasp of the nuances of meaning. Where we thought it important, the explanations also contain hints on stylistic and even syntactic usage of the synonyms concerned. As for the sentences contained in the exercises, these are all based on actual frequent experience of such usage. Now it may well be true that some Englishmen have never used a particular expression in the context given. But the reader may rest assured that very many others *have* so used them, and that these usages are sufficiently common to put him on the right road to success if he masters them. Whilst the book lays no claim whatever to contain all wisdom on the subject, it should, properly used, provide the basis for a better grasp of the different usages of similar words. It is in that spirit of modest confidence that we place this small offering before the public.

Hans Löffler, Leipzig/Leonard Goldman, Brighton

ABBREVIATIONS

Adj.	adjective	Adjektiv
Adv.	adverb	Adverb
Am.	American (English)	Amerikanisches Englisch
colloq.	colloquial	umgangssprachlich
e.g.	for instance (exempli gratia)	zum Beispiel
esp.	especially	besonders
fig.	figuratively	im übertragenen Sinn
i. allg.	commonly	im allgemeinen
i.e.	that is (id est)	das heißt, bedeutet
N.	noun	Substantiv
sl.	slang	Slang
s.o.	someone	jemand
s.th.	something	etwas
V.	verb	Verb

CONTENTS

1
ähnlich
resembling, similar, alike, like

resembling: I've never seen anything resembling a cricket pitch on the continent.
"Any resemblance to persons living or dead is purely coincidental."
Der äußeren Erscheinungsform nach ähnlich; bezieht sich auf Personen und Dinge.

Resembling usually suggests that several things or persons have some external characteristic in common. Appearance is important here. It can be used only after the noun or pronoun it qualifies. (N.: *resemblance*)

similar: The two tunes are strikingly similar (to each other).
There is a striking similarity between the two characters.
Collocations: similar in appearance.

Similar bezeichnet nicht nur die äußere, sondern auch die wesensmäßige Ähnlichkeit.

Similar often denotes not only 'surface likeness' but also closer resemblance in character. (to be *similar* ***to*** sth.; N.: *similarity*)

(a)like: They are so much alike that it is difficult to tell them apart.
She treats all her children alike.
James and his brother are very like. Like thinking produces like ideas.
Collocations: somewhat alike; not a bit alike; very much alike; alike as two peas; very like; like things/ideas, etc., and the like (=und dergleichen).

Alike (prädikativ gebrauchtes Adj. und Adv.) und *like* (prädikativ und attributiv gebrauchtes Adj.) können soviel wie 'fast gleich' bedeuten und bezeichnen damit einen noch höheren Grad von Ähnlichkeit als *similar.*

Alike (predicative adj. and adv.) and *like* (predicative and attributive adj.) can mean *being almost the same* and, thus, indicate an even more comprehensive correspondence than similar. (N.: *likeness*)

Exercise 1 (A) Complete the sentences inserting *resembling, similar,* or *(a)like.*

1. I met a woman . . . my mother.
2. Soccer and rugby are . . . games.
3. Mary and her mother are not a bit . . .
4. He gave us a . . . answer.
5. Chess and draughts are, in some ways, . . .
6. Anyone . . . a film star was immediately mobbed.
7. He wrote some books on the preservation of wildlife, the running of national parks and . . . subjects.
8. Have you this cloth in stock, or anything of a . . . nature?

9. The two brothers are more . . . than I expected.
10. The twins are . . . in appearance.
11. The swan and the goose are . . .
12. I saw an Indian . . . Gandhi.
13. Our teachers and our parents gave us . . . advice.
14. The twins are . . . as two peas.
15. He slithered through the mud, . . . a giant lizard, rather than a footballer.
16. The design of the two houses is somewhat . . .
17. The two paintings do not portray the same person, but two different personalities . . . each other very strongly.
18. Did you ever see the . . .?
19. Their handwriting is strikingly . . .
20. This is a . . . case to the one Sherlock Holmes solved.
21. They are all . . . those Smiths.
22. The picture is not a good . . . of him.

2
alt
old, elderly, aged, ancient, antique

old: You are as old as you feel, they say.

Der allgemeinste Ausdruck für alt (Gegensatz: *young*; *new*).

Advanced in years or life; the most general term (opposite: *young*; *new*).

elderly: The elderly couple still dressed smartly.

Ältlich, älter (mit Bezug auf Personen).

Between middle and old age.

aged: I had three aged serving men. (old song)

Collocations: an aged man/tree; the aged (=alte Leute).

Hochbetagt, vorgeschrittenen Alters; gealtert.

Extreme old age; having existed long. (Pronunciation: [ˈeɪdʒɪd])

ancient: The pyramids are ancient monuments.

Collocations: the ancient Romans/Greeks; ancient history/customs.

Einer lange vergangenen Zeit oder dem Altertum zugehörig.

Belonging to a time long past, to some remote period (esp. before the end of the Western Roman Empire).

antique: He likes antique vases.

Collocations: antique furniture; an antique shop.

Von antikem Stil oder antiken Stil nachahmend.

Of ancient style.

Exercise 2 (A) Complete the sentences inserting the best suitable term, *old, elderly, aged, ancient,* or *antique.*

1. The couple were . . . but they danced well.
2. . . . Greece reached a high level of civilisation.
3. But it was . . . Rome that spread this civilisation.
4. The . . . part of the town was built 200 years ago.
5. The . . . couple were nearing the end of Life's journey.
6. . . . wine is better than new.
7. . . . furniture fetches high prices.
8. But not so much as . . . jewellery or . . . porcelain.
9. Was . . . man freer than we are today?
10. He is past his prime. He's getting . . .
11. After his harrowing experiences, he looks very . . .
12. It is considered more polite to call someone . . . , rather than old.
13. I'm tired out already. I must be getting . . .
14. . . . dealers frequently sell fakes.
15. I'm sixty next birthday. That's not considered . . . these days.
16. I hadn't seen him for 30 years. How . . . he looked!
17. My . . . partner was nearing retirement.
18. The . . . man was on his last legs.
19. I love to examine . . . tools and weapons.
20. I know of a factory where they have special implements for banging new furniture to make it look . . . !

3
ändern
to change, to alter, to modify, to vary

to change: His face has changed beyond recognition.

Collocations: to change one's mind; to change one's opinion; to change the subject; to change one's clothes / the train.

In wesentlicher Beziehung ändern; austauschen, wechseln.

To change suggests 'making or becoming different in an essential way'. The idea of substitution of one thing for another may also be implied, i.e. to exchange. (N.: *change*)

to alter: Could you alter my trousers (so that they fit better)?

Collocations: to alter a suit / dress, etc.

Teilweise verändern, abändern. *To alter* und *to change* sind jedoch häufig austauschbar.

To alter denotes a partial change. However, *to change* and *to alter* are often interchangeable. (N.: *alteration*)

to modify: By and large I approve of the contract. There are just some minor modifications I would like to suggest.

Collocations: to modify the words used; to modify a law.

Kleinere Abänderungen durchführen, besonders um zu verbessern, zu mildern oder abzuschwächen.

To modify often indicates a minor difference or the idea of making less strong or severe whilst retaining the fundamentals. It may also suggest an improvement from what had been unsatisfactory. (N.: *modification*)

to vary: The resourceful teacher knows how to vary his methods.

Collocations: to vary from time to time; to vary one's diet/method/style; the charm of variety; variations of temperature.

Abwechseln, variieren.

To vary denotes the idea of shifting from one to the other and back again if necessary. (N.: *variation*; *variety*)

Exercise 3 (A) Fill in the best suitable terms: *to change, to alter, to modify, to vary,* or a term closely related.

1. I want you to . . . these trousers. Take them in two inches at the waist.
2. I like to . . . my reading.
3. It is no good trying to . . . the weather. Only nature can do that.
4. Will you, please, . . . this dress? It's too tight.
5. I think we should . . . the design of the house.
6. You'll have to . . . the expression before it is printed.
7. It is not easy to . . . people's habits.
8. They want to . . . the whole school system.
9. A girl . . . her name when she gets married.
10. Always try to . . . a child's diet.
11. Notice outside a tailor's shop: We do . . .
12. I hope you are not going to . . . your mind.
13. Here is the . . . version of the script you asked for.
14. I don't want you to . . . I love you as you are.
15. His performances . . . from night to night. He's most erratic.
16. They have . . . the length of coats that year by introducing the "maxi".
17. His sermons never . . .
18. He has . . . considerably since I saw him last.

Exercise 3 (B)

1. If things don't . . . , they'll stay as they are. (old saying)
2. The treaty was . . . to suit all signatories.
3. "What history syllabus is used in England?"–"It . . . from school to school."
4. Our plan will have to be . . . a little.
5. He always . . . his tone when he talks to me.
6. I refuse to . . . the portrait to suit your vanity.
7. To . . . conditions is not always to improve them.
8. Try to . . . the syllabus. It covers too much ground.
9. I've decided to . . . the arrangements.
10. After I told him off, he . . . his behaviour considerably.

4
Arbeit
work, labour, toil, drudgery, grind, job, task

work: How far have you gone with your work?
This bookcase is a fine piece of work.

Collocations: hard work; out of work; in work; to look for/seek work; avoid work; (to make) quick work (of s.th.); a work of art.

Work bezieht sich sowohl auf die Tätigkeit als auch auf das Arbeitsergebnis.

Work refers to both the application or effort and the result (i.e. product) of it.

labour: Clearing the Augean stables was among the twelve labours of Hercules.
The criminal was sentenced to ten years hard labour.

Collocations: the labours of Hercules; farm/unskilled labourer; capital and labour; labour force; horny-handed sons of labour; a labour of love; the Labour Party.

Labour bezeichnet angestrengtere körperliche oder geistige Arbeit. Es wird als gewählterer Ausdruck auch für *work* verwendet.

Labour may suggest strenuous physical or intellectual activity. It may also be used in literary style.

toil: She looked pale and haggard from too much toil.

Collocations: endless/base/weary toil; sons of toil.

Ermüdende, eventuell auch zugleich unangenehme Arbeit.

Highly fatiguing (possibly at the same time unpleasant) work.
Toil sometimes indicates formal or literary English. (V.: *to toil*)

drudgery: Washing dishes for ten hours a day was awful drudgery.

Collocations: household drudgery; sheer drudgery.

Langweilige, mit Widerwillen verrichtete Arbeit.

Dull, disgusting work. *Drudgery* is not used in plural. It does not normally take an indefinite article.

grind: He had little interest in languages, so memorizing irregular verbs was a mere grind for him.

Collocations: the daily grind; to be one long grind; an endless/a real grind; to grind away (at s.th.).

Ein umgangssprachlicher Ausdruck für uninteressante, ermüdende Arbeit. *Grind* impliziert den Gedanken ständiger Wiederholung.

A colloquial term for uninteresting, exhausting work. It may imply the idea of trying to the nerves. *Grind* is not used in plural. *Grind* implies a repetitive idea.

job: He is looking for another job because he cannot make ends meet any more.

Collocations: to apply for/to finish a job; a well/badly paid job.

Arbeit im Sinne von Posten, Anstellung (umgangssprachlicher Ausdruck); eine einzelne Arbeit, Aufgabe.

Job is the colloquial expression for post or position, i.e. employment. It may also mean a single piece of work one has to do.

task: Your task, Bob, is to water the flowers.

Collocations: to set s.o. a task; a difficult/pleasant/easy task.

Arbeit im Sinne von Aufgabe.

A piece of work allocated to someone by some authority, e.g. a teacher, or held to be necessary.

Exercise 4 (A) Fill in *work, labour, toil, drudgery, grind, job,* or *task,* as suitable.

1. When you have finished that . . . , I'll give you another one.
2. I was ordered to peel three sacks of potatoes, an unpleasant . . .
3. My . . . is very pleasant. I'm a wine taster.
4. Capital and . . . are the two elements in production.
5. . . . are rather scarce these days. Unemployment is rising.
6. I have been out of . . . for several weeks.
7. I'm fed up with it here. Anyone can have my . . .
8. All Youth Hostellers are given a . . . to do before they leave.
9. The daily . . . was beginning to get him down.
10. He hated the . . . of washing decks continuously all day long.
11. This bridge was the product of six months . . .
12. Did you do that . . . the boss asked you to do yesterday?
13. The housemaid resented the . . . of her work.
14. The children were given their . . . for the day.
15. Weary with . . . , he lay down to sleep.
16. All the . . . parts of the machine must be regularly oiled.
17. His inner contentment at the success of his . . . shone forth from his eyes.
18. That old writing-desk is a . . . of art.

Exercise 4 (B)

1. Learning grammar is a . . .
2. This is not man-made; it is a . . . of nature.
3. When your work becomes a . . . , change your job.
4. The mental strain of concentrating on straight lines all the time made his job a . . .
5. Fancy copying another man's work all day long and nothing else! What . . . !
6. The endless interruptions and obstacles made her work a . . .
7. I don't mind doing this; it's a . . . of love.
8. They loved their painstaking work, so it never became a . . .
9. It was . . . , emptying slop-pails all day and every day.
10. He counted the telegraph poles as they flashed past, until it became a . . .
11. Studying law is one long . . .
12. I like English and History but I find Maths just . . .

5
aufhören, enden; beenden
to stop, to cease, to end, to discontinue, to finish, to conclude

to stop: Stop the bus. We want to get off here.
Look, the rain has stopped. We can go out again.

Collocations: to stop talking/nagging; to stop a fight/the traffic; to come to a full stop; to put a stop to s.th.

Anhalten, unterbrechen; aufhören. Die meist mehr oder weniger schnelle, plötzliche Unterbrechung einer Handlung oder eines Vorganges.

To halt an action or progress abruptly; to come to an end. (N.: *stop*)

to cease: It has ceased (or stopped) raining.
That noble heart has ceased to beat.
He has ceased driving a car (i.e. he is no longer a car driver).

Collocations: to cease publication; to cease one's idle chatter (This collocation is a mock poetic or dramatic exclamation. The point is that *cease* often has a facetious tone.).

Cease wird als Ausdruck höherer Stilebene für *stop* verwendet. In der Umgangssprache wird *cease* immer mehr von *stop* verdrängt. *Cease* kann die Vorstellung eines allmählichen Nachlassens implizieren. Doch auch ... *ceased abruptly* ist nicht ungewöhnlich.

Cease is used as a literary expression for stop. In everyday language it is increasingly replaced by *stop*. *Cease* can imply the idea of a gradual ending of some state or activity. However, the collocation ... *ceased abruptly* is not at all uncommon. (N.: *cessation*)

to end: The performance will end (or finish) at about 11 o'clock.
The war ended in 1945.
The game ended in a quarrel.

Collocations: to end up as; to end one's life (either suicide or to spend the last years of one's life).

Zu Ende gehen, schließen. Der Gedanke der Endgültigkeit spielt gewöhnlich eine Rolle. Einer Sache ein Ende setzen.

To reach its end, to result in something; to cause to come to an end. *To end* usually suggests finality. (N.: *end*)

to discontinue: The meetings of the committee have discontinued.

Collocations: to discontinue publication/a regular series/a scheme; to discontinue a line (of merchandise).

Nicht weiterführen, einstellen. Eine gewohnheitsmäßige Handlung nicht weiter fortsetzen. *Discontinue* gehört der gehobenen Stilebene an.

To give up a practice or habit or some (till then) regular or constant activity or performance. *Discontinue* tends to suggest formal English. (N.: *discontinuance*)

to finish: Finish your supper and go to bed.

Have you finished your work yet?

Collocations: to finish a meal/game; to be finished with s.th. (i.e. have no further use for it); to be finished with s.o. (have nothing further to do with s.o.); to put the finishing touches to.

Zu Ende führen, beenden. Die letzten Einzelaktionen eines Gesamtvorganges erledigen.

To carry out or go through the final stages of some action, to complete it. (N.: *finish*)

to conclude: The concert concluded with the national anthem.

He concluded by saying that he would not accept such conditions.

Collocations: to conclude a piece of music/a speech/an essay; '... to conclude, ...' (end of a speech, letter, etc.).

Ähnlich *to end*, aber gehobenere Stilebene. Es wird oft mit Bezug auf eine Rede, Abhandlung, Sitzung u. ä. verwendet.

Similar in meaning to *end* but more formal. It is often used with reference to a speech, an essay, a meeting, performance and the like. It indicates a feeling of rounding off or completion. (N.: *conclusion*)

Exercise 5 (A) Fill in a suitable term of the above group.

1. The game ... in a draw.
2. Oh, do ... chattering! I want to read.
3. I'm waiting for him to ... the painting.
4. The orchestra ... the concert to loud applause.
5. I'm not going to ... nagging you, till you give in.
6. School ... at 4 p.m.
7. Some people just don't know when to ... talking.
8. Haven't you ... the game of chess yet?
9. Why did you ... your regular walks?
10. They both ... their driving lessons at the same time.
11. Wars have been going on for centuries. Will they ever ...?
12. I wish to ... by thanking the organisers of the rally.
13. The defeat ... all our hopes.
14. We must put a ... to that right away.
15. What? Smoking again? I thought you had ... that habit.
16. The crash ... his career as a racing driver.

Exercise 5 (B)

1. This series has been ...
2. The sobbing ...; all was quiet in the room again.
3. "And now, to ..., I shall summarise the main points."
4. The regular publication of statistics has been ...
5. Miracles have long since ...
6. When he took the floor, all argument ...
7. He has ... complaining.
8. The noise ... for a moment before starting again.
9. The ... bars of the symphony were just dying away.
10. My joy has gone; it has ... for ever.

6
aufschieben, verschieben, verzögern
to put off, to postpone, to defer, to delay, to procrastinate

to put off: Never put off till tomorrow what you can do today.

Collocations: to put off an appointment.

Umgangssprachlicher Ausdruck für aufschieben, verschieben. (Manchmal als Euphemismus für 'annullieren').

In everyday use for shifting some action, event, etc. to a later time. (Sometimes a euphemism for 'cancel completely'.)

to postpone: The meeting has been postponed until next Friday.

Collocations: to postpone a decision / project / sporting fixture (football match, etc.); to postpone sine die (=indefinitely).

Der Hauptunterschied zwischen *postpone* und *put off* liegt darin, daß ersteres in der Amtssprache bevorzugt wird, während letzteres mehr der Umgangssprache zugehört: Etwas bereits Festgelegtes auf einen späteren Zeitpunkt verschieben (häufig in bezug auf Versammlungen oder einen Termin verwendet).

The main difference between *postpone* and *put off* is one of style, the former being more official language but the latter colloquial. To shift to some later date (most often meetings, an appointment and the like) what has already been fixed. Sometimes it is used evasively by officialdom. (N.: *postponement*)

to defer: The session of the committee will have to be deferred.
The judge decided to defer judgement.

Collocations: to defer an arrangement / a decision / a payment / the sitting of a court.

Gewählter, eleganter Ausdruck für 'aufschieben'. Vorzugsweise in amtlicher, offizieller Sprache (in noch höherem Maße als *postpone*).

To delay temporarily (a promise is more or less implied to do it later). It is used in official, elegant language, even more so than postpone. Often *to a later date* is added. (N.: *deferment*)

to delay: Sorry we're late. A policeman delayed us.
Delay may be fatal.

Collocations: to delay an operation; to delay answering a letter.

Hinauszögern, verzögern (aus Unlust u. ä.); verschieben, aufhalten, (be)hindern, weil etwas Hemmendes dazwischentritt.

To be tardy, act slowly (because of unwillingness, etc.); to keep back an action because of interference of something that hinders progress. (N.: *delay*)

to procrastinate: The government procrastinated in the hope of allaying public anger.
Life is short, my friend. Do not procrastinate.

Tadelnswertes oder unentschuldbares Hinauszögern einer Handlung (aus Gleichgültigkeit, Faulheit etc.). Gewählter Ausdruck.

To delay in a blameworthy or inexcusable way (out of indifference, laziness, etc.). Used in literary language. (N.: *procrastination*; *procrastinator*)

Exercise 6 (A) Fill in a suitable expression of the above group.

1. I can't understand why they . . . the conference.
2. The ship was . . . by engine trouble.
3. I've decided to . . . my application. I've got cold feet.
4. It's long past midnight. What . . . you?
5. "Hallo! Back so soon?"–"Yes, the dance has been . . . ."
6. An accident on the line caused great . . .
7. The kick-off was . . . until 3.30 p.m.
8. The excursion was . . . until the weather improved.
9. His Majesty has decided to . . . the ceremony.
10. As the chairman had failed to arrive, a . . . was necessary.
11. Why does he always . . . making decisions? Is it cowardice?
12. The meeting was . . . sine die.
13. There was three days' . . . in the post.
14. We shall have to . . . the visit for a while.
15. The visit of the Lord Mayor was . . . owing to his illness.

Exercise 6 (B)

1. His incurable . . . has cost him his job.
2. To . . . things now might be dangerous. Press on!
3. Dear Sir, we apologise for the . . . in answering your letter.
4. If you continue to . . . , we shall be unable to get a booking.
5. His final success was . . . by bad management.
6. He had brought . . . to a fine art.
7. . . . cannot be avoided in stormy weather.
8. I shall . . . my assessment until I have further information.
9. I'm a born . . . I've opted out of the rat race.
10. The project was . . . for a month because of a technical hitch.
11. I don't want to . . . so important a decision much longer.
12. ". . . is the thief of time. Collar him!" (Dickens)

7
aufstehen, sich erheben
to get up, to stand up, to rise

to get up: I usually get up at five in the morning.
He could not get up from his chair.

To get up ohne weiteren Zusatz bedeutet häufig 'sich aus dem Bett erheben'. Es wird auch als (ziemlich scharfe) Aufforderung verwendet. *Get up* ist der häufigste umgangssprachliche Ausdruck der Gruppe.

To get up without any further specification often means 'to get out of bed'. It is also used as a (rather rude) command. *Get up* is the most colloquial expression of this group.

to stand up: The audience stood up when the soloist entered the stage.

Aufstehen aus sitzender, kniender oder liegender Stellung. Als Aufforderung etwas neutraler als *to get up.*

To get to one's feet from a sitting, kneeling, or lying posture. As a command stand up is more neutral than *get up.*

to rise: She rose from her chair to answer the door.
The rocks rise steeply from the valley.
The people rose (up) against the usurper.

To rise ist der am wenigsten umgangssprachliche Ausdruck dieser Gruppe. Er gehört mehr der Schriftsprache an und bezeichnet eine langsamere Aufwärtsbewegung als *get up* und *stand up. Get up* und *rise* werden oft von *from* gefolgt, nicht aber *stand up.*

To rise is the least colloquial term of the group. It suggests slower movement than *get up* and *stand up. Get up* and *rise* are often used with *from,* but not *stand up. Rise* is also used in the sense of to rebel.

Exercise 7 (A) Fill in a suitable term of the above group.

1. We usually . . . when the national anthem is played.
2. My daughter has just . . . after a long illness.
3. He . . . to his full height and glared at me threateningly.
4. They always . . . when I enter the room.
5. The audience . . . as one man, and cheered him to the echo.
6. (Teacher:) ". . . all those who want to play football."
7. (Angry officer:) ". . . when I enter the room!"
8. Come on, it's time to . . .
9. Exercise, exercise, every morning when you . . .
10. The castle . . . majestically before us.
11. I had eaten so much I could not . . . from my seat.
12. Everybody . . . and drank a toast to the bride.
13. I . . . an hour before my wife.
14. The orator . . . to his feet and commenced his speech.
15. I can just reach the top shelf when I . . . and stretch.
16. After a short rest, we . . . and continued our walk.
17. The boxer tried to . . . but was unable to do so.
18. The boxer tried to . . . off the floor but was unable to do so.
19. . . . and fight, you coward!
20. He . . . slowly and walked to the door.
21. The peasants . . . against their masters.
22. I wanted to . . . off the sofa, but was unable to do so.
23. . . . , like lions after slumber. (Shelley)
24. When the bomb went off, we all . . . quickly and left our seats. (old joke)

8
ausführen, durchführen
to carry out, to perform, to execute, to accomplish, to effect

to carry out: These measures should not be carried out (or through).
You should never make a promise which you are not ready to carry out.

Allgemeiner Ausdruck für (Maßnahmen, Pläne usw.) aus-, durchführen.

General term for putting a plan or measure into practice.

to perform: The mayor performed the opening ceremony last night.
The way he has performed his duties deserves praise.

Collocations: to perform an operation / a duty / a ceremony / a task; to perform at a concert; to perform on the piano; to perform s.th. well.

Perform bezieht sich vor allem auf Tätigkeiten, die besonderes Geschick, besondere Fähigkeit, Anstrengung, Bemühung verlangen oder gar zeremoniellen Charakter aufweisen. *Perform* gehört im Vergleich zu *carry out* einer gehobeneren Stilebene an.

To perform applies specially to the carrying out of things which ask for special skill, effort, aptitude, or may be ceremonial in character. In comparison with *carry out, perform* is a relatively formal expression. (N.: *performance*)

to execute: Your order will be executed without further delay.

Collocations: to execute a piece of music / a plan / an order / a manoeuvre / gymnastic feat.

Einen Befehl, eine Anweisung ausführen; einen Plan, ein Projekt verwirklichen, etwas Beabsichtigtes durchführen. *Execute* findet sich auch häufig mit Bezug auf physische Aktivitäten (Sport, Militär u. ä.). Es kann auch im Sinne von *perform* verwendet werden.

To execute an order, plan, programme, something intended. Execute is also often used in connection with physical movement (sport, military drill, etc.) or even artistic creation (similar *to perform*). (N.: *execution*)

to accomplish: He begins everything but accomplishes nothing.

Collocations: to accomplish one's purpose / s.th. desired / a task / one's mission / a promise.

Erfolgreich zu Ende führen. Der Nachdruck liegt also auf der vollen Durchführung des Begonnenen.

To finish successfully. The term denotes the carrying through to its definite end. It indicates a sense of achievement. (N.: *accomplishment*)

to effect: After years of intensive research the scientists effected the first chain reaction.

Etwas bewerkstelligen bei gleichzeitiger Überwindung von Hindernissen. Unterschwellig wirkt auch die Vorstellung von der zur Auslösung kommenden Kraft mit.

To bring about by overcoming obstacles. The term suggests also the force inherent in the doer. (N.: *effect*)

Exercise 8 (A) Fill in a suitable term of the above group of synonyms.

1. The customer's orders were rapidly . . . .
2. He . . . his tasks to the letter.
3. The new doctor . . . a cure where the others had failed.
4. You have to . . . this operation with great care.
5. Please . . . the instructions carefully.
6. We do not . . . orders until we receive payment.
7. The burglars . . . an entry.
8. The military manoeuvres were cleverly . . . .
9. We managed to . . . an improvement in our circumstances.
10. You'll never . . . anything at that pace.
11. First . . . my request, then you'll be paid.
12. The batsman . . . a classic stroke.
13. One case could have . . . a spread of the disease.
14. Are you likely to . . . what you set out to do?
15. He is friendly, but only if you . . . his wishes.
16. The priest . . . the wedding ceremony.
17. What you desire seems less desirable once it is . . . .
18. It should be a pleasure to . . . such a rewarding task.

Exercise 8 (B)

1. The government . . . a complete volte face.
2. He . . . his functions most efficiently.
3. Congratulations! You have almost . . . a miracle.
4. I have . . . my life's ambition.
5. The pianist . . . the Beethoven sonata brilliantly.
6. The figure was . . . in stone, by the sculptor.
7. A painting of such beauty is a great . . . .
8. The registrar . . . the marriage ceremony.
9. His task was to repair the delicate machinery and he . . . it well.
10. He showed little interest in the . . . of his duties.

9
Bad, baden
bath, bathe, swim

bath: You can't see Tom now, he is just having a bath.
She had to bath the baby in the wash-tub because the bath in the bathroom was broken.

Das Bad, das man (im Badezimmer) zur Reinigung oder zur Erfrischung des Körpers nimmt. Auch im Sinne von Badewanne, Badehaus.

To wash the whole body, or refresh it, usually by total immersion in a *bath*. *Bath* can also mean the large basin in which one baths. (Note: a *Turkish bath*)

bathe: Let's go for a bathe (or a swim) in the river.

My eyes are itching, that's why I must bathe them in fennel tea.

Collocations: bathed in / with sweat.

Das Baden im Freien (Fluß, See); Heilbäder nehmen. Auch im Sinne von 'überzogen mit', 'eingetaucht in etwas' (z. B. Schweiß, Licht) und im übertragenen Sinne verwendet.

One *bathes* in a river, lake, etc. The term is also used in the sense of applying water, etc. to some wound or the like, to cleanse medically, usually with antiseptic some sore part of the body. Also in the sense of spread over with water, light, mist, or sweat. It is also used figuratively.

to swim: I went to the (swimming-)baths to have a swim.

Let's go for a swim in the lake.

Baden gehen im Sinne von 'schwimmen gehen' ähnlich *to bathe.* (*Bathe* schließt jedoch nicht eigentlich das Schwimmen mit ein.)

To propel oneself along in the water by means of one of a number of 'strokes' (breast, crawl, etc.).

Exercise 9 (A) Complete the sentences inserting a suitable term, *bath, bathe,* or *swim.*

1. My finger was sore, so I . . . it in very hot water.
2. He smells as though he hasn't had a . . . for months.
3. They . . . and sunbathed alternately.
4. . . . is forbidden when the red flag is flying.
5. I can't stop now. I'm just going to . . . the baby.
6. I always feel fresh after a . . .
7. Take the children for a . . . See if you can teach them to swim.
8. . . . in this river is forbidden. It is too dangerous.
9. I'm all sweaty from gardening. I must have a . . .
10. I've been . . . too long and got sunburnt.
11. I love . . . in the warm waters of the Mediterranean.
12. I can't even . . . myself in peace; someone always knocks at the door.
13. They were . . . in the sea all day long.
14. I started . . . in the sea, long before I could swim.
15. You can't . . . now, the . . . is broken.
16. Let's all go for a . . .
17. The Friday night . . . is quite a tradition in some homes.
18. He'd been running up the hill and was . . . in perspiration.
19. We . . . in the warmth of their welcome.
20. You're covered in mud. Go and have a good . . .
21. . . . in the sea is fun, but keep out of the way of the swimmers.
22. Hurry up in the bathroom. I want a . . .
23. The whole party went . . .
24. The top of the mountain was . . . in mist.

10
behaupten, erklären
to assert, to contend, to maintain, to claim, to allege, to pretend

to assert: The Prime Minister asserted that the economy was improving.

Collocations: to assert positively; to assert without proof; an unproven / unsupported assertion.

Voll innerer Überzeugung etwas feststellen, mit Nachdruck behaupten, ohne daß ein objektiver Beweis vorliegen muß.

To state forcefully, with personal conviction. (An *assertive person* is one with strong convictions and personality, able to persuade people into his point of view.) (N.: *assertion*)

to contend: She contends that the statement made by the witness is not true. Winters are getting colder and summers hotter, they contend.

Argumentierend oder streitend etwas behaupten, eine gegenteilige Behauptung aufstellen. Das Streben nach Überwindung einer entgegengesetzten Meinung ist immer mit im Spiel.

Contend suggests argument, dispute, the desire to overcome that which is opposed. (N.: *contention*)

to maintain: Do you still maintain that you've never seen him in your life?

Collocations: to maintain one's point of view.

Bei einer Behauptung bleiben, auf etwas beharren.

To make and uphold some statement, possibly in defiance of opposition.

to claim: He claims he has solved the problem.

Collocations: to claim that s.th. is yours / that you are right / that s.o. is wrong.

Behaupten im Sinne von (die Anerkennung eines konstatierten Sachverhalts oder auch eines Rechtes) beanspruchen. Zuweilen dem deutschen 'jemanden etwas glauben machen wollen' ähnlich.

To make a statement and demand its recognition as a fact, possibly against denial. (N.: *claim*)

to allege: She alleged that her husband had hit her on the head.

Collocations: the alleged criminal; he is alleged to . . . (= man behauptet von ihm, daß er . . .); a false / serious allegation; to refute / to prove an allegation.

Bei *allege* schwingt gewöhnlich der Zweifel an der Richtigkeit der Behauptung mit. *Allege* wird oft von Journalisten gebraucht, um sich davor zu schützen, falsche Behauptungen aufgestellt zu haben.

To state, declare, or accuse without proof. *Allege* is often used by journalists to avoid libel actions. It suggests formal English. (N.: *allegation*)

to pretend: They pretended to be political refugees.

Collocations: to pretend to be what one is not; to be always pretending; a shallow pretence.

Wider besseres Wissen behaupten, zu Unrecht behaupten, vorgeben.

To make a false statement. *Pretend* is a form of lying, it always involves deceit, albeit either in fun, or in relatively unimportant things. (N.: *pretence*)

Exercise 10 (A) Complete the sentences inserting a suitable term of the above group of synonyms.

1. She . . . to be lame.
2. You can . . . that you are right till you burst. I'll never agree.
3. I can positively . . . that no further harm will come to you.
4. You cannot prove that . . .
5. She only . . .ed to love him.
6. With the utmost sincerity they . . . that they would support us.
7. Once I have said it is so, I will always . . . it.
8. It was . . . ed in the article that he was a liar and a cheat.
9. In order to leave I . . .ed to be sick.
10. It's silly to continue to . . . that which has been proven wrong.
11. Does she . . . that her garden is better than yours?
12. There was a time when it was . . . that the Earth was flat.
13. But Columbus . . . that it was round.
14. You must . . . it with all your force or you will not be believed.
15. The newspaper . . . that Brown had led the riot.
16. She . . . that the seas may one day dry up.
17. I still . . . that we could have won.
18. Why did you . . . to be upset?
19. He . . . that he had won. (His opponent thought otherwise!)
20. Don't just . . . it with such conviction–prove it!

Exercise 10 (B)

1. You . . . that you were wronged. Can you prove it?
2. She . . . that Sally had robbed her.
3. Those who . . . that mankind is doomed are pessimists.
4. The pundits used to . . . that no man would ever fly.
5. I saw through his . . . He was no policeman.
6. She . . . that she was their long-lost daughter.
7. I do not . . . that I am always right, but . . . . . .
8. You . . . that all is well? I know differently.
9. The foreign minister . . . that Ruritania was about to attack them.
10. "You can take it from me", he . . .ed, "this is the man."

11

bekommen

to get, to obtain, to receive

to get: He got a handful of mud for his pains.

Collocations: to get a shock / a surprise / a good hiding / a good telling off; to get your train / a letter / good marks, etc.

To get ist der allgemeinste Ausdruck für bekommen, erlangen, erhalten. Es kann sowohl für *receive* als auch für *obtain* verwendet werden und entspricht oft dem deutschen 'kriegen'.

To get is the most general term of this group. It may suggest acquisition through or without any effort.

to obtain: If you wish to obtain a licence, apply to the ministry. (officialese)

Collocations: to obtain a post / a licence / an information / a copy of a book (with difficulty).

To obtain beinhaltet ein gewisses Maß an Aktivität, Hoffnung, Absicht oder Wunsch. *Obtain* ist weniger umgangssprachlich als *get*.

To obtain implies a certain amount of activity, hope, intent, or desire. *Obtain* is more stylish than *get*. It may sound a little mannered in ordinary speech and somehow "official".

to receive: Will you sign this form to show that you have received the parcel?

Collocations: to receive a message / a letter / an invitation.

Erhalten, bekommen ohne eigenes Bemühen. Im allgemeinen etwas gewählter als *get*.

This term implies passiveness. To get something without intentional effort. In general it is less colloquial than *get*.

Exercise 11 (A) Fill in a suitable term of the above group of synonyms.

1. When did you . . . payment for your work?
2. Where did you . . . that hat?
3. I . . . a terrible shock when I saw her.
4. I could not . . . the information I required.
5. Where can I . . . a dress suit? (to buy is suggested)
6. I . . . your letter today. (i.e. through the post)
7. I . . . my degree at Oxford.
8. (Student to friend): I . . . a "one" in History.
9. (Student to prospective employer): I . . . a "one" in History.
10. (Professor to friend): Three of my students . . . "one's" in History. (i.e. I gave)
11. I . . . my train, but only by running for it.
12. Your message . . . Over. (radio message)
13. I have . . . hundreds of phone calls this week.
14. Can one . . . a drink after 10 p.m. in your country?
15. Waiter, when do I . . . my beefsteak?

16. He only . . . a ticket with very great difficulty.
17. I . . . my wages early this week.
18. I . . . the last instalment yesterday.
19. Those who wish to ... a certificate should call at this office before 4.30. (officialese)
20. You'll . . . a good hiding if you're not careful.
21. To be on the . . .ing end of one of those punches was painful.
22. I've been trying very hard to . . . a copy of this book.

12
beleidigen
to offend, to insult, to affront, to abuse, to outrage

to offend: Don't be offended, but would you mind if I go there on my own?
Please, forgive me if I've offended you.

Collocations: to be careful not to offend; to give offence; an offensive remark; no offence intended.

To offend ist der übliche und relativ schwächste Ausdruck für beleidigen, verletzen. Er kann sich auf beabsichtigte und unbeabsichtigte Beleidigungen beziehen.

To offend is the usual and weakest term for to hurt someone's feelings (with or without intention, by words or by actions). (N.: *offence*)

to insult: The tearing down of their flag was a grave insult to their country.
They grossly insulted him, calling him a liar.

Collocations: to insult s.o.'s memory/intelligence; to add insult to injury.

Jemanden gröblich, in unverschämter Weise und böswillig beleidigen.

To offend someone wantonly and in a very rude way, can be by words or actions. An *insult* is very definite and usually easily recognised. An *offence* may be vague and less easily defined. (N.: *insult*)

to affront: He affronted him by sneering at his wife in public.

Collocations: to affront s.o.'s dignity; to feel affronted.

In der Öffentlichkeit beleidigen, bloßstellen oder provozieren. *Affront* wird verhältnismäßig selten gebraucht.

To show disrespect of a person in public. (N.: *affront*)

to abuse: Don't just abuse the government, tell us what *you* would do in their place.

Collocations: to abuse one's opponents; to abuse roundly; vulgar abuse; personal abuse.

Jemanden mit Worten in schwerer, unflätiger Weise beleidigen, jemanden beschimpfen, schmähen. *Abuse* beinhaltet auch physisches Leid, das jemandem zugefügt wird.

To attack someone violently with contemptuous, disgraceful language. *Abuse* may also be physical. (N.: *abuse*)

to outrage: His gross misbehaviour outrages the feelings of all present.

Collocations: outraged feelings; to outrage all decency; to outrage s.o.'s sense of justice; to outrage the whole company; to commit an outrage.

Eine alles Maß überschreitende, gröblichste Verletzung von Gefühlen, Anstand, Gerechtigkeitssinn, Recht und Gesetz. *Outrage* ist häufig mit Gewalttätigkeit verbunden.

Outrage suggests a disregard of people's feelings, sense of justice, decency, of human dignity, right and law so extreme in its nature that it exceeds all bounds. *Outrage* often implies the use of violence. (N.: *outrage*)

Exercise 12 (A) Complete the sentences inserting a suitable term of the above group of synonyms.

1. He suffered no physical harm, but it was an . . . to his dignity.
2. I tried not to . . . him, but it was very difficult.
3. After . . .ing her roundly for having let the cakes burn she made her clean up the mess.
4. His friends were . . . at the treatment he received in prison.
5. She . . . us with a string of invectives.
6. I just cannot understand why he felt . . .
7. No . . . meant, I assure you.
8. A politician has to get used to . . .
9. She . . . him by her refusal.
10. Some people take . . . at the slightest opposition to their wishes.
11. It is the practice of some politicians to . . . their opponents instead of criticising their policies.
12. Even when he accused me falsely in public, I was not really . . .
13. I'm afraid I . . . him without really meaning to.
14. My neighbour hurled . . . at me because my tree obstructed his view.
15. Try not to . . . him. We need his help.
16. Those who have no reasoned answer to your arguments, fall back on . . .
17. He was always . . . me by some public exposure of my vices.
18. You can . . . him as much as you like, he won't take . . .

Exercise 12 (B)

1. He . . . them all by smashing the crockery and the furniture.
2. Personal . . . is no substitute for reasoned analysis.
3. Sir, you have . . . the memory of my dead father! Come outside!
4. I tried to explain why I cannot help them, but the only reply I got was . . .
5. She . . .ed the assembled company by flying into a temper, storming out and slamming the door behind her.
6. You can't . . . him–he's too ignorant.
7. The pompous old man was always receiving imaginary . . .
8. He . . . me right and left, but I turned the other cheek.
9. Sticking your tongue out at someone is regarded as an . . .
10. He pushed me into the swimming pool, fully clothed. What an . . .!

11. In the old days, when one gentleman slapped another in the face with a glove, an . . . of that nature always led to a duel.
12. He . . . me by seating me at one of the lower tables.

13

bemerken, wahrnehmen

to notice, to observe, to perceive

to notice: "Who was in the room at the time?"–"I didn't notice."
If you keep it covered, nobody will notice.

Collocations: to notice the obvious / an omission / what s.o. is wearing; to notice in passing; to take notice (of).

(Flüchtig) bemerken, Notiz nehmen von; wahrnehmen, sehen. *Notice* drückt ein mehr oder weniger zufälliges, müheloses Sehen oder Wahrnehmen aus.

To see or become aware of something in an accidental or effortless way. *Notice* may involve more than passive awareness, however, e.g. He doesn't miss a thing. He notices everything. (N.: *notice*; Adj.: *noticeable*)

to observe: Observe him at table, how fussy he is with his food.
He was observed entering the bank.

Collocations: to observe closely / secretly / scientifically; to observe the details / a scene / an act of some kind.

(Aufmerksam) beobachten; feststellen. *Observe* und *notice* können häufig in der gleichen Situation verwendet werden. *Observe* bezeichnet aber i. allg. eine größere Bewußtheit und Zielgerichtetheit in der Wahrnehmung als *notice*.

To watch something carefully; become conscious of, perceive. *Observe* and *notice* can often be used in the same situations. The former, however, may imply a higher degree of conscious attention and more concentration. (N.: *observation*; Adj.: *observant*)

to perceive: A three weeks old baby can see persons but hardly ever perceives them as distinct individuals.
"I knew he was guilty from the start!"–"Really? How very perceptive."

Collocations: to perceive a motive / reason / difference; to perceive at a glance; to perceive through the senses.

Erkennen, begreifen. *Perceive* impliziert einen noch höheren Grad von Bewußtheit im Wahrnehmungsprozeß als *observe*. Außerdem gehört es der gehobenen Stilebene an.

To recognise and understand something through the use of our senses or the mind. *Perceive* is, however, qualitatively much higher than observe and more literary than the latter. (N.: *perception*; Adj.: *perceptive*)

Exercise 13 (A) Complete the sentences inserting a suitable term of the above group of synonyms.

1. From our hiding place, it was possible to . . . their every movement.
2. They . . . that she seemed quieter than usual.
3. I was unable to . . . the reason for his strange action.
4. My . . . had been dulled by too much alcohol.
5. He suffers from a squint in one eye, which is rather . . .
6. You did not suspect him? Where is your . . .?
7. She . . . a smell of burning as she entered the kitchen.
8. I want you to . . . how the conjurer's patter distracts your attention from what his hands are doing.
9. You were late today.–Yes, did anyone . . .?
10. We can only experience that which we . . . through the senses.
11. Some people have a kind of sixth sense which sharpens their . . .
12. I . . . a fox prowling round the hen house.
13. Did you . . . the way he looked up as we came in?
14. Did you . . . the man who just passed us?

Exercise 13 (B)

1. They can . . . a great deal with a minimum of evidence.
2. With her woman's instinct, she . . .ed everything at a glance.
3. I saw a hawk hovering in the sky today.–Really, how . . .!
4. You may have . . . that I dislike dishonesty.
5. You're a fine detective! You didn't even . . . the hat he was wearing.
6. Keen . . . is the mark of the scientist.
7. Do you . . . any difference in his behaviour?
8. From his clothing and bearing I . . . he had suffered much.
9. Look at the cat. . . . how it stalks its prey.
10. I . . . you don't try to defend yourself.
11. I have not . . . any change in your behaviour.
12. It was impossible to . . . everything that was going on.
13. I . . . you've had your hair cut.
14. Ha, I . . . we are going to get on very well together.

14
Beruf
trade, profession, occupation, vocation, calling

trade: He is a plumber (locksmith, butcher, etc.) by trade.

Collocations: the weaver's/brewer's/carpenter's trade; to learn/to follow a trade.

Der praktische Beruf (Handwerker u. ä.)

A skilled craft, i.e. *trade* involves skilled manual labour.

profession: He is a lawyer (an engineer, a journalist, etc.) by profession.

Collocations: the medical/legal/teaching, etc. profession; an honoured/ ancient profession; to practice a profession.

In erster Linie der Beruf, der ein Studium voraussetzt.

Profession usually refers to an occupation requiring years of study (but also *professional sportsmen, artists*).

occupation: It says on this form: Please state your occupation.

He has no fixed occupation. He is an odd-job man.

Collocations: a hazardous/boring/an absorbing, etc. occupation; occupational therapy/hazards, etc.

Occupation ist ein allgemeiner Ausdruck für Beruf oder für eine zeitweilige oder dauernde Beschäftigung.

Occupation is a general term for a person's temporary or permanent employment.

vocation: Don't try teaching unless you have a vocation for it.

Collocations: vocational training (i.e. training for whatever trade or profession the trainee may enter but usually suggesting a manual trade); to follow a vocation.

Die innere Berufung und ausgesprochene Neigung zu einer beruflichen Tätigkeit.

The natural fitness for and positive attraction towards some career.

calling: Teaching wasn't simply his vocation, it was his calling.

Collocations: not just a profession/trade but a positive calling.

Calling wird in ähnlicher Weise wie *vocation* verwendet, ist jedoch gefühlsbetonter. Es hebt das Gefühl des inneren Zwangs hervor.

Calling is used in a similar way to *vocation*, it is, however, more emotional and poetic. It suggests inner compulsion.

Exercise 14 (A) Fill in a suitable term of the above group of synonyms.

1. The medical ... has a great responsibility.
2. He seems to have a mysterious ... Nobody knows what he does.
3. The ... of cooper is rapidly dying out.
4. "What is your ...?"–"I'm doing clerical work at the moment."
5. The lawyer hadn't been in the ... very long, and you could see it.
6. What a fine piece of work! Where did you learn your ...?
7. When you apply for a new job, you are usually asked your present ...
8. ... footballers can earn high salaries in England.
9. What ... do you train the boys for in this factory?
10. What a wonderful singer! Why doesn't she take it up as a ...?

Exercise 14 (B)

1. Preaching was certainly his ...
2. I've always felt that my ... was for the Arts.
3. He is a highly skilled man, so he knows his ... well.
4. His last ... was that of a clerk.
5. Those who feel they have a ... should follow it.

6. Both men were of the same . . . (Close sympathy is suggested.)
7. Fixing washers on taps is part of a plumber's . . .
8. She follows her . . . with fanatical zeal.
9. Painting is a very risky . . . financially.
10. She suffers from an . . . disease.

15

beschließen, entscheiden

to decide, to resolve, to settle, to make up one's mind

to decide: If you and I agree, who shall decide otherwise?

Collocations: to decide an issue; to decide for/against/in favour of; to make a decision; to come to a decision; the deciding factor.

Sich klar für die eine oder die andere Seite entscheiden; einen (endgültigen) Beschluß oder Entschluß fassen.

To settle a question promptly and clearly as to what shall be done. (etymologically, *decide* = cut off.) (N.: *decision*)

to resolve: After much thought, I resolved to try again.
She resolved that she would work harder.
I resolved on making an early start.

Collocations: to resolve firmly; to resolve a problem; ". . . be it resolved that . . .".

Nach einer Zeit der Überlegung, Beratung, ausführlicher Diskussion zu einer Schlußfolgerung und damit zu einem Entschluß kommen. Daher oft mit Bezug auf die Beschlußfassung seitens eines Ausschusses, Komitees u. ä. verwendet. Zugleich wird auch die Festigkeit der Absicht zum Ausdruck gebracht.

Resolve indicates a process of considerable thought or discussion and so it is often used in connection with committees, assemblies and the like. At the same time, *resolve* suggests firmness of purpose. (N.: *resolution*)

to settle: I'll be glad when it is all settled.
The question of our contract is as good as settled.
"There are no more tickets available."—"That settles the matter. We'll have to stay at home."

Collocations: to settle an argument / a quarrel / a question; to settle s.th. finally / satisfactorily; to settle on (or for) s.th. (to settle for or on suggests compromise).

To settle, im Sinne von beschließen, entscheiden, impliziert den Gedanken oder das Gefühl der Beruhigung nach einem Zustand innerer Unruhe oder Ungewißheit. Daher: eine Angelegenheit regeln, eine Übereinkunft erzielen.

To settle implies the idea of bringing to an end a state of uncertainty, worry, or wavering. So it suggests arrival at some agreement about a matter and to arrange something. (N.: *settlement*)

to make up one's mind: Don't dillydally so much. You really must make up your mind.

Collocations: to try to make up one's mind; not to be able to make up one's mind.

Einen Zustand der Unentschlossenheit, des Zögerns überwinden und sich schließlich, endlich zu etwas entscheiden. Umgangssprachlicher Ausdruck.

A colloquial term which means to arrive at some decision after some hesitation or indecision.

Exercise 15 (A) Complete the sentences filling in a suitable term.

1. However hard I tried, I just couldn't . . .
2. A directors' meeting . . . that the company go into liquidation.
3. The referee's . . . is final.
4. It's time you . . .ed the argument.
5. A woman can often make up her face quicker than she can . . .
6. Tomorrow's results will . . . the question.
7. The jury . . . to free the prisoner.
8. I thought the matter over carefully and . . . to fight for my rights.
9. "W-e-l-l, I'm not quite sure".–"For heaven's sake . . .!"
10. My . . . didn't falter despite this setback.
11. When will they finally . . . that business?
12. "It is unanimously . . . that this meeting believes that . . . . ."
13. Jack Brown scored the . . . goal.
14. The judge . . . in my favour.
15. "I've looked through the menu, but I don't know what to order."–"Well, . . . it's nearly 2 o'clock."

Exercise 15 (B)

1. At one time she had . . . to run away, but changed her mind.
2. We finally . . . for a holiday in Ireland.
3. I didn't want to . . . anything without your advice.
4. I just can't . . . what to do.
5. After weeks of wrangling they . . . to split up the partnership.
6. I'm glad my son's career is . . . now. It's been a worry.
7. Once he's . . . nothing will change it.
8. He . . .ed to be held back by nothing.
9. He had at last . . . the matter in his own mind.
10. I hope the matter will be . . . tomorrow.
11. The origin of man was . . ., once and for all, by Darwin.
12. The workers . . . to take it up with the management.
13. I don't want to have to . . . on my own.
14. The whole question was . . . in my absence.

16
beständig, ununterbrochen, andauernd
continual, continuous, constant, permanent, perpetual

continual: I was disturbed by the continual ringing of the telephone.
I was continually asked the same questions.

Collocations: continual struggle / ebb and flow.

Unaufhörlich, ständig, fortwährend. Bezeichnet die fortwährende, schnell aufeinander folgende Wiederholung oder etwas, das praktisch ununterbrochen vor sich geht. Oft mit Bezug auf irgendeine negative oder unangenehme Erfahrung.

Suggests very frequent recurrence or something which is going on practically incessantly. (Usually there are pauses in between.) Often with reference to some negative or unpleasant experience.

continuous: What does this continuous tone mean?
She keeps up a continuous commentary when we are watching TV.

Collocations: a continuous line / noise / commentary / traffic / flow.

Zeitlich wie räumlich ununterbrochen; betont die durchgehende Verbindung.

Uninterrupted in time or space, without cessation. *Continuous* stresses unbroken connection.

constant: I could not stand their constant whispering.
I constantly chased that cat away from my garden, but it returned again and again.

Collocations: constant interruption / nuisance / lover / admirer / attention / endeavour / help (in time of need) / headache.

Konstant, unveränderlich. *Constant* hebt den Gedanken der Gleichförmigkeit, Unveränderlichkeit, Unwandelbarkeit (auch Zuverlässigkeit) hervor.

This term stresses the idea of uniformity, invariability, also reliability.

permanent: This is not a temporary appointment but a permanent one.
His hearing was permanently damaged by the din.

Collocations: a permanent reminder / feature / structure / wave (hairdressing); a permanent crick in the neck; to endure permanently.

Permanent hebt die unbegrenzte Fortdauer eines Zustandes oder bestimmter Verhältnisse hervor. (Gegensatz: zeitweilig)

Permanent stresses the idea that something is not liable to change, that it is lasting. (Opposite: *temporary*)

perpetual: Perpetual dripping of water will wear away the hardest stone.

Collocations: perpetual motion / nuisance / nature / snows / cold.

Perpetual hebt hervor, daß sich etwas mit unfehlbarer Gewißheit wiederholen oder für immer andauern wird. Es ist gefühlsbetonter als z. B. *permanent.*

It suggests that something will recur unfailingly or go on for ever. *Perpetual* is more emphatic than e.g. *permanent*. (N.: *perpetuity*)

Exercise 16 (A) Complete the sentences filling in a suitable term of the above group of synonyms.

1. I'll have a haircut and a . . . wave.
2. You were my . . . help in time of need.
3. It isn't very solid. Is it meant as a . . . structure?
4. Our lives are but temporary journeys in . . . time.
5. They are . . .ly on hand with advice and a kind word.
6. . . . pressure may irritate, but it brings results.
7. This nail varnish is . . . ; I can't get it off.
8. This land is granted to you and yours in . . .
9. A . . . high-pitched buzz indicates "number unobtainable".
10. His determination remained . . . throughout the years.
11. They were . . . companions.
12. No scientist has ever discovered the secret of . . . motion.
13. That experience has . . . spoilt the place for me.
14. He waged . . . warfare against the insects in his greenhouse.
15. The noise was . . .–it never stopped.
16. Rheumatism has been a . . . nuisance to me all my life.
17. They were . . . knocking on my door to borrow the lawn mower.
18. "Do you have trouble with greenfly?"–". . ."
19. There was a . . . murmur from the audience.
20. We shan't fell that tree; it's become a . . . feature of the landscape.

Exercise 16 (B)

1. Life is a . . . struggle to adjust to new situations.
2. They kept up a . . . chatter.
3. Small boys are . . . ringing my doorbell.
4. The . . . snows of Everest were a . . . magnet to me.
5. There was a . . . stream of visitors to her bedside.
6. The noise of the traffic is a . . . nuisance.
7. San Francisco is noted for its . . . fog.
8. Mountain streams flow . . . in spring.
9. I'm . . . telling him about it but he continues to irritate me.
10. They are . . . eating sweets. It will ruin their teeth.

17
besuchen
to call (on), to visit, to attend, to frequent

to call (on): The doctor called whilst you were out.
A friend of mine called on me in the afternoon.
Collocations: to pay or make a call on s.o.; to call at s.o.'s house.

Einen kurzen oder auch zwanglosen Besuch abstatten; vorsprechen bei jemandem. Im Vergleich zu *visit* ist *call on* umgangssprachlicher.

To pay a short visit to someone.–*Call on* sounds more casual and is nearer *to drop in* (=vorbeikommen) than *to visit* which sounds more serious.

to visit: We visited Madame Tussaud's when we were in London.
How often did the doctor visit you?

Collocations: to pay a visit to; to go on a visit.

To visit bedeutet normalerweise einen offiziellen oder amtlichen Besuch abstatten oder besuchen im Sinne von besichtigen. *Visit* kann sich auf einen längeren oder auch kurzen Besuch von Personen oder Lokalitäten beziehen.

To pay an official visit or inspection; to see some place of interest. To go to some person or place and stay there for any length of time. *To visit* indicates a higher stylistic level than *call on.*

to attend: Did you attend the conference?
The meeting was well attended.

Besuchen im Sinne von teilnehmen an (einer Versammlung, Vorstellung, Vorlesung etc.)

To attend something means to be present at some meeting, performance, lecture, etc. (N.: *attendance*)

to frequent: He frequents the pub at the corner.
The Dolphinarium at Brighton is a much frequented place.

To frequent bedeutet (einen Ort) häufig besuchen. Es verbindet sich gewöhnlich mit der Vorstellung einer speziellen persönlichen Neigung. Eine Lokalität in geradezu genießerischer Weise immer wieder aufsuchen.

This term means to go often to some place, esp. places of amusement. *To frequent* has a certain rakish air about it (e.g. frequent the Low Dives in a town).

Exercise 17 (A) Fill in suitable terms of the above group.

1. Have you ever . . . New York?
2. Those who did not . . . the meeting felt they had missed something.
3. He always . . . us when he's around this way.
4. . . . at school is compulsory.
5. His lectures are well . . .
6. Please, don't . . . between 10 and 11.30 a.m.
7. The . . .ing surgeon took great interest in my case.
8. Music lovers . . . orchestral concerts regularly.
9. The mysterious . . . stayed for some time in the village.
10. When *he* plays, . . . goes up considerably.
11. Brighton attracts . . . from all over the world.
12. She loves to . . . the fashionable shopping centres.
13. I haven't . . . him since we quarrelled.
14. Shall we . . . a quick . . . on auntie, now we're here?
15. She . . . all the Low Dives in town.

16. . . . to London often find the city very confusing.
17. When in Paris, we . . . Montmartre. It fascinated us.
18. The class . . . on . . . to a local factory.
19. Which course do you think I should . . .?
20. Their . . . at concerts was most irregular.

Exercise 17 (B)

1. I'd love to see you any time you're in the neighbourhood. Do . . .
2. I do not . . . such unsavoury places.
3. We only . . . the "poshest" places.
4. . . . relatives can be very tiring at times.
5. I am a . . . of all art galleries in town.
6. Whenever we received a . . . from the higher-ups, we trembled.
7. The inspector . . . our school.
8. If there is a ring at the door, ask the . . . into the lounge.
9. . . . the National Gallery and soak up some culture.
10. When I was young, an unexpected . . . was always an event.

18

bewahren, aufbewahren, (bei)behalten

to keep, to preserve, to retain, to maintain

to keep: Keep this money until I return.

You'd better not eat all the oranges now, keep some for tomorrow.

Collocations: to have s.th. to keep (or for keeps); to keep warm / alive / cheerful / going; to keep a shop / promise; to keep s.th. (i.e. to store it).

Der allgemeinste Ausdruck für (auf)bewahren, in einem bestimmten Zustand erhalten.

The most general term for to continue to have in one's possession or to cause to remain in a given state, place, or position.

to preserve: I painted the woodwork to preserve it.

Collocations: to preserve a calm exterior; to preserve fruit / vegetables; the preservation of wildlife.

Vor Zerstörung, Zersetzung oder Schäden bewahren.

To protect something from decomposition, decay, or harm. (N.: *preservation*)

to retain: This material will retain its colour.

A lot of German villages and towns have retained the root of their former Slavonic names.

Collocations: to retain a (tight) hold (e.g. on one's emotions); to retain a custom/one's tickets; a retentive memory.

Beibehalten, bewahren. Hier steht der Gedanke der fortgesetzten Erhaltung eines Besitzes oder Zustandes gegen drohenden oder möglichen Verlust im Vordergrund. *Retain* gehört einer etwas höheren Stilebene an als *keep*.

Retain stresses the idea of continued possession or usage of something, particularly as against possible or threatening loss. To continue to have some quality. *Retain* is a somewhat higher register than *keep*. (N.: *retention*; Adj.; *retentive*)

to maintain: More money should be spent on the maintenance of roads.
The police help to maintain law and order.
Our government wants to maintain good relations with all nations.

Collocations: to maintain a house / a car / one's family / a railway line / a road / one's health / one's position / an army; to carry out maintenance.

Aufrechterhalten; unterhalten. Etwas durch aktive Bemühungen in einem bestimmten gegebenen Zustand erhalten; die weitere Gebrauchsfähigkeit und Wirksamkeit sicherstellen.

To keep something in due condition so as to allow further existence, action, or usage. A colloquial rendering of *maintain* would be "keep something going". (N.: *maintenance*)

Exercise 18 (A) Fill in a suitable term of the above group.

1. You can . . . it. I don't want it.
2. She was sixty, but well-. . .
3. The caretaker . . . the school in good order.
4. I . . . all my working clothes in this cupboard.
5. Nature's abundant gifts to man should be . . .
6. Will this coat . . . its waterproof qualities?
7. You'll have to grease it if you want to . . . it.
8. Would you . . . my car for me on a regular basis?
9. Did he give it to you to . . . or does he want it back?
10. No one had taken steps to . . . it, so it rusted away.
11. Where do you . . . your scissors?
12. Self-. . . is said to be the strongest instinct.
13. . . . your seats, please.
14. "Will it . . .?"–"Yes, if you . . . it in a fridge."
15. It was only with difficulty that we . . . his service.
16. Britain . . . an army to protect her shores.
17. Those will be difficult to . . . in this climate.
18. It's the game warden's duty to . . . the wildlife here.
19. Here's some money to buy me a paper. You can . . . the change.
20. This is very valuable. . . . it somewhere safe.

Exercise 18 (B)

1. He . . .ed a permanent grin, even when things went wrong.
2. The responsible authorities have . . . much of the Lake District's natural charm.
3. This is our . . . man; he . . . the wheels turning.
4. He . . .ed his old photographs with loving care.
5. She . . .ed her habit of listening, and talking little. (literary)

6. They . . . a fleet of motor boats.
7. All tickets should be . . . for inspection.
8. A man is legally bound to . . . his family.
9. You have to have a . . . memory for this job.
10. You'd better . . . those sandwiches, in case we get lost. (i.e. Don't eat them or let them be eaten now.)

19
bleiben
to stay, to stop, to remain

to stay: I stayed up till 5 a.m. to watch the football match on TV.
"Stay where you are or I'll shoot!"

Collocations: to stay at home; to stay away from school; to stay behind (=zurückbleiben); to stay out; to stay up.

Bleiben in lokaler Beziehung (für längere oder kurze Zeit) und mit Bezug auf einen Besuch. (Fast ausschließlich von Personen gebraucht.)

To remain in some place or situation (for any length of time); also with reference to paying a visit to someone. (It is almost always used of persons.)

to stop: Let's stop here for a couple of minutes and wait for him.
We stopped at a delightful little restaurant in the country.

To stop wird nicht selten umgangssprachlich für *to stay* gebraucht.

This term is quite often used in colloquial language in the sense of *to stay*.
Note the following word play:
"Where are you going for your holiday?"–"(I'm going to) 'Stoppertham'." (i.e. Stop-at-home!)

to remain: You can remain where you are.[1]
I took all those that remained.[2]
Everyone was chattering away; only Tim remained silent.[3]

[1]dableiben, nicht weggehen (wie *to stay*); [2]übrigbleiben; [3]weiterhin in einem bestimmten Zustand verharren.

[1]not to go away; [2]to be left over; [3]to continue to be in a given state or condition.

Exercise 19 (A) Fill in a suitable term from the above group.
1. He . . . standing on the same spot for hours.
2. Half a wall was all that . . . of the castle.
3. A . . . in the country will do you good.
4. He . . . ed thunderstruck.
5. They ... here whenever they passed through the village.
6. They . . . cheerful to the end.
7. We . . . there another three days. (i.e. on our way elsewhere)

8. And what has . . . of your fortune? Nothing!
9. You were the only friend that . . . by my side during the crisis.
10. We . . . at Reigate, on our way from London to Brighton.
11. He was sorry he couldn't . . ., but he left his card.
12. Nothing . . .ed but to grin and bear it.
13. (Judge:) He shall . . . in custody until we decide what to do with him.
14. I . . . in the shop, whilst she went home for the money.

Exercise 19 (B)

1. He's a very restive boy. He can't . . . still for a minute.
2. Don't . . . there all night. Come straight home as soon as it's over.
3. Only five coins . . . in my purse.
4. I liked Brighton so much that I . . . there longer than I intended.
5. The property which . . . in my possession was valuable.
6. . . .! . . .! but if you needs must go, we pray thee, gentle maiden, come again. (poetic)
7. This is a mistake.—Never mind, let it . . . in.
8. Just . . . where I put you, and don't move.
9. He is so unsettled that he never . . . in one house for long.
10. She . . . motionless to avoid discovery.
11. Don't . . . at Ronnie's too long, they also have supper early.
12. She . . .ed an enigma to the last.

20
Blick, blicken
look, glance, glimpse, gaze, stare

look: Let me have a look at your sore throat.
He gave me an astonished look.

Collocations: to take a look / a good hard look (i.e. in great detail) at; to give s.o. a look; to look at / into / out / round, etc.

Look ist der allgemeine und neutrale Ausdruck für Blick, blicken.

Look is the general, neutral term. It is more deliberate than glimpse and glance. (V.: *to look*)

glance: I saw at a glance that something was wrong.
I glanced at her face and saw at once that she was ill.

Collocations: at a glance; a quick / fleeting glance; to give s.o. a glance; to be worth a second glance.

Ein rascher, kurzer Blick, den man absichtlich auf etwas wirft.

A quick, brief look. Something you do intentionally. (V.: *to glance*)

glimpse: As the car raced along the motorway, I just caught a glimpse of its driver but I did not recognise him.

Collocations: to get / catch a glimpse.

Ein kurzer Blick, der nur einen flüchtigen Eindruck vermittelt, ohne daß man absichtlich hinschaut.

A brief sight which gives only a fleeting impression of what one has seen. Something you receive irrespective of intention. (V.: *to glimpse*)

gaze: When she realised his gaze was upon her, she turned away.

Collocations: a fond / dreamy / enraptured / sightless gaze; to gaze into the far distance / into nothingness

Ein aufmerksamer, interessierter Blick.

An interested, steady look. Softer and gentler than *stare.*

stare: He looked at me with an absent-minded stare.

Collocations: a rude / penetrating / open-mouthed stare.

Der starre, stierende Blick mit weit geöffneten Augen.

A steady, hard, fixed look with eyes wide open. *To stare / a stare* often imply rudeness or impoliteness. (V.: *to stare*)

Exercise 20 (A) Fill in suitable terms of the above group.

1. I just got a . . . through the curtains.
2. . . . what I've got!
3. I could . . . at the sunset for hours.
4. Her blue eyes . . .ed dreamily at her wedding dress.
5. You have to be lucky to catch a . . . of them.
6. Take a . . . at the documents whilst you are here.
7. They . . .ed in open astonishment.
8. A quick . . . was all I needed to reassure myself.
9. The villagers always . . . at strangers.
10. He came and went like a whirlwind. I didn't really get a . . . of him.
11. We shall have to take a good hard . . . at the problem.
12. By looking through the tent flap I got a . . . of the elephants.
13. One . . . was enough to send him hurrying to the police.
14. I haven't much time, I'm afraid.–Well, just . . . through it then.
15. Her presence left him in a daze; all that he could do was . . .
16. Her quick . . . could not conceal her interest.
17. He . . .ed at me in his piercing way and my legs turned to jelly.
18. His . . . went through me like an arrow.
19. Tourists . . . at Niagara Falls for hours on end.
20. Don't stand there . . .ing all day. Get some work done!

Exercise 20 (B)

1. . . . is considered bad manners.
2. I stood there for hours but didn't get a . . . of the Lord Mayor.
3. I like to . . . through my notes before giving a lecture.
4. He can . . . as much as he likes. It does not embarrass me.
5. I . . .ed up at the clock and saw that it was late.
6. The . . . that passed between them gave them away.
7. I . . .ed at the view stretched out before us.

8. What was she like?–Oh, I only . . . at her in passing.
9. . . . can speak volumes.
10. They just . . . him as he flashed past.

21
blühen, gedeihen
to bloom, to blossom, to flourish, to prosper

to bloom: These flowers bloom in early spring.
Water makes the desert bloom.

To bloom bezieht sich vor allem auf das Blühen von Blumen. Es wird auch im übertragenen Sinne verwendet.

Refers usually to plants grown for their beauty (flowers, etc.). It is also used in a figurative sense. (N.: *a bloom*)

to blossom: My cherry-tree is in full blossom at present. (or: it is blossoming now).

To blossom wird i. allg. auf das Blühen fruchttragender Pflanzen (Obstbäume etc.), sowie auf das frühe Stadium des Blühens bezogen und im übertragenen Sinne verwendet.

This term is usually used with reference to trees bearing fruit. It also suggests an early stage of the flower, to open into flower. Sometimes also used in a figurative sense. (N.: *a blossom*)

to flourish and **to prosper:** His business is flourishing.
Drama flourished in Shakespeare's time.
He did good business, so he prospered.

Beide Verben werden im Sinne von gedeihen, sich erfolgreich entwickeln gebraucht, wobei *flourish* der umfassendere Ausdruck ist. *To prosper* bezieht sich vor allem auf wirtschaftlichen Erfolg und damit auf Personen.

Both verbs mean to develop successfully. *To flourish* is used in a more comprehensive sense. *To prosper* usually refers to economic or financial success. (N.: *prosperity*)

Exercise 21 (A) Fill in suitable terms of the above group.
1. Where are your daffodils?–They are not . . . this year.
2. Work hard, save hard, live soberly, and you will . . .
3. The monarchy . . . in the Middle Ages.
4. After a difficult start the settlers . . .
5. Happiness does not always come with . . .
6. The country that makes the best use of its resources will . . .
7. The area was rocky, but the pioneers made it . . .
8. His cacti . . .ed despite the damp climate.
9. The Puritans of the 17th century had the recipe for . . .
10. Roses are . . . in Picardy. (English ballad)
11. The once . . .ing town looked dirty and uncared-for.

12. The oak tree has always . . . in England.
13. Wasteland will still . . . (newspaper headline)
14. Poetry has not really . . . this century.

Exercise 21 (B)

1. The daughter begins to . . . , before the mother can be content to fade. (Johnson)
2. You'll be mine in apple . . . time. (old song)
3. My young son does a . . . trade with stamps.
4. The first . . . were out in the hedgerows.
5. If you have business acumen, you will . . .
6. The dog-rose . . . early.
7. The . . . has gone off these violets.
8. How is your family?–. . .!
9. . . . time fills the valley with gorgeous colour and perfume.
10. When do you expect these buds to . . .?

22
Boden, Grund
ground, soil, bottom

ground: The snow covered the ground like a white carpet.

Collocations: on firm / slippery ground; to fall on / to the ground; a piece of ground; a football ground; a playground.

Erdboden, Erdoberfläche; der Boden, auf dem man steht; das Gelände.

The surface of the earth; an area on the earth's surface; firm, solid land.

soil: The soil has lost its humus.

Collocations: fertile soil; a handful of soil; loose soil; a soil sample; to dig / fertilise / plough the soil; native soil.

Boden als Nährstoffgrundlage für Pflanzen; auch der heimatliche Boden.

That layer of the earth's surface in which plants grow; the ground of one's native land.

bottom: There was a leak at the bottom of the barrel.

Collocations: the bottom of the page / the sea / the river; from top to bottom; at the bottom of the class.

Der unterste Teil eines Gefäßes, Gewässers, Berges etc. Auch im übertragenen Sinne.

The lowest part of any container, body of water, mountain, etc. Also used in a figurative sense.

Exercise 22 (A) Fill in a suitable term of the above group.

1. Some of the . . . came away on our boots.
2. The . . . of the cake is a little too dry.
3. The . . . is too wet for football.

4. He sat on the . . . and waited for a sign from me.
5. The peasant bent down and picked up a handful of . . .
6. I wrestled with my opponent and threw him to the . . .
7. I found it at last, right at the . . . of my drawer.
8. The . . . of the pot was rusty.
9. A good yield of fruit largely depends on the . . . in which the trees grow.
10. She fell to the . . . and broke her leg.
11. The new fashion is gaining (or losing) . . .
12. The . . . was fertile.
13. We stamped on the . . . to keep our feet warm.
14. Please send a sample of the . . . to our laboratory.
15. I jumped down to the . . . of the ditch.
16. We dug the . . . up in order to plant more deeply.
17. The . . . was too clayey for those flowers.
18. There was a small coin at the . . . of the purse.
19. That . . . is reserved for children to play on.
20. The . . . of the lake could be seen through the clear water.

Exercise 22 (B)

1. We've really reached rock . . .
2. I drained the glass right down to the . . .
3. The . . . rose steeply and we were soon out of breath.
4. Debris from the wrecked plane lay all over the . . .
5. We descended the pit for half an hour until we reached the . . .
6. The tulips did not come up very well although I had planted them in rich . . .
7. They had to leave their native . . .
8. The . . . on which we stand belongs to the company.
9. When the bomb dropped, the . . . flew in all directions.
10. Peasants are sometimes called 'sons of the . . .'.

23
bringen
to bring, to take

to bring: Waiter, bring me a cup of tea, please.
I wonder what the future will bring.

Herbringen, d. h. zum Ort der sprechenden Person oder zu dem Ort, an dem sich die angesprochene Person befindet (dann also = hinbringen).

To carry to the place of the person speaking or to a place where the person spoken to is supposed to be. *See* note after *to take*.

to take: Take this message to Mrs. Jones, right away.
Take it back there!
Im Sinne von fortschaffen, fortbringen.

Used in the sense of carry away from the place of the person speaking.

Note the following sentences:
I'll *bring* the things to your place. (If the person addressed is expected to be at his place when the things are brought.)

I'll *take* the things to your place. (If the person addressed is not expected to be at his place when the things arrive.)

The job *brought* them a lot of trouble. (If the direct object is represented by an abstract noun, only *bring* is possible.)

Exercise 23 (A) Fill in a suitable term of the above group.

1. Our milkman . . . the milk every morning.
2. My daughter . . . me the morning paper.
3. . . . this letter to Mr. Smith, please.
4. I'll . . . the parcel to you.
5. Please, . . . these books back to the library.
6. The cat . . . in a dead mouse.
7. May I . . . my sister to your party?
8. I . . . the things to your house whilst you were out.
9. Please, . . . these dishes into the kitchen.
10. Let's see what tomorrow . . .
11. . . . my luggage upstairs, please.
12. . . . me my luggage.
13. I will . . . you home.
14. He . . . his hoard to a secret place.
15. . . . this postcard to the post.
16. I've . . . you a present; I hope you like it.
17. George, go and . . . me some beer from the fridge, please.
18. For heaven's sake, . . . this rubbish away.
19. Hallo, what have you . . . me today?
20. . . . those trousers to the cleaner's.

24
Brust
breast, chest, bosom

breast: When the baby started crying, she gave it the breast.[1]
He had some scars on his breast.[2]
He doesn't seem to have a heart in his breast.[3]

Collocations: a double/single-breasted jacket (or coat); to beat one's breast; to make a clean breast of it.

[1]Die weibliche Brust; [2]der Vorderteil des Brustkorbes; [3]die Brust als Sitz der Gefühle.

[1]One of the milk-producing organs of the female body; [2]the upper front part of the human body, of a coat or dress; [3]the seat of emotions.

chest: The chest encloses the heart and the lungs.
Doctor, I have a pain in my chest.
Collocations: to have phlegm on the chest; a sore chest; a chesty cough; a hairy/manly chest; chest measurements (tailoring).
Der Brustkorb, Brustkasten.
The trunk of the body between the neck and the belly. The term tends to be used for men, where *breast* might be used for women.

bosom: I returned to the bosom of my people.
Collocations: in the bosom of one's family; to clasp s.o. to one's bosom.
Die menschliche Brust in poetischer Sprache (Busen).
The breast of a human being, esp. in poetic and polite language.

Exercise 24 (A) Fill in a suitable term of the above group.

1. Regular gymnastics will develop your ...
2. He expanded his manly ... (by using a patent ...-expander).
3. The mother's ... were sore after feeding her baby.
4. I spent Christmas in the ... of my family.
5. She had very fat legs and a huge ...
6. The cold has gone onto my ...
7. We sometimes joke about a man with a pot belly, and say: Your ... has slipped.
8. Double-... jackets are in fashion again.
9. She keeps her handkerchief tucked into her ...
10. "Who gave you the black eye?"–"The wife of my ...!"
11. She was embarrassed at having to bare her ... at the doctor's.
12. Some men have hairy ...
13. ...-beating is not a habit of mine. (i.e. to confess sin)
14. His ... got terribly sunburnt.
15. They were ... friends.
16. He was a barrel-... man of medium height.
17. Come to my ..., little one, and be comforted.
18. (Fashion note:) ... are "out" this year. (i.e. not to be emphasised)
19. The doctor listened-in to my ... with his stethoscope.
20. The little boy had a sore ...
21. I bared my ... before him. (i.e. told him my whole story)
22. Within my ... my boding heart pants. (Shakespeare)

25
Ehe, Hochzeit, Heirat
marriage, matrimony, wedlock, wedding

marriage: When is the marriage to take place?
Their marriage was a most happy one.
Collocations: a happy/unhappy/perfect/secret marriage; a marriage of like minds; a marriage of convenience.

Eheschließung, Hochzeit, Trauung; Ehe, Ehestand.

The legal act, the ceremony by which a man and a woman are made husband and wife. The state of living together as husband and wife. Also used in a figurative meaning. (V.: *to marry*)

matrimony: Helen and Bob have now had two years' experience of matrimony.

Collocations: to contemplate matrimony; the question of matrimony/ difficulty of matrimony.

Gewählter Ausdruck für Ehestand. (Relativ selten gebraucht.)

Formal term for marriage (second meaning). Far less used than marriage. (Adj.: *matrimonial*)

wedlock: Charles was born out of wedlock.

Collocations: to be joined in/born out of wedlock; holy wedlock; in a state of wedlock.

Der juristische und in gewählter Sprache verwendete Ausdruck für Ehestand, Ehebund. (Manchmal auch ironisch).

The legal term for marriage (second meaning). It is also used in literary style and sometimes ironically: Holy deadlock.

wedding: I was not present at their wedding.

Collocations: wedding party/guest/ceremony/dress/day/ring.

In der Umgangssprache und im literarischen Stil üblicher Ausdruck für Hochzeit, Trauung. *Wedding* bezieht sich vor allem auf den Tag der Festlichkeit.

Both formal and informal term for the marriage ceremony and its festivities (specific to the *day* or anniversary). (V.: *to wed*; Adj.: *wedding*)

Exercise 25 (A) Fill in a suitable term of the above group.

1. I've been . . . for nine years.
2. Where is the . . . going to be?
3. He made a disastrous . . .
4. I danced all night at my brother's . . .
5. The whole question of . . . is dealt with thoroughly in this book.
6. To be born out of . . . is no disgrace.
7. What a gorgeous . . . dress!
8. The difficulties that arise in . . . are usually mutual.
9. Their . . . was blessed with three fine children.
10. The . . . commenced punctually at 11 a.m.
11. Though joined in . . . these 40 years, they cherished each other still.
12. Her . . . was a most expensive affair, it nearly ruined her father.
13. They were . . . in church.
14. After the . . . comes the honeymoon.
15. We kept our . . . secret for three years.
16. The night before the . . . is often a sleepless one.
17. . . . is a lottery. (old saying)
18. "My dear girl", said my maiden aunt, ". . . is a serious matter."

19. The . . . guests were all assembled.
20. . . . are made in heaven. (old saying)

Exercise 25 (B)

1. . . . bliss is dreamed of by many a single girl–and man.
2. (Judge:) "And how long have you lived in a state of . . .?"
3. ". . . should not be taken lightly", said the speaker.
4. (Priest:) "I join this man and woman in holy . . .".
5. His judgement was a perfect . . . of justice and mercy.
6. . . . difficulties fill the law courts.
7. How often doth . . . lead to deadlock!
8. Do . . . agencies fill a real need?
9. (Lawyer:) "Here is the evidence that they were in a state of . . ."
10. "Her . . . beggared description."–"Yes, and it nearly beggared her father!"

26
Eigenschaft
quality, property

quality: She is not only a first class mathematician but has a number of excellent qualities as a housewife as well.

These shoes are of rather poor quality.

Collocations: medium / poor / high / low/excellent quality; of the finest quality; first class quality.

Quality bezieht sich auf das Wesen, die innere Beschaffenheit, die Eigenschaften von Personen. Darüber hinaus wird es mit Bezug auf Dinge in der Bedeutung von Qualität gebraucht.

With reference to persons *quality* denotes the true, inherent character. With reference to things it usually indicates the degree of excellence.

property: Tensile strength is one of the main properties of reinforced concrete.

Collocations: distinctive / fundamental properties; one of its many properties; a property of matter.

Sollen die speziellen (oft physikalischen oder chemischen) Merkmale angegeben werden, die einer Sache eigen sind, so wird vorzugsweise *property* gebraucht.

If the distinctive characteristics of things (as distinct from persons) are to be pointed out, one usually uses *property.*

Exercise 26 (A) Fill in a suitable term of the above group.

1. Hardness is a . . . of steel.
2. I like the . . . of her cooking.
3. What . . . does a good salesgirl require?
4. One of its many other . . . is durability.
5. Humility is a very fine (but rare) . . .

6. He possesses all the . . . of a good husband that I lack.
7. A fundamental . . . . of fire is heat.
8. (Teacher:) What are the . . . of a circle?
9. Her good . . . are sometimes overlooked.
10. If the price is low, you can hardly expect good . . .
11. The . . . of rubber make it ideal for rainproof material.
12. He has the disturbing . . . of complete honesty.
13. He showed his . . . by knocking his man out in the first round.
14. They sell medium . . . furniture.
15. (Notice in a shop window:) . . . shoes at bargain prices.
16. I've heard of plutonium but I couldn't detail its . . .
17. They made an inquiry into the . . . of several rare substances.
18. Her virtuous . . . commended her to him.
19. We examined the metal under a microscope to try and detect its . . .
20. She showed me the best . . . overcoat they had in the store.

27
einfach
simple, plain

simple: The problem is not as simple as that.[1]
I am not simple enough to take that propaganda at its face value.[2]
[1]Einfach = unkompliziert; leicht zu machen; [2]von Personen: einfältig.
[1]Uncomplicated; easy to do or to make; [2]of persons: easily deceived. (N.: *simplicity*; Adv.: *simply*)

plain: The matter is as plain as can be.[1]
To be plain with you, I think you are telling lies.[2]
She prefers plain cloth.[3]
She's by no means pretty; in fact, she's quite plain.[4]
[1]Einfach = leicht zu verstehen, klar; [2]offen (und ehrlich), ohne Umschweife; [3]schlicht, natürlich, unverfälscht; [4]von Personen: unschön, unansehnlich; schlicht.
[1]Easy to understand; [2]downright, absolute; frank; [3]ordinary, unadorned, unrefined; [4]of persons: almost ugly; without special merits, unsophisticated. (N.: *plainness*)

Exercise 27 (A) Fill in a suitable term from the above group.
1. The reason is quite . . .
2. I'll tell him . . . that I've changed my mind.
3. Your duty is . . .: you must go back to him.
4. The frontage was of a very . . . design.
5. The solution turned out to be quite . . ., in the end.
6. Her intentions were . . . for all to see.
7. It's as . . . as the nose on your face. (old saying)
8. He's not so . . . as he looks.

9. "... Words" is the title of a book giving advice (originally to civil servants) on how to use–and not to use–English.
10. Don't be ornate in your expressions. Write ...
11. It ... won't do. You must try again.
12. Remember–you are writing for ... men and women.
13. You really believe that? ..., you were deceived.
14. The house was modestly furnished in ... style (or: ... furnished).
15. His habits were ... and frugal.
16. Can't you give a ... answer to a ... question?
17. In some respects she's ...; in others wise.
18. It is ... a question of adding 2 and 2 together.

28

Eingang, Eintritt, Zutritt

entrance, entry, access, admission, admittance

entrance: Use the front entrance (back entrance), please.[1]
He prepared carefully for the entrance examination.[2]
Entrance to the hall is by ticket only.[2]
(Producer:) You make your entrance from the left.[3]

Collocations: the main / front / back side entrance; the entrance money or fee (to join a club); to make one's entrance.

[1]Der Eingang eines Gebäudes; [2]der Eintritt, das Recht auf Eintritt; [3]das Eintreten.

[1]The doorway or gate by which a place may be entered; [2]the right to enter; [3]the act of entering.

entry: The entry of Great Britain into the war took place on September 3, 1939.[1]
We watched the triumphal entry of the champions into the stadium.[2]
The burglers forced an entry into the church by night.[2]
The entry to his house was long, wide and impressive.[3]

Collocations: entry into a profession; a triumphal entry; the entry of Britain into the EEC; the entry of the U.S. into world politics, etc.

[1]Eintritt in übertragender Bedeutung; [2]als förmlicherer Ausdruck für den Akt des Eintretens; [3]im Sinne von Zugang, Einfahrt(stor); Vorhalle, Flur.

[1]To enter in a figurative sense; [2]as a more formal term for the act of entering; [3]a passage or way approaching the entrance.

access: He obtained access to the secret files of the ministry.

Collocations: to gain / obtain access; to be permitted / refused access; to give access; easy (of) access; (not) readily accessible; an access of fever, etc.; access to files / documents / books, etc.

Der Zugang zu einer Person oder Sache. Das Herankommen, die Annäherung an eine Sache oder Person steht im Mittelpunkt durch Überwindung irgendwelcher Schranken oder Hindernisse. (Während *admission* mehr die Gewährung einer Erlaubnis impliziert.)

Access signifies the possibility of approaching a person or place. (*Admission* suggests the granting of some right or permission, whereas *access* implies the overcoming of some obstacle or barrier.) Also in the meaning of a sudden oncoming of an illness or condition.

admission: We gained admission to the president's office.
What's the price of admission?

Collocations: No admission (to the public); admission fee; to gain or to grant admission to a college / university / profession.

Zulassung, Aufnahme, Zutritt; auch Eintrittspreis. *Admission* impliziert den Begriff der Erlaubnis.

Being admitted to a person or place. *Admission* involves permission, someone's consent.

admittance: Admittance was barred to all journalists.

Zutritt zu einer Lokalität. (Relativ selten gebraucht)

Usually permission to enter some place. *Admittance* is more formal than *admission.*

Exercise 28 (A) Fill in a suitable term of the above group.

1. The front door's locked, let's go round to the side . . .
2. . . . was free on the first night.
3. Don't stand there, you're blocking the . . .
4. There are only a few channels which give . . . to the island.
5. To get more customers they reduced the price of . . .
6. The . . . was crowded. We had to elbow our way in.
7. . . . to university is granted only to those with the necessary qualifications.
8. We stopped at the . . . to the tunnel.
9. He had . . . to a considerable fortune.
10. We've 200 . . . to university this year.
11. The burglar obtained . . . by forcing the door.
12. The guilds of the Middle Ages restricted . . . to their trades.
13. Times of . . . to the museum: 9.30 a.m.–6 p.m. daily.
14. The . . . to the cave was littered with bones.
15. . . . to the concert was free.
16. . . . to the fortress is by a hazardous route.
17. (Notice:) No . . . during rehearsals.
18. The . . . of Moscow by Napoleon's troops was a disaster for him.
19. . . . to university is difficult.
20. . . . to our profession was high this year.

Exercise 28 (B)

1. . . . to the manager's office was only possible after seeing the secretary.
2. We celebrated his . . . into man's estate.
3. Wait until the party is at its height, then we'll make our . . .

4. . . . to the Stock Exchange is open to members only.
5. (Notice:) No . . . except on business.
6. Our attempt to gain . . . to the star's hotel room was baulked by her bodyguard.
7. . . . into the legal profession is difficult.
8. He owed his . . . into the coterie to her generosity.
9. I've had no . . . to him since he was locked up.
10. Their . . . into the battle proved decisive.

29
Empfang
receipt, reception

receipt: He jumped for joy on receipt of the telegram.

Collocations: to acknowledge a receipt; on receipt of . . . , to be in receipt of; a receipt for the goods/money.

Der Empfang, Erhalt von (übersandten oder übergebenen) Sachen; auch im Sinne von Empfangsbescheinigung, Quittung.

The act of receiving things (sent or delivered); a bill, invoice containing the statement and signature confirming that something has been paid.

reception: A host of guests were present at the wedding reception.

Collocations: to get an excellent / a tumultuous / poor / royal / favourable / hostile reception; wedding reception; to hold a reception; radio reception.

Der Empfang von Personen, bes. mit Bezug auf die Art und Weise ihrer Aufnahme; im übertragenen Sinn die Aufnahme von Ideen, Publikationen etc. durch die Öffentlichkeit etc.; der offizielle, feierliche Empfang von Personen; der Rundfunkempfang.

The act of receiving persons and the manner of such *reception*; figuratively referring to ideas, publications, etc. A ceremonious, formal receiving of persons on special occasions. Also the quality of a radio broadcast.

Exercise 29 (A) Complete the sentences inserting *receipt* or *reception.*

1. Please report to the . . . desk on arrival.
2. His . . . was less enthusiastic than I had expected.
3. I hereby acknowledge . . . of your letter, dated . . . . . .
4. On . . . of the news, he sat down and mopped his brow.
5. I couldn't hear the concert clearly as the . . . on my radio was poor.
6. I always issue a . . . for goods delivered.
7. The cup-winning team returned home to a tumultuous . . .
8. The mayor held a civic . . . for them.
9. If you want to exchange the goods, you must produce the . . .
10. There was a . . . after the performance.

11. Many foreign trade organisations hold . . . during the Leipzig Fair.
12. May I have a . . . for the money?
13. His . . . of the news was jubilant.
14. I don't envy him the . . . he got at her hands!
15. Thank you, Sir. Here is the shirt and this is the . . .
16. This . . . also acts as your guarantee.
17. He is in . . . of a monthly allowance.
18. There was a most unfavourable . . . for the plan.
19. The . . . of the plan was hostile.
20. Evidence of postage will not be accepted as evidence of . . .

30

entdecken

to discover, to detect

to discover: I have never discovered his secret.
She discovered that he loved her.

Collocations: to discover the reason; difficult to discover; remarkable discovery; The Age of Discovery.

Etwas bisher schon Bestehendes durch Forschung oder Zufall erstmalig erkennen oder plötzlich wahrnehmen.

To realize or find for the first time what has so far remained unknown or hidden, or beyond sight, i.e. it had already existed. (N.: *discovery*)

to detect: After careful examination, I detected a slight crack in the rock.
I couldn't detect a trace of guilt in his behaviour.

Collocations: to detect a difference; difficult to detect; do you detect . . . ?

Eine meist unangenehme Entdeckung machen; auch zur Bezeichnung einer Wahrnehmung nach sorgfältiger Beobachtung oder Untersuchung. *Detect* wird zuweilen auch ironisch gebraucht.

To become aware of something disagreeable or unpleasant; to find something out after careful observation or investigation. *Detect* sometimes suggests irony. (N.: *detection*; *detective*)

Exercise 30 (A) Fill in a suitable term of the above group.

1. Columbus thought he had . . . a new route to India but it was later . . . that it was America he had . . .
2. You've been searching a long time; what have you . . . ?
3. They're not supposed to be the same, but I couldn't . . . any difference.
4. The . . . of how to make synthetic rubber was of paramount importance.
5. The theft was . . . by a shop-assistant.
6. Do I . . . a hint of irony behind that remark?
7. I . . . that water is wet at an early age.
8. I . . . a slight cooling of the temperature.
9. Under a microscope, I could just . . . a tiny spot on the surface.
10. The . . . sent him into ecstasies of joy.

11. I . . . that he was mean and hypocritical.
12. He . . . a slight difference in the wording of the two contracts.
13. When was America first . . .?
14. There are hundreds of new things to be . . . every day.
15. We . . . a beautiful cove on the other side of the island.
16. They were unable to . . . why they had been attacked.
17. By reasoning from the clues, he was able to . . . the culprit.
18. You've been . . . , my lad. You might as well own up.
19. She . . . a remarkable stone under the sand.
20. From the top of the cliff I . . . the eagle's nest.

31

entlassen

to dismiss, to discharge, to release, to sack

to dismiss: The firm will not dismiss its skilled workers, even when business is slack.

The sergeant dismissed the platoon when the parade was over.

Collocations: to be dismissed from a firm; to be dismissed by an employer; to dismiss a class at school (implies end of lesson and leaving the room); to dismiss a company/a squad, etc. (at the end of a parade or the day).

Dismiss wird vorzugsweise in bezug auf die berufliche Tätigkeit, das Geschäftsleben verwendet (auch im Sinne einer unfreiwilligen Entlassung).

Dismiss is the usual term with regard to business life in the sense of to send away from employment. It is also used in the sense of to allow to go (*see* above collocations). The idea of forcing to go unwillingly is often implied. (N.: *dismissal*)

to discharge: After serving his sentence the prisoner was discharged.

When we found out about his unreliability, we discharged him out of hand.

Collocations: to discharge from hospital/prison/from the army; an honourable/ignominious discharge; to discharge out of hand; to discharge without a stain on his character (legal).

Discharge wird vor allem auf die Entlassung aus dem Krankenhaus, Gefängnis, der Armee bezogen. Außerhalb dieser Bereiche wird es gelegentlich auch als ein etwas schärferer Ausdruck als *dismiss* verwendet.

This term usually refers to hospital, imprisonment, or military service. If used outside this sphere it can sound harsher than *dismiss.* (N.: *discharge*)

to release: The police released him on bail.

Release the prisoner; there is no case against him.

Collocations: to release a prisoner (but usually *before* completion of sentence); to release from confinement; released from one's duties; to release on bail (legal); to release from bondage; to get one's release.

Auf freien Fuß setzen. *Release* bezeichnet eine weniger offizielle Art von Entlassung als *discharge* und wird darum eher auf Gewahrsam, Haft bezogen als auf die Entlassung aus dem Gefängnis.

Release usually refers to the setting free of a person who was held captive. However, it sounds less official than *discharge*. That is why it is more likely to refer to custody before trial than to prison. (N.: *release*)

to sack: The manager sacked twenty workers when business was bad.
I got the sack today.

Collocations: to give s.o. the sack; to get the sack; mass sackings.

To sack ist ein umgangssprachlicher Ausdruck für 'entlassen' mit Bezug auf berufliche Tätigkeit.

A colloquial term for dismissing from his job or losing one's employment. It is less formal than *dismiss*.

Exercise 31 (A) Insert a suitable term of the above group. (To *get the sack* or *give the sack* are looked upon as one expression in this exercise, so only one blank space is provided for them.)

1. What did you do when you were . . . from the Navy?
2. I shall not . . . her, she's too good a typist.
3. The next time you're late, I'll . . .!
4. I'm still rather weak. I was only . . . from hospital yesterday.
5. When the firm nearly went bankrupt, there were many . . .
6. She . . . for smoking at work.
7. (Prisoner:) I expect to be . . . six months earlier for good conduct.
8. I used to be in the Army, and I've got my . . . papers to prove it.
9. As a punishment, the class were not . . . for break.
10. There was a tremendous flutter of wings as thousands of doves were . . .
11. We've had to . . . most of our office staff.
12. It wasn't really violence, just a . . . of energy.
13. The law says a worker must be given a week's notice before . . .
14. Only the registrar can . . . you from hospital.
15. The accused was . . . on £ 100 bail.
16. He received an honourable . . . from the Army.
17. (Police sergeant at a police station:) Hold that one for questioning. . . . the others.
18. He was . . . by his firm for disciplinary reasons.
19. They tried to . . . the shop steward for calling a strike.
20. I had to . . . him for insolence.

Exercise 31 (B)

1. As soon as I was . . . from school, I ran straight home.
2. You're all . . .! The lot of you!
3. He took his . . . calmly.
4. After he had spoken there was a great . . . of tension.
5. The Prime Minister "..." one of his junior ministers for leaking the report.

6. (She:) "Please, . . . my hand, you're hurting it."
7. We are . . . ten a week, until we reach our planned maximum.
8. She . . . her servant from the room.
9. Captain Brown, you're . . . the service for ungentlemanly conduct.
10. They . . . the tool-room operatives, one by one.

32

sich erinnern

to remember, to recollect, to recall, to remind

to remember: I remember posting the letter.
I met him once, but I don't remember his name.

Collocations: try to remember; I can't remember (whether/ what, etc.); remember me to the family.

Sich an etwas erinnern, sich entsinnen.

To keep something in one's memory. (N.: *remembrance*)

to recollect: Do you recollect borrowing 5p. from me?
I can't recollect which day it happened.

Sich erinnern im Sinne von wieder ins Bewußtsein heben. Mit *recollect* verbindet sich in stärkerem Maße ein bewußtes Bemühen, als das bei *remember* der Fall ist.

To bring back to one's mind. *Recollect* presupposes some effort in contradistinction to remember which does not usually suggest conscious effort. (N.: *recollection*)

to recall: Can you recall the pattern of her dress?
She recalled the incident to mind.

Collocations: to recall to mind; to recall an incident; still recall; beyond recall.

Sich erinnern unter bewußtem Einsatz des Willens ähnlich *recollect*; ins Gedächtnis zurückrufen. *Recall* ist der gewählteste Ausdruck der Gruppe.

To call back to one's memory. This term implies volition similar to *recollect*. But *recall* is the most literary term of this group. Sometimes it is used sentimentally. (N.: *recall*)

to remind: I may forget to pay back the money if you don't remind me.
I had to remind him of his promise.
Remind me to leave a message for him.
Oh, that reminds me!

Collocations: I need hardly remind you that . . . ; that reminds me, . . .; it reminds me of . . .; give s.o. a reminder.

Jemanden an etwas erinnern; dem Gedächtnis nachhelfen.

To recall something to somebody's mind; to jog somebody's memory. (N.: *reminder*)

Exercise 32 (A) Fill in a suitable term of the above group.

1. You mustn't forget to . . . me of my appointment.
2. Do you . . . that chap we met in Paris last year?
3. I shall . . . that evening till my dying day.
4. I always tie a knot in my handkerchief to . . . me of what I have to do.
5. . . . the beautiful view from the top of Snowdon?
6. His biography is called: My . . .
7. Look Mum, a hippopotamus!–Ah, that . . . me; I must buy your father a birthday present.
8. . . .! I expect you to be back before midnight.
9. If my . . . is correct, you always go there in the summer.
10. . . . me to post that letter when we're in town.
11. I need hardly . . . you that we are over half an hour late.
12. I have no . . . of ever having been there.
13. He still hasn't paid. We must send him a . . .
14. Why didn't you . . . me to book the tickets?

Exercise 32 (B)

1. We always used to celebrate November 11th as . . . Day.
2. The mind often refuses to . . . unpleasant or painful experiences.
3. I . . . vaguely what happened, but cannot . . . the exact details.
4. Do you . . . the end of the story?
5. I tried hard to . . . , but couldn't.
6. As far as I can . . . , I left them in the kitchen.
7. We asked him to try to . . . his boyhood memories.
8. They are all dead; gone beyond . . .
9. Can you . . . exactly what he looked like?
10. I can't . . . the colour of her eyes.
11. Train your memory, and you won't always need . . . of such simple things.
12. She was able to . . . the incident many years later.
13. Where did you put the camera?–I can't . . .
14. I cannot . . . any other occasion, when agreement was so widespread.

33
erklären, erläutern
to explain, to elucidate, to expound, to interpret, to account for

to explain: He explained a number of idiomatic phrases to us.
He explained to me how to operate the machine.

Collocations: to explain a situation / a problem / a process / an obscure point / one's behaviour / the meaning of; to explain why . . . ; to be unable to explain; to explain patiently.

Erläutern, was bisher noch nicht bekannt war, nicht richtig verstanden wurde oder nur schwer zu verstehen ist.

To cause a person to understand what was not known or not properly understood, to make clear, to render intelligible. (N.: *explanation*)

to elucidate: He elucidated his statement by adding a commentary.
Some examples will elucidate the meaning of this difficult passage.

Collocations: to elucidate a difficult problem / text; let me elucidate.

Durch anschauliche Darstellung, zusätzlichen Kommentar aufhellen, deutlich machen, was verworren oder unklar ist, erläutern. *Elucidate* gehört der gehobenen Stilebene an.

To make lucid, clear what was obscure and dark before, especially by additional commentary, illustration, etc.; to throw light on something. *Elucidate* suggests formal English. (N.: *elucidation*)

to expound: He expounded the theory of atomic chain reaction.
The passage from the Bible was well expounded by the clergymen.

Collocations: to expound a point of law; to expound a theory / a philosophy / a doctrine, etc.

Etwas mit besonderer Sorgfalt, Punkt für Punkt und oft mit wissenschaftlicher Gründlichkeit in einem Vortrag, Buch etc. auseinandersetzen. *Expound* impliziert inneres Engagement.

To give a careful, scholarly, methodical explanation in a lecture, book, argument, debate. *Expound* implies commitment to what is being expounded.

to interpret: The teacher interpreted the poem to his students.
A conductor has to interpret a symphony.

Collocations: to interpret a piece of music / a dramatic work; to interpret a dream / an omen / s.o.'s remarks.

Entspricht dem deutschen interpretieren, deuten, auslegen.

To explain the underlying meaning of words, a passage of a book, etc. by paraphrase involving one's personal opinion. (N.: *interpretation*)

to account for: Some urgent business accounts for her absence.
I cannot account for her refusal.

Collocations: Ah, that accounts for (it); how do you account for (that)?; there's no accounting for (it); I simply can't account for (it).

Erklären durch Angabe des Grundes, der Ursache.

To explain the cause of, or reason for something.

Exercise 33 (A) Fill in a suitable term from the above group.

1. He patiently . . . the workings of the machine.
2. "I've had toothache for days."–"So that . . . your silence!"
3. I demand an . . . of his atrocious behaviour.
4. Pianists give their own . . . of Chopin.
5. "Why did he interrupt so rudely?"–"I simply can't . . . it."
6. Brecht's . . . of Shakespeare is quite revolutionary.
7. There's no . . . tastes. (a popular saying)
8. How do you . . . her strange behaviour?

9. The guide . . . why they were unable to visit the tomb.
10. Oracles in ancient times claimed they could . . . omens.
11. There's no . . . the actions of a neurotic.
12. The doctor . . . why I should go into hospital.
13. "Modern" art takes some . . .!
14. After his . . . the problem was perfectly clear to me.

Exercise 33 (B)

1. The Hyde Park orator loved to . . . his doctrines at great length.
2. Despite the wealth of detail, the theory defied . . .
3. His lawyer was just . . . a point, when the judge interrupted him.
4. Your point is not quite clear. Would you, please, . . .?
5. I can't . . . the lies he's been telling recently. He's always been so honest.
6. She's fond of . . . her ideas to all who will listen.
7. Even the professor wasn't able to . . . the problem satisfactorily.
8. "Your work is deteriorating."–"I've been ill."–"That . . . it."
9. This theory will have to be . . . in great detail.
10. How do you . . . these marks on the table?
11. It is not an easy problem to . . .
12. Line drawings and diagrams were used to . . . the plan.
13. "You'd better have your answers ready."–"Don't worry, I can . . . everything."
14. To . . . a philosophy convincingly, you have to believe in it.
15. His clear outline of the problem needed no . . .

34
erklären, sagen
to declare, to proclaim, to pronounce, to state

to declare: Great Britain declared war on Germany on August 4, 1914.
He declared himself in favour of the proposal.

Collocations: to declare oneself for (in favour of) or against s.th. or a person; to declare s.th. to be false; to declare s.th. null and void; to declare s.o. or oneself guilty; to declare s.o. the winner of the contest; to declare one's love/one's intention; to declare war.

Etwas mit Bestimmtheit und Nachdruck erklären; auch offiziell verkünden.

To state something emphatically, sometimes with authoritative force and in a formal manner. (N.: *declaration*)

to proclaim: On July 4, 1776, the U.S.A. proclaimed itself an independent republic.

Collocations: to proclaim s.o. a traitor; to proclaim s.o. president/king; to issue a proclamation; a royal/papal/governmental proclamation.

Proklamieren, etwas öffentlich verkünden. *Declare* ist persönlicher, *pro-*

claim neutraler. *Declare, proclaim* und *pronounce* sind relativ gewählte Ausdrücke, wenn sie in der Umgangssprache gebraucht werden.

To announce something officially and sometimes loudly and ceremoniously in a public place or to the public. (N.: *proclamation*)

to pronounce: He was found guilty and sentence of death was pronounced. The judges pronounced in my favour.

Collocations: to pronounce judgement; to pronounce (two people) man and wife; to pronounce a person who is seriously ill out of danger; to pronounce sentence of death; to pronounce in favour of or against s.th. or s.o.

Etwas mit gewisser Feierlichkeit erklären (vor allem in der gehobenen Schriftsprache).

To utter something in a solemn way. *Pronounce* is preferable in formal English. (N.: *pronouncement*)

to state: He always stated his opinions forcefully.

Collocations: to state one's opinion / views / reasons; to state a case (einen Fall darlegen); to state s.th. in one's defence (= etwas zu seiner Verteidigung vorbringen); to state facts (= Tatsachen anführen); to state full particulars (= alle Einzelheiten angeben); to make a statement, i.e. to the police or officially to the public; to issue a statement.

Etwas mündlich oder schriftlich im einzelnen darlegen; feststellen, äußern, auseinandersetzen.

To set forth in due detail in written form or orally. (N.: *statement*)

Exercise 34 (A) Fill in a suitable term of the above group.

1. (Policeman:) "Do you wish to make a . . .?"
2. A . . . of war is a serious matter.
3. He . . . his devotion to her.
4. He was . . . king, when his father died.
5. She . . . her reasons for refusing the offer.
6. The government made a . . . , clarifying its position.
7. I hereby . . . this 21st International Philatelists' Conference open.
8. It was . . . in the prisoner's defence that he had acted under provocation.
9. He was . . . ruler over all the island.
10. They refused to collaborate with me but they didn't . . . their reasons.
11. The other side will now . . . its case.
12. He . . . his love in passionate terms.
13. An official . . . was issued to the public the next morning.
14. The papal . . . was read to the multitude outside the palace.
15. "I refuse to be browbeaten!" he . . . indignantly.
16. India was . . . a republic soon after independence.
17. They . . . their intention of staying up all night.
18. You are requested to . . . your name, address and date of birth.
19. They . . . her Queen of the May.
20. The French sailors . . . for England, and joined the British Navy.

Exercise 34 (B)

1. She was . . . thoroughly fit again.
2. He . . . that when he returned home, she had vanished.
3. The registrar was about to . . . them man and wife, when the wedding ring dropped on the floor.
4. The governor had his order . . . throughout the land.
5. You may . . . me a traitor, but the people will not be deceived.
6. An M. P. or local councillor must . . . any material interest he may have in any project under discussion.
7. The political party issued a . . . of its policy. (i.e. a manifesto)
8. The judge's . . . was received in stunned silence.
9. Please . . . the facts clearly and without emotion.
10. The government issued a . . . of intent.

35
erlauben
to allow, to permit, to admit of

to allow: People are not allowed to smoke in the auditorium.
Allow me to help you with your case, madam.

Collocations: Allow me to tell you . . . Not allowed. Allow me. (When about to help s.o., e.g. to lift s.th.)

Erlauben =geschehen lassen, zulassen.

Allow means not to try to prevent, let a person do s.th. (N.: *allowance*)

to permit: "That may be tacitly allowed which is not expressly permitted." (Webster)
Who do you have to go to, to get permission?

Collocations: if circumstances permit; to permit an inspection of accounts; to refuse/grant/obtain permission; weather permitting.

Permit hebt i. allg. die ausdrückliche Zustimmung, Einwilligung hervor. Auch im Sinne von ermöglichen verwendet.

Permit often implies express authorization, i.e. to give permission; also in the sense of 'to make something possible'. (N.: *permission*; *permit* = Durchlaßschein, Passierschein)

to admit of: The balance of payments did not admit of any further imports.
This case did not admit of public discussion.

Collocations: circumstances may (or may not) admit or permit of some action; a sentence/passage, etc. admits of some interpretation.

Erlauben im Sinne von: (mit Bezug auf irgendwelche Umstände) eine Gelegenheit bieten, Raum lassen für, zulassen.

(With reference to circumstances) to render possible, to leave room for some improvement, doubt, conclusions, etc.

Exercise 35 (A) Fill in a suitable term of the above group.

1. My mother would never . . . us to talk to strangers.
2. After allowing him entry, I . . . him to stay.
3. He applied for leave of absence, but . . . was refused (or not granted).
4. The situation . . . no delay.
5. I . . . my children to choose their own friends.
6. He obtained . . . to leave the room by feigning sickness.
7. Smoking is only . . . in the foyer.
8. Fair judgement . . . no partiality.
9. Dogmatism . . . no error.
10. I simply cannot . . . him to get away with it.
11. You were expressly refused . . . to go there–and you went!
12. He showed his . . . and the doorkeeper reluctantly . . . him to enter.
13. This theory . . . various interpretations.
14. We are . . . to walk on the grass.

Exercise 35 (B)

1. There are no rules; but some things are tacitly . . . and some are not.
2. (Soldier:) ". . . to smoke, sir?"–(Officer:) "Yes, you may."
3. This is a classical dilemma: it . . . two possible solutions.
4. The cat was not . . . into the kitchen.
5. I cannot possibly . . . you to take such liberties!
6. The matter is urgent. It . . . no further delay.
7. The case is clear; it . . . but one verdict.
8. They were . . . to wander as far as they liked.
9. "Is it really . . .?"–"Well, they turn a blind eye to it."
10. If you have a banker's card, you are . . . to pay by cheque.
11. Genius . . . no monotony.
12. I shall not . . . you to pay for your own lunch; you are my guest.
13. The circumstances seemed to . . . various possibilities.
14. His circumstances . . . no luxuries.

36

erleichtern, mildern, abschwächen

to lighten, to ease, to relieve, to alleviate, to allay, to mitigate, to facilitate

to lighten: I took one of the suitcases from Bob to lighten his load.

I was marking papers and I lightened the work by tuning in to some music.

Collocations: to lighten a load / task / punishment; to lighten taxes / one's heart.

Das Gewicht vermindern; eine Bürde, etwas Niederdrückendes mildern. Mit *lighten* verbindet sich auch gelegentlich der Gedanke der Aufheiterung.

To make lighter (in its literal meaning); to make less burdensome or oppressive. *Lighten* can also connote a cheering influence.

to ease: This medicine will ease your pain.

This policy will contribute towards the easing of international tension.

Collocations: to ease pain (also figuratively) / worry / cares / trouble(s) / anxiety / one's mind, etc.; to ease pressure / tension / strain / a burden; to ease someone's work / a problem / a difficulty / the situation.

Etwas Schwieriges leichter machen; die Spannung vermindern, entspannen; Schmerz lindern.

To lessen what causes tension; to render less severe; to make less difficult or more comfortable. *Ease* can suggest slowness or gradualness.

to relieve: He was greatly relieved when he had got his divorce.

Good nursing gave the patient relief but could not cure him.

Collocations: be (greatly) relieved; be relieved by (some news); to relieve the misery / poverty / distress of . . .; to relieve pain / headaches / fear / dullness / monotony; to relieve oneself (euphemistic and formal for emptying the bladder or bowels); to relieve someone of his purse (facetious).

Relieve ist oft mit der Vorstellung der Befreiung von irgendeiner Art von (geistigem oder physischem) Empfindungsstau verbunden. Also von etwas Bedrückendem befreien; etwas (wenigstens) zeitweise erträglicher machen; eine (oft durch Katastrophen verursachte) Not lindern.

Relieve often suggests outlet of feeling; make some misery caused by disaster more bearable, endurable; to free at least temporarily from something oppressive or unpleasant. (N.: *relief*)

to alleviate: The plight of the poverty-stricken population was alleviated by relief supplies from abroad.

Collocations: to alleviate sorrows / misery / poverty / suffering / woes / one's lot, etc.

Alleviate hebt das Zeitweilige der Abschwächung einer Belastung hervor. Es ist ein relativ gewählter Ausdruck.

Alleviate stresses the temporary character of the lightening of some mental burden, pain or suffering. It does not suggest removal or cure. *Alleviate* is not usable about persons, only situations, conditions, e.g. pain, unhappiness, etc. It is a relatively formal expression. (N.: *alleviation*)

to allay: The good news allayed his anxiety.

I pleaded with him, but could not allay his wrath.

Collocations: to allay anxiety / fears / agitation / excitement / suspicions / thirst / hunger / anger / wrath.

Zustände negativer Erregung (siehe Kollokationen) wirksam mildern, abschwächen; beschwichtigen, beruhigen.

To lessen effectively what distresses, disquiets; to soothe, pacify a person. *Allay* suggests formal English.

to mitigate: After hearing further evidence, the judge mitigated his sentence.

The poultice mitigated the swelling on his wound.

Collocations: to mitigate an offence / a punishment / harsh conditions / the severity of climate / of cold / of a winter, etc.

Die Härte oder Intensität von etwas abschwächen, das uns auferlegt ist oder von uns verursacht wird; irgend etwas Böses, Schädliches oder Falsches, das begangen wurde, mildern.

To lessen the seriousness of something inflicted or of something evil, harmful, or wrong done by someone. *Mitigate* is a formal *expression.* (N.: *mitigation*)

to facilitate: Computers greatly facilitate every kind of calculation.

Access to his library facilitated my work at the university.

Collocations: to facilitate some work / negotiations / the learning of a foreign language, etc.

Die Schwierigkeit einer Arbeit, eines Vorganges etc. verringern.

To make less difficult; to help, promote some action, work, process.

Exercise 36 (A) Fill in a suitable term of the above group.

1. We're through at last! What a . . .!
2. I delivered the heaviest parcel first to . . . my load.
3. This new piece of equipment . . . the process.
4. His intervention greatly . . . our situation.
5. It . . . ed my heart to see her looking so well.
6. Labour-saving equipment has . . . the task of the housewife.
7. His assistance . . . my task considerably.
8. Here is an aspirin to . . . the pain.
9. The . . . of tension which his words produced was dramatic.
10. His . . . at the news was written all over his face.
11. We must reduce the strain and . . . his burden of work.
12. Relax, and . . . the strain.
13. I was greatly . . . to hear that he was safe and sound.
14. It will not cure but only . . . the pain.
15. Ability to concentrate . . . study.
16. They . . . my task by providing me with better tools.
17. The work of the pioneers . . . advances in science.
18. The pickpocket . . . him of his watch.
19. By kind words and real help she . . . his misery.
20. We bathed their wounds in an attempt to . . . their suffering.

Exercise 36 (B)

1. Supplies from abroad . . . their misery for a time.
2. Drugs may raise the spirits and . . . suffering but they are a dangerous expedient.
3. The sight of such strong defences was enough to . . . their fears.
4. Sleep brought temporary . . . of his woes.
5. Your anger at the loss of your wallet does not . . . your crime.
6. Nought could . . . that mental torture.
7. His profuse apology somewhat . . . the offence.
8. We shall need large sums if we are to . . . their poverty.

9. Do not let him . . . your anger with honeyed words.
10. Here is her letter. It will . . . your pain.
11. The government tends to . . . taxation.
12. His early successes . . . his rise to fame.

37
Ernte
crop, harvest

crop: We have an excellent crop of raspberries in our garden every year.
The crops were already stacked in the warehouse.
The wheat crop is promising this year.

Collocations: a fine / poor crop; to sell one's crop; to save / ruin the crop; a crop failure; potato / coffee / tobacco / cotton / apple / rice crop; wheat crop or wheat harvest.

Der alltägliche Ausdruck (auch im Geschäftsleben) für Ernte im Sinne von Ernteertrag und Feldfrucht. Gelegentlich auch im übertragenen Sinne, z. B. *a fine crop of students this year.*

The common and commercial term for the yield of some cultivated produce of the ground; the produce itself as grain or fruit. (Also: *a fine crop of students this year.*) (V.: *to crop*)

harvest: After the harvest some fields used to lie fallow.
Harvest time is when the various crops are harvested.

Collocations: to reap the harvest; a bumper harvest; harvest (time); harvest festival; harvest-weather.

Die Erntezeit; die Erntearbeiten; vor allem bei Getreide auch im Sinne von Ernteertrag. *Harvest* ist gewählter als *crop.*

The season for reaping the crops; the gathering of crops; sometimes the yield itself, esp. of grain. *Harvest* suggests a somewhat higher stylistic level than *crop.* (V.: *to harvest*)

Exercise 37 (A) Fill in a suitable term of the above group.
1. As I looked at the field, the . . . were swaying in the breeze.
2. How much do you think your . . . will fetch on the open market?
3. . . . your . . . before you start spending the proceeds! (i.e. Don't count your chickens before they are hatched.)
4. The men are . . . the wheat today.
5. We had a fine . . . of pupils last year.
6. The potato . . . was ruined this year.
7. We expect a good . . . of wheat this autumn.
8. Despite the drought, we managed to save most of the . . .
9. We always take on extra hands at . . . (time).
10. A complete . . . failure was narrowly averted.
11. Fish are sometimes referred to as the . . . of the sea.

12. The peas . . . ed well this year.
13. He looked the . . . over with a professional eye.
14. After . . . the wheat, we tied it in sheaves.
15. We had a wonderful . . . of apples to show for our pains.
16. He has worked hard all his life, and now he's reaping the . . .
17. He has not made much profit on the rice . . . , since he started.
18. *We* worked and sweated, but *he* reaped the . . .
19. What a wonderful . . . we had that year!

38
ersticken
to suffocate, to stifle, to smother, to choke

to suffocate: If you don't weed the garden soon, the plants will be suffocated.
I smashed the window to prevent us all from suffocating.

Collocations: to be suffocated by smoke/fumes/some unbearable atmosphere; to be suffocated by anxiety/fear/some excitement; to be suffocated with the loss of breath (because of fast running); weeds may suffocate plants; suffocating air.

Durch Verunreinigung der umgebenden Luft ersticken; durch irgendwelche Emotionen das Gefühl des Erstickens verursachen oder empfinden.

To prevent or cause difficulty in breathing by lack of air, due to fumes, gas, smoke, etc.; to cause the sensation of suffocation owing to some kind of excitement (rage, anxiety, grief, etc.) (N.: *suffocation*)

to stifle: The steamy atmosphere nearly stifled me.
It's so hot and smoky, I feel stifled in here. (or: it's suffocating)

Collocations: stifling heat/smoke/atmosphere; to stifle a yawn/a sigh/a groan/a cry, etc.; to stifle the flames/one's grief; to stifle a revolt.

1. wie bei *suffocate* durch Rauch, Dämpfe, bes. Hitze, zu wenig Raum zum Atmen ersticken (jedoch meist mit folgendem Objekt und oft in der ing-Form als attributives Adjektiv);
2. ein Geräusch (Lachen, Schreien, Gähnen, Schluchzen etc.) unterdrücken;
3. im übertragenen Sinne ein Geschehen, eine Entwicklung, Ideen, das Bekanntwerden einer Tatsache etc. unterbinden.

1. to impede respiration by smoke, fumes, heat, too little room for breathing (mostly used as a transitive verb).
2. to prevent the emission of some utterance (laughter, a cry, a yawn, sobs, etc.)
3. to suppress some development, idea, publication of facts, etc.

to smother: He tried to smother her by pressing a cushion down on her face.

Collocations: to smother a person (by covering his face); to smother a fire/a sound; to smother a person with embraces/kisses/presents; to smother (up) a scandal; to be smothered in/with shame.

Behinderung der Atmung oder töten durch Bedecken des ganzen Gesichtes; durch flächenhaftes Zudecken oder Überhäufen mit etwas behindern, einhüllen oder im übertragenen Sinne ersticken. Eine Gefühlsäußerung unterdrücken.

To hamper or stop respiration by covering the whole face. To overwhelm with something; to repress full utterance of a feeling.

to choke: The murderer pressed his hands around his victim's throat and choked him.

The food was so dry, we nearly choked over it.

Collocations: to be choked to death; to choke off a discussion; to choke back (angry words, etc.); to choke over s.th.; to choke (up) some pipe/channel.

Ersticken im Sinne von würgen, erwürgen, das heißt also durch Abschnürung der Luftröhre von außen oder auch durch Versperrung der Luftwege von innen. Das Gefühl der Erstickung kann auch durch seelische Erregung verursacht werden.

To stop respiration by strangling or squeezing from without, by blocking the breathing passages. Also to struggle to breathe due to ırritation, excessive excitement, etc.

Exercise 38 (A) Fill in a suitable term of the above group.

1. The overjoyed mother . . . her baby with kisses.
2. The food went down the wrong way and nearly . . . him.
3. After two hours in his company, I could hardly . . . a yawn.
4. I had to . . . a cry when I saw the huge spider.
5. One way to put out a fire is to . . . it with a blanket.
6. Don't press my windpipe like that; you'll . . . me.
7. Hang this heavy curtain across the door, to . . . the sound.
8. He tried to . . . her, but she prized his hands loose.
9. She left her parents' house, because the atmosphere was . . .
10. Put out that smoky fire, or we shall all be . . .
11. Wet heat is enervating; dry heat is . . .
12. The noose round a condemned murderer's neck is intended to . . . him.
13. . . . by fear, he could hardly speak as he staggered into the room.
14. I heard him approach although he tried to . . . his cough.
15. My tie was so tight that I nearly . . .
16. I tried to . . . my laughter so as not to annoy him.
17. Place a cloth over the end of the trumpet to . . . the sound.
18. With a great effort of will I . . . back my curses.

Exercise 38 (B)

1. The low-lying trees were . . . in dense fog.
2. I felt . . . because I wasn't able to express myself freely.
3. The harsh discipline produced a . . . atmosphere.
4. She . . . back her tears.
5. She nearly . . . the poor little dog with her hugs.
6. Three firemen had to come out for fear of . . .
7. She tried unsuccessfully to . . . her sobs.

8. She was . . . with grief.
9. I could not . . . my grief and let out a low moan.
10. He nearly . . . himself by swallowing a fish-bone.
11. The authorities . . . all criticism relentlessly.
12. A . . . mist arose as we filed through the valley.

39

erwarten

to expect, to look forward to, to await, to anticipate

to expect: I expect you to do your duty.
I did not expect it of him.

Collocations: to expect a visitor / a visit / a letter / a child, etc.; to expect s.o. to do s.th.; beyond expectation; to fall short of s.o.'s expectations; an expectant mother.

Mit etwas rechnen, mit relativer Gewißheit etwas erwarten.

To have good reasons to believe or to think that something will happen. (N.: *expectation*)

to look forward to: We're looking forward to our hiking tour along the south coast next spring.
I'm looking forward to another three years of hard work. (slightly ironical)

Mit angenehmen (zuweilen auch unangenehmen) Empfindungen erwarten, sich auf etwas freuen.

To await something pleasant (sometimes unpleasant).

to await: We sat for our exams last week and now we are awaiting (or waiting for) the results.

Collocations: to await an answer / a reply / the news / s.o.'s instructions, etc.

Abwarten, mit gewisser Geduld auf etwas warten. Das Subjekt kann sich auch auf Dinge oder Abstrakta beziehen, z. B. *A warm welcome awaits you.* (Häufig wird für *await* in der Umgangssprache *wait for* verwendet.)

Often patiently to look for something to happen, to be mentally ready for something to happen. With reference to things or abstract nouns: *to be in store for somebody.*

to anticipate: A good footballer always anticipates a pass before it happens.

Collocations: to anticipate s.th. with pleasure; with pleasant anticipation; in anticipation of s.th. (formal).

Das Herannahen eines Geschehnisses deutlich vor sich sehen, vorausahnen. Häufig wird das gefühlsbetonte Erwarten eines Ereignisses bezeichnet.

To foresee or foretaste the approach of some occurrence, to picture it in one's mind, to realize beforehand. (N.: *anticipation*)

Exercise (39) A Fill in a suitable term of the above group.

1. The children are . . . their holidays.
2. You have made a promise, and I . . . you to keep it.
3. I've been . . . meeting you.
4. A hot meal . . . her when she returned.
5. They are not . . . the encounter at all.
6. Those with great . . . are often disappointed.
7. "Where is your husband?"–"I . . . him home any minute."
8. I . . .ed her phone call with growing impatience.
9. We always used to . . . Christmas.
10. He . . . their action and took the necessary precautions.
11. The prisoner calmly . . . the verdict.
12. "Hallo, *you*'re up early!"–"Yes, I'm . . . a visitor."
13. My partner was . . . me in the hall.
14. She's . . . her party tonight.
15. I waited for her with pleasant . . .
16. He's . . . to win a prize. I'm afraid he's going to be disappointed.
17. Are you . . . your retirement?
18. . . . is sometimes sweeter than actual enjoyment.
19. Now, Jean, I . . . you to behave yourself.
20. You don't seem to be . . . getting married.

Exercise 39 (B)

1. The art of goal-keeping is . . .
2. Mrs. Jones is . . . her third child in June.
3. He . . . her answer with a delicious sense of . . .
4. "Who shall I say called?"–"The man they've been . . ."
5. I wonder what fate . . . him.
6. We respectfully . . . your instructions. (Business letter)
7. A smile of . . . hovered round his lips.
8. I don't really . . . any trouble.
9. Children tend to achieve what they know is . . . of them.
10. The dog's mouth watered in ...

40

erziehen, ausbilden; aufziehen; züchten

to bring up, to rear, to educate, to breed, to train

to bring up: They have brought up their children very well.

Collocations: well/ badly brought up; a strict upbringing.

Kinder (in der Familie) großziehen. (Der üblichste Ausdruck).

To care for in the family until grown-up. The commonest term for what parents do to their children. (N.: *upbringing*)

to rear: They rear chicken(s) for a living.

He was reared amidst squalor and poverty.

Collocations: to rear cattle / poultry / plants.

Im Sinne von Tiere oder Pflanzen züchten gehört *to rear* der Alltagssprache an. Im Sinne von Kinder erziehen wird es ähnlich gebraucht wie *to bring up*, ist jedoch im brit. Englisch weniger häufig als im amerikanischen.

In the sense of *to breed* or *raise* animals or crops it is a term of everyday English. Used in the sense of *to bring up* children, however, it has an American flavour and is less usual in British English, even a bit old-fashioned.

to educate: It is the task of teachers to educate children.

Collocations: to be educated at school / university, etc.; to educate s.o. for s.th. or to do s.th.; an educated person.

Durch Unterricht und Erziehung (oder durch Erfahrung) die geistig-sittlichen Anlagen des Menschen ausbilden.

To develop, bring out the intellectual and moral powers of a person by instructions, teaching, or experience. (N.: *education*)

to breed: Some farmers specialize in cattle breeding.

Collocations: to breed sheep / dogs, etc.; selective breeding; a well-bred / ill-bred man; bad breeding (= schlechte Manieren).

Tiere (bes. Rassen, Sorten) züchten. (*Rear* hingegen bedeutet lediglich soviel wie die Tiere versorgen und großziehen.) *Breeding* bezieht sich auf die Tätigkeit eines ausgebildeten Züchters, während *rear* mit Bezug auf einfache Tierhaltung verwendet wird. – In bezug auf Menschen: vor allem hinsichtlich der Umgangsformen und im Einklang mit den gegebenen Traditionen „erzogen sein".

To raise livestock. *Breed* indicates the process of reproduction und usually improvement thereby. (Whereas *rear* is simply to look after animals and to bring to satisfactory maturity.) Breeding is done by a skilled breeder, whereas a mere cattleman rears the cattle.
To cultivate someone's manners in accordance with tradition; sometimes in the sense of to prepare for some career by education and instruction. (N.: *breed*)

to train: He is a trained teacher of languages.

Collocations: to train soldiers / a child to do s.th. / an athlete or sportsman; to train a dog; to train for some competition; fully / well-trained; a trained teacher / nurse, etc.

Zu einem bestimmten Leistungsniveau hinführen, in der Anlage vorhandene Fähigkeiten weiterentwickeln. Mit Bezug auf Mensch und Tier gebraucht.

To bring a person or animal to some desired level of efficiency, to further develop powers that already exist. (N.: *training*)

Exercise 40 (A) Fill in a suitable term of the above group.

1. She . . . her children under difficult circumstances.
2. The wealthy send their sons to public schools to be . . .
3. You can always tell a well-. . . man by his manners.

4. . . . sheep develops the leg muscles.
5. But . . . cattle requires much less walking.
6. He . . . the finest cattle in the country.
7. To watch him act is an . . . in itself.
8. The herd has been improved by selective . . .
9. He was . . . in the countryside.
10. He's remarkably arrogant for an . . . man.
11. The soldiers had six hours hard . . . per day.
12. It was once thought dangerous to . . . the masses.
13. What . . . of sheep are they?
14. She was . . . by her grandparents.
15. It takes three years to . . . a teacher.
16. The worst housewife . . . the best pigs. (old saying)
17. . . . is more than mere learning by rote.
18. I'm trying to . . . my dog to jump fences.
19. Robert Bakewell was famous for . . . Leicester Shorthorns, a new . . . of sheep.
20. You have . . . your children to be a credit to you, Mrs. Jones.

Exercise 40 (B)

1. Foster parents often make a good job of . . . their charges.
2. I . . . the bird from a chick.
3. Familiarity . . . contempt. (old saying)
4. Dog . . . abound in England. We are a nation of dog lovers.
5. My little daughter took over the . . . of the puppy.
6. She is . . . to be a nurse.
7. One look at him and I could tell the . . .! (pejorative)
8. We were . . . to stand life's harshness.
9. "Where were you . . .?"–"At a teachers' . . . college."
10. He was . . . under heartbreaking conditions.

41
fähig
able, capable, apt

able: He is an able minister.

Collocations: an able mathematician / doctor/student, etc; able-bodied (= körperlich leistungsfähig, kerngesund).

Bei attributivem Gebrauch bezeichnet *able* deutlich über dem Durchschnitt liegende Fähigkeiten, Veranlagung, meisterhaftes Können. Es bezieht sich auf weiter gefaßte, gehobenere Fähigkeiten als *capable.* (Bei prädikativem Gebrauch bezieht sich *able* auf das bloße Vermögen = in der Lage sein etwas zu tun.)

Used attributively: to be talented in a conspicuous way, to have unusual intellectual qualifications, the power for outstanding practical performance. It suggests broader and more elevated abilities than *capable.* (Used predicatively it merely suggests skill, power to do something.) (N.: *ability*)

capable: He is a capable craftsman; he'll tackle any job and do it well.
He has proved himself capable of doing difficult translations.

Collocations: a capable nurse/teacher/doctor/housewife, etc.; to have great capabilities; to be capable of doing s.th.

Gut veranlagt zur Erfüllung üblicher Anforderungen; tüchtig (ähnlich *able* aber i. allg. auf etwas niedrigerer, einfacherer Stufe, z. B. Fleiß, Findigkeit, allg. Leistungsvermögen). *Capable* of s.th.: imstande sein zu etwas (auch im negativen Sinne).

Capable implies the fulfilment of more ordinary demands and requirements than *able* (such as diligence, resourcefulness, efficiency, etc.). *Capable of anything* denotes the fitness for doing anything (from good to bad, evil, or even vicious). (N.: *capability*)

apt: An apt student learns easily and quickly.

Collocations: an apt child/pupil, etc.; to be apt at doing things (learning languages, devising new machines, methods, etc.)

Über eine rasche Auffassungsgabe verfügend, befähigt, scharfsinnig. *Aptitude* impliziert eine Neigung in eine bestimmte Richtung und wird gern näher bestimmt, z. B. *aptitude for woodwork.*

Quick to learn, quick-witted; skilful. *Aptitude* is a leaning (in a certain direction) perhaps a liking for something. It tends to be specific, e.g. an *aptitude for woodwork,* i.e. a fitness, natural propensity, whereas *ability/capability* are more general. (N.: *aptitude* or *aptness*)

Exercise 41 (A) Fill in a suitable term of the above group.

1. He picks up things quickly. He's an ... pupil.
2. My mother was a very ... housewife.
3. I was operated on by a very ... surgeon.
4. The work has clearly been done by very ... bricklayers.
5. Mr. Jones is an ... administrator.
6. She proved a ... cook.
7. I am not very ... at mathematics.
8. Our butcher is a very ... businessman.
9. She was not ... to overcome her difficulties.
10. Those decorators were not very ... workmen.
11. He has the ... alright; but has he the temperament?
12. Intellectual ... is no guarantee for practical ...
13. Einstein was one of the most ... thinkers of our age.
14. George Washington, they say, wasn't ... of telling a lie.
15. I didn't think you ... of such a despicable act.
16. "Have you really tried?"–"Well, I've done it to the best of my ..."
17. She is ... at understanding difficult problems.
18. She may only be nine, but she's quite ... washing the dishes.
19. To succeed as a manager you have to be an ... organiser.
20. "Did he break it?"–"I wouldn't put it past him. He's ... anything."

Exercise 41 (B)

1. There are various ways of testing . . . for mechanical work.
2. Teachers are now challenging the old idea of fixed . . . in children.
3. You may be . . . in one subject, but not necessarily in others.
4. He is an . . . punster, but not a real wit.
5. Your . . . at cards will never win you a fortune.
6. ". . . was I ere I saw Elba." (palindrome attributed to Napoleon)
7. They are far too . . . picking up bad habits.
8. His . . . for lengthy sermons drove his friends away.
9. Your assistant may have been . . . , but he was dishonest.
10. She is . . . mimicking her elders.

42

fahren, reisen
to drive, to ride, to travel, to go

to drive: She drove her Jaguar into the garage.
If you do not drive carefully, you may get into trouble.

Collocations: To drive a car/lorry/van/coach/horse and cart/tram; to drive carelessly/carefully; to drive away/back/off; to go for a drive; to have/take a drive; a driving-licence; a driving-instructor.

Ein Fahrzeug fahren (=steuern). *Drive* wird gewöhnlich transitiv verwendet. Es kann jedoch auch gebraucht werden, wenn das Objekt nicht genannt wird.

To act as the driver of a car (or train). The term is mainly used transitively. It may also be used where the object is unspoken. (N.: *a drive*)

to ride: When I saw him, he was riding his bicycle. Do you wish to walk or ride? Shall we ride home on a bus? Did you enjoy your ride in his new car? I sometimes ride in a taxi.

Collocations: to ride a bicycle/motorcycle; to ride in a train/car/tram, etc.; a tram/bus/car ride.

In einem (öffentlichen) Verkehrsmittel fahren; Fahrrad, Motorrad fahren; als Fahrgast fahren.

To be carried along in any kind of (public) conveyance (without being the driver); to travel on a bike. (N.: *a ride*)

to travel: We shall travel from Edinburgh to Blair Atholl by coach or by train.
His car was travelling at 70 miles per hour when he lost control of it.

Collocations: to travel by boat/rail, etc.; to travel slowly/fast/first class/at . . . m.p.h.; to travel in great style.

Fahren, reisen, sich von einem Ort zum andern fortbewegen; sich auf bestimmte Weise fortbewegen.

To move from one place to another; to move or go in some specified manner, at some specified speed, etc.

to go: Will you go by steamer or by plane?
Where are you going?
We were going fast when we noticed a roadblock in front of us.
Collocations: to go by bus/train/rail/tram/air/taxi, etc.
Der allgemeine Ausdruck für fahren; entweder ohne Zusatz oder mit folgender Angabe des benutzten Verkehrsmittels.
The general term. It is used either without or with indication of the means of conveyance.

Note the following sentences:
Take me to Piccadilly Circus, please. (=Fahren Sie mich zum . . .)
He gave me a lift. (=Er hat mich mit seinem Auto mitgenommen.)
When does the train leave? (=Wann fährt der Zug?)
The train only runs on Sundays. (=Der Zug fährt nur sonntags.)
The Queen Elizabeth is bound for New York. (=Die Q. E. fährt nach N. Y.)
The steamer sails between Rostock and Hull. (=Das Schiff verkehrt zwischen . . .)

Exercise 42 (A) Fill in a suitable term of the above group.

1. We . . . along on the crest of the wave. (also fig. meaning)
2. Where did you . . . for your holidays?
3. . . . broadens the mind.
4. If you . . . too fast, you'll be fined.
5. The train . . . saw the signal just in time.
6. What speed were you . . . at?
7. I like to . . . in front, beside the driver.
8. I . . . to Italy last year.
9. . . . should be considerate to pedestrians.
10. We had a lovely coach-. . . into the country.
11. We shall . . . by boat and train.
12. I was sick when we . . . to London.
13. I'll . . . , I'm sure you're tired after your journey.
14. We . . . from the station to the airport in 20 minutes.
15. In our local pageant I . . . on a float.
16. I took her for a . . . along the front. (The passenger might say: I went for a . . . with him.)
17. Please . . . into town and buy me a packet of cigarettes.
18. You'll have to . . . far to find a better view than this.
19. ". . . carefully–We love our children." (sign outside an American town)
20. Can you . . . a bicycle?
21. My wife went for a . . . test yesterday.
22. They were . . . in great style, on the back seat of a Rolls Royce.
23. She passed and obtained her . . . licence.
24. A sleigh-. . . is very enjoyable.
25. The taxi driver . . . slowly so that I could see the sights.

43
fehlen
to want, to lack, to be absent, to be missing

to want: She wants three years for her pension.
He is wanting in experience.
Collocations: to be in want of; want for nothing (He wanted for nothing = Es fehlte ihm an nichts.); to be tried in the balance and found wanting.

Mangel haben an etwas oder eine Sache völlig entbehren. *Want* wird gewöhnlich in der Verlaufsform des Präsens gebraucht, wenn es von der Präposition *in* gefolgt wird. *Want* klingt zuweilen ein wenig altmodisch.

To be short of something or to be without something. *Want* is normally used in present progressive tense, especially when used with *in* (but not with *of* or *for*). *Want* (used in this sense) sometimes has a somewhat old-fashioned ring about it. (N.: *want*)

to lack: The only thing he lacks is patience.
They are lacking in practice.
The house lacks central heating.
Collocations: to be lacking in s.th.; to lack s.th.; a lack of s.th.; for lack of; no lack of; lack-lustre.

Bezeichnet (gleich *want*) entweder den völligen Mangel oder die Knappheit an etwas.

Similar to *want* it suggests 'to be in short supply of something or not to have'. (N.: *lack*)

to be absent: She was absent from school because she was ill.
Collocations: absent without leave; (to drink to) absent friends.

Abwesend sein (vor allem mit Bezug auf Personen).

Not to be present (chiefly used of persons). (N.: *absence*)

to be missing: There are some pages missing in the dictionary.
Collocations: missing persons (police expression); reported missing; the dead and missing (military expression).

An der Vollständigkeit fehlen (von Personen und Dingen), etwas vermissen.

Used of persons and things: what is lacking to make something complete; what one does not find in its place.

Exercise 43 (A) Fill in a suitable term of the above group.

1. All that he . . . is a little education.
2. All her jewels were . . .
3. How many children are . . . this morning?
4. There was an . . . of warmth in his character.
5. The . . . man turned up unexpectedly.
6. There is no . . . of rain in the tropics.

7. He certainly did not . . . courage.
8. If John weren't . . . , the whole family would have been there.
9. Where have you been? You've been . . . for a long time.
10. There's a book . . . from this shelf.
11. She is pretty, but she . . . charm.
12. They were . . . when we assembled for the journey.
13. Where's the dog? He's been . . . for days.
14. There was a complete . . . of inhibitions among the children.
15. She was . . . from home when the burglary occurred.
16. The plant died through . . . of moisture.
17. Three soldiers were . . . without leave.
18. I think your behaviour is . . . in courtesy.
19. They died in thousands through . . . of nourishment.
20. If you are in . . . of anything, just let me know.

Exercise 43 (B)

1. They were tried in the balance and found . . .
2. The . . . of any explanation was annoying, to say the least.
3. It . . . just one more provocation to put him in a rage.
4. He is . . . in a little tact.
5. I'm going to desert. When they call the roll, I'll be . . .
6. I . . . an interesting companion with whom I could chatter.
7. Have a good look round and tell me what is . . .
8. I've examined their equipment; they have everything, there's nothing . . .
9. Oh, he's well off. He doesn't . . . for anything.
10. She will see to it that we do not . . . for anything.

44
Fehler
mistake, error, blunder, slip, fault, failing, flaw

mistake: How many mistakes did you make in the examination?

It is a mistake to be too modest in your demands.

Collocations: to make a mistake; by mistake (=aus Versehen); and no mistake (i.e. without the slightest doubt); a slight/bad/serious/silly mistake.

Der Fehler im Denken und Handeln, der Mißgriff, Irrtum

An error in thought or action, a wrong decision. (V.: *to mistake*)

error: I've spotted a number of errors in your work.

You have to allow a margin of error in your calculation.

Collocations: to make an error (in one's calculations); to avoid an error; to be (or to stand) in error; an error of judgement; an error of observation.

An error ist das Gleiche wie *a mistake*, jedoch ist *error* gewählter als *mistake* und wird nicht so häufig gebraucht wie letzteres. Darüber hinaus kann *error* aber auch eine moralische Kategorie bezeichnen: *the errors of one's youth* (=Verirrungen). Hier wäre *mistake* unmöglich.

An *error* is the same as a *mistake.* It is, however, a slightly formal term and not so often used as *mistake. Error* can also adopt a moral quality: e.g. *the errors of one's youth. Mistake* would be impossible here. (V.: to *err*)

blunder: You've operated on the wrong man! What a blunder!

Ein schwerer Fehler, der aus Fahrlässigkeit oder Dummheit gemacht wird.

A bad or stupid mistake. (V.: *to blunder*)

slip: That was only a minor slip.
You've made a slip in this sum.

Collocations: a slip of the tongue/of the pen.

Ein kleines Versehen, ein kleiner Fehler, der aus mangelnder Konzentration oder Unachtsamkeit begangen wird. Ein "Ausrutscher".

A small, careless mistake.

fault: The accident was his fault: he wasn't looking where he was going.
Great men have great faults.

Collocations: to find fault with; with all his faults (=bei all seinen Fehlern); whose fault is it? (=wessen Schuld ist es?); to be at fault (=sich irren).

Fehler im Sinne von Schuld, Verschulden oder Vergehen; der in der Natur der Sache oder Person liegende Fehler oder Mangel.

Fault may imply either the responsibility for something wrong or it may refer to some natural imperfection in persons or things.

failing: Unpunctuality can be a serious failing.
It is surprising how readily one can excuse one's own failings.

Die Fehler, (verzeihlichen) Schwächen des Menschen, die in ihm von Natur aus liegen und deren man sich u. U. gar nicht voll bewußt ist. *Failing* ist ein milderer Ausdruck als *fault.*

A weakness of character, shortcoming, or imperfection in a person that may be pardoned. *Failing* often suggests that one is not entirely responsible for the fault.

flaw: I noticed a flaw in the china plate.
You may point out the flaws in my scheme, but have you a better one?
The work of art was flawless.

Collocations: a flaw in a jewel/in an argument/in s.o.'s character

Der Materialfehler, z. B. ein Sprung oder Riß; der Fehler in der Struktur einer Sache; der (Form)Fehler, der die Rechtskräftigkeit eines Dokumentes beeinträchtigt.

A defect in quality caused by imperfect structure; a weak spot of any kind, as a fissure or crack. A defect which diminishes the validity of a document or the like.

Exercise 44 (A) Fill in a suitable term of the above group.

1. We all have our little . . . , don't we?
2. I noticed a tiny . . . in the pattern.
3. It is not my . . . that this instrument doesn't function.
4. You are always finding . . . with people.
5. You've made a . . . in this sum. (a small, careless mistake is meant)
6. He must have been drunk to make such a . . .
7. It is amazing how many . . . they make, even when they're copying.
8. Laziness is no . . . of mine.
9. I can't accept this report; it's simply full of . . .
10. His behaviour was . . .
11. The cleverest people have their little . . . .
12. To . . . is human; to forgive divine. (saying)
13. You must pay for your . . .
14. The biggest . . . was to trust him.
15. Even his . . . endeared him to us.
16. Some . . . can be rectified; others can't.
17. You . . .ing fool! You've ruined everything!
18. He will replace any cloth which has a . . . in it.
19. You keep making the same . . . It must be psychological.
20. A flea and a fly were imprisoned in a flue.
    Said the flea: "Let us fly";
    Said the fly: "Let us flee".
    So they flew through a . . . in the flue. (old rhyme)

Exercise 44 (B)

1. You must always allow for human . . .
2. She is generous to a . . .
3. The cleverest people are at . . . sometimes.
4. If everything works so well, where is the . . . in his theory?
5. If you think I'm going to put up with this, you are . . .
6. It is the . . . of others that are so irritating.
7. It is an . . . to think that money can buy happiness.
8. You can lay the . . . at my door, if you like.
9. There is a . . . in this document which renders it valueless.
10. In war . . . cost lives.

45
Fest
feast, festival, festivity, fête

feast: She was a wonderful cook, and made every meal a feast.
The music and the dancing provided a feast for the senses.
Collocations: the feast of Resurrection; the feast of Passover; the Chinese feast of lanterns; feast days; to feast one's eyes on s.th. (=to

look with enjoyment at); an (im)movable feast; to feast s.o. (i.e. to wine and dine s.o.); to feast on s.th. (i.e. to have a specially good meal).

Ein üppiges Mahl; im übertragenen Sinne ein Hochgenuß für Intellekt oder Sinne; ein (jährlich wiederkehrendes) religiöses Fest. Man verwende *feast* nicht in der alltäglichen Unterhaltung, außer z. B. einem Priester gegenüber oder in einer ernsthaften Diskussion über religiöse Fragen.

A grand meal; any delight to intellect or emotions. A (periodical) religious celebration. Don't use *feast* in ordinary conversation, unless you are talking to, say, a priest or official or having a serious religious conversation.
Note that without the specific name the *feasts* are called *festivals*, e.g., *What festival are you celebrating?* But: *The feast of Passover.* (V.: *to feast*)

festival: Religious festivals are celebrated throughout the year.
The Eisteddfod is a Welsh festival of song, music and poetry.

Collocations: a national festival; a harvest festival; a music festival; a festival committee; a family festival; the festival of Christmas; religious festivals.

Eine weltliche Festlichkeit, besonders musikalischer, sportlicher Natur; auch für religiöse Feste gebraucht, betont aber weniger die streng kirchliche Art des Feierns als vielmehr die weltlich volkstümliche.

An occasion of public, sometimes private, joyful celebration esp. with regard to music, sports, etc.; but also for religious feasts (it suggests, however, the popular character of celebration rather than the religious).

festivity: He is the one who organises all our family festivities.

Collocations: a festive occasion.

Festlichkeit, festliches Treiben; Feststimmung.

Any kind of rejoicing or gaiety. *Festivity* suggests activity. (Adj.: *festive*)

fête (or **fete**): We all enjoyed the fête, and it raised £ 20 for the school funds.
Volunteer carpenters set up stands for the charity fête.

Collocations: garden fête, school fête; church fête; charity fête.

Heute gewöhnlich im Sinne von Wohltätigkeitsveranstaltung gebraucht, die meist im Freien durchgeführt wird. Darüber hinaus auch (Garten-, Familien-) Fest.

A festive entertainment, usually for charitable purposes and out of doors, if weather permits. (V.: *to fête*)

Exercise 45 (A) Fill in a suitable term of the above group.

1. The harvest . . . follows the harvest.
2. Our garden . . . was ruined by bad weather.
3. After the hectic days of the . . . life resumed its humdrum routine.
4. H'm, sausage and mashed potatoes–hardly a . . .
5. Our play group is holding a . . . in the grounds, to raise money.
6. And who is going to pay for all this . . .?

7. We are putting on a . . . of music, dance and drama.
8. The . . . of Passover commemorates an authentic, historic occasion.
9. We attended several shows during the . . .
10. My stomach was upset for days after the . . .
11. The vicar opened the . . . by releasing balloons.
12. She had decorated the table and made it look most . . .
13. When the . . . was at its height, he flung open the door dramatically.
14. Our local sports . . . was rained off this year.
15. A wonderful . . . was spread out before us.
16. The Brighton . . . lasts two weeks. It includes music, drama, films, etc.
17. Christmas . . . seem to begin earlier and earlier each year.
18. Don't forget your routine tasks amid the . . .
19. . . . committees sprang up overnight, when we heard the news.
20. And what do you wear on . . . occasions?

Exercise 45 (B)

1. He . . .ed me well last year and now I must return the compliment.
2. Would you care to run a stall at our church . . .?
3. After the fast comes the . . .
4. What . . . are you planning when your prodigal son returns?
5. It is . . . time in the city just now.
6. He . . . his eyes on the beautiful girl sitting opposite.
7. They . . . their visitor until they discovered that he was a fake.
8. The club . . . was opened by a film star.
9. Our . . . were interrupted by a loud clap of thunder.
10. I'd like to hold a . . . for the old age pensioners.

46
fest
fast, fixed, firm, solid, steady

fast: The door is shut fast.

The ship has stuck fast in the mud.

Collocations: to make a knot fast; fast friends/friendship; fast asleep; (bus-conductor to standing passengers:) hold fast; fast colour.

Unbeweglich, gut befestigt, nicht lose; auch im übertragenen Sinne gebraucht.

Unmovable, not loose, securely attached, tied; permanent, lasting. (N.: *fastness*)

fixed: He gets a fixed salary.

He stared fixedly at her.

Collocations: a fixed sum/intention; fixed prices; a fixed star; a fixed idea; fixed landing gear.

Festgelegt; starr, nicht wechselnd; unveränderlich.

Permanently placed, not subject to change; not changeable; not changing, not moving. (V.: *to fix*)

firm: To ensure a firm foundation, you must first dig a deep pit.
The jelly has not set firm yet.

Collocations: firm foundations (of a building); a firm voice / hand / grip / promise / decision / conviction / intention; firm principles/friends, etc.; to have a firm grasp of s.th.

Von solider Substanz oder Struktur; nicht schwankend; unwandelbar, unbeugsam.

Of a comparatively solid substance or structure; not shaking; unalterable (in belief, etc.), determined. (N.: *firmness*)

solid: The lake has frozen solid.
Have you any really solid reasons for refusing my offer?

Collocations: a solid structure / foundation / ground; a solid constitution / alliance; solid reasons; a solid body (i.e. neither liquid nor gaseous; with reference to human body = a healthy, strong body); solid particles (in a liquid substance); a solid fabric.

Hart, fest, stabil, solid; zuverlässig, dauerhaft; fester Aggregatzustand; nicht hohl, gediegen.

Of stable shape, well grounded; compact or hard in substance; opposite to hollow; also in the sense of reliable. (N.: *solidity*)

steady: That chair isn't steady. One of its legs is broken.
After the illness, I wasn't steady on my legs for some time.

Collocations: a steady chair / table / shelf / ladder; steady prices; a steady job; a steady boy (or girl) friend; to be steady (or unsteady) on one's legs; going steady (i.e. with a view to marriage).

Das Gleichgewicht wahrend, fest auf den Beinen stehend; zuverlässig gleichbleibend.

Not to lose equilibrium, well balanced; constant in conduct or mind.

Exercise 46 (A) Fill in a suitable term of the above group.

1. We have been . . . friends for years.
2. The post was fixed . . . in the ground.
3. Prices have not remained . . . since the war.
4. Make the door . . . before you leave the house.
5. The rope held me . . . I couldn't move an inch.
6. He's over eighty, but he still has a . . . grip.
7. Tie up the boat. Make it . . . to the jetty.
8. You can't bargain with *them.* They have . . . prices.
9. You made a . . . promise–and you broke it.
10. Why don't you get yourself a . . . job? You're always changing.
11. As soon as he had eaten he fell . . . asleep.
12. That was quite a . . . agreement and I intend to act upon it.
13. Is your daughter going . . . with that boy?
14. The Pole Star is the only one which appears to us to be . . .

15. I tried to take my hand away, but he held it . . .
16. "Are you sure this material is . . . colour?"–"Oh, yes, madam."
17. His voice was friendly but . . .
18. "Is that hollow?"–"No, it's . . ."
19. One must be loving but . . . with children.
20. He may look thin, but he's . . . muscle. (or: but he's all . . . m.)

Exercise 46 (B)

1. Instant coffee is made of "soluble . . . of pure coffee".
2. I've had this idea . . . in my mind for quite some time.
3. Now take a . . . hold of yourself, I've got some unpleasant news for you.
4. The temperature in this room has remained . . . all day.
5. It's a prefabricated construction, but it looks very . . .
6. They tried to argue us out of it, but we stood . . .
7. He used to be most untrustworthy, but he's become a . . . citizen.
8. Hold . . . there; we're about to move off.
9. He . . . them with his glittering eyes.
10. It is my . . . intention to get married before I'm thirty.

47
Fleck
spot, speck, patch, blot, stain

spot: I'd rather have the tie with the yellow spots.

Collocations: a spot of rust / paint / grease; a sun spot.

(Schmutz, Rost, Farb etc.)-Fleck; Farbtupfen; Makel, Stelle.

A mark caused by some substance, such as dirt, mud, rust, colour, grease, etc.; a dot, a blemish; a locality. (Adj.: *spotted, spotty*)

speck: A tiny speck of dirt got into my eyes.

The ant looked like a tiny brown speck on the grass.

Collocations: a speck of light / dirt.

Ein kleiner Fleck, ein Pünktchen; ein kleines oder winziges Teilchen einer Substanz.

A tiny spot; a particle of some substance. (Adj.: *speckled*)

patch: The large oily patch on the sea gradually spread, as the tanker broke up.

She sewed a patch on his trousers.

Collocations: a cabbage patch; an eye patch / a patch over one eye; patch-pockets; cloud patches.

Ein relativ großer, unregelmäßiger Fleck; ein Stück Material (Stoff, Metall, Gummi etc.), das zur Ausbesserung eines Loches oder zur Verstärkung einer schwachen Stelle, zur Bedeckung einer Wunde etc. verwendet wird; ein kleines Stück Land.

A relatively large or irregular area on some surface; a piece of material (cloth, metal, rubber, etc.) used to mend a hole, strengthen a weak spot, protect a wound, an eye, etc.; a piece of ground. (Adj.: *patched, patchy*; V.: *to patch*)

blot: Write this exercise out again. There are blots all over it!

Collocations: to make a blot; a blot of ink; a blot on one's character / on one's escutcheon; to blot one's copybook; to blot s.th. out (i.e. destroy it).

Klecks; charakterlicher Makel.

A (dark) spot (of ink, etc.) spoiling the surface; moral blemish. (Adj.: *blotted*; V.: *to blot*)

stain: Coffee-stains are difficult to remove.

Collocations: a blood-stain; a tea-stain, etc.; stain-remover; a stain on one's reputation; stainless steel; stained-glass (in a church).

Schmutz-, Farbfleck (gewöhnlich durch verschüttete Flüssigkeit, Abfärben etc.); farbig; Makel ernsterer Art.

A mark of colour caused by contact with, or absorption of, foreign matter; a grave blemish on a person's character or reputation. (Adj.: *stained*; *stainless*; V.: *to stain*)

Exercise 47 (A) Fill in a suitable term of the above group.

1. We picnicked in a very pleasant . . . beside the lake.
2. (Customer, at the cleaner's:) Can you remove this . . .?
3. The cow had black . . . on its face and rump.
4. You've made a . . . on your letter.
5. There's a tea-. . . on the table-cloth.
6. The cat had got a large brown . . . on its back.
7. A . . . of dust on the lens impaired the quality of the photo.
8. A monument marks the . . . where the general was wounded.
9. A large, ugly . . . spread halfway across the paper.
10. A tiny . . . of blood on his shirt betrayed him.
11. Sometimes washing removes . . . better than cleaning.
12. A . . . of dirt on the cloth does no harm.
13. The blood-. . . led us to the murderer.
14. What you have done is a . . . on the family escutcheon.
15. I've tried several . . .-removers on it, but without success.
16. When I'm bilious, I see . . . before my eyes.
17. This is just the . . . I should choose for my retirement.
18. The . . .ed hen was a good layer.
19. The garment was covered with small grease . . .
20. His rear light gradually became a . . . of red receding in the distance.

Exercise 47 (B)

1. The curtain was badly . . .ed.
2. In adolescence, a boy's face becomes . . .
3. His arm was . . . with tiny pin-points of blood.

4. The layman often refers to dalmatians as . . . dogs.
5. The tramp's clothes were all . . . and ragged.
6. You leave this court without a . . . on your character.
7. "Look at the mud on your skirt!"–"Oh, it's only a . . ."
8. There's nothing left of your jacket; it's all . . .
9. I can't write with this pen, it . . .
10. Some modern fabrics just don't . . .

48
Fleisch
flesh, meat

flesh: He is lean; he has hardly any flesh on his bones.
The spirit is willing, but the flesh is weak. (saying)
The lion is a flesh-eating animal.

Collocations: a flesh-wound; flesh-coloured stockings; one's own flesh and blood; weakness of the flesh; more than human flesh can / will bear; the flesh-pots (i.e. a place supplying good food and material comfort); to gain (or put on)/to lose flesh.

Fleisch als Substanz des menschlichen oder tierischen Körpers, das lebende Fleisch; im übertragenen Sinne das Fleisch im Gegensatz zum Geist, die menschliche Natur.

The soft part of the body of an animal or a human being; human nature with its weaknesses or the body as opposed to spirit or soul.

meat: The meat we were served for dinner was excellent.

Collocations: raw / roast / boiled / fresh / tough / tender / frozen meat; the meat course (in a meal).

Tierisches Fleisch als Nahrung für den Menschen.

Animal flesh for human consumption.

Exercise 48 (A) Fill in a suitable term of the above group.
1. The wound went deep into his . . .
2. To think that my own . . . and blood should turn against me!
3. During the war restaurants had . . . less days, as . . . was rationed.
4. I must have . . . , at least once a day.
5. You'll have to feed him up; he's losing . . .
6. We all received a weekly ration of . . .
7. He needs exercise; his . . . is flabby.
8. The waiter brought on the . . . course.
9. The . . . was tender but the vegetables were hard cooked.
10. I once ate elephant-. . . , in Africa, when there was nothing else.
11. We were delighted to return to the . . .-pots of civilisation.
12. I've had enough! It's more then human . . . can stand!
13. Whale-. . . was popular during the war.

14. Would you like the . . . well done or underdone?
15. His . . . was all wasted by the disease.
16. I don't condemn them for weaknesses of the . . . We've all got them.
17. Her . . . quivered at his touch.
18. He's one of the best judges of horse . . . in the county.

49
Frau
woman, wife, lady, madam

woman: Women are playing a greater role in public life.

Collocations: a single/married woman; a pretty/plain-looking/ugly woman; a woman-hater; women's page (in a paper); women's wiles; woman-of-the-world.

Die Frau ganz allgemein (im Gegensatz zum Mann).

An adult female.

wife: I should like to make her my wife.

Collocations: man and wife; to take s.o. as one's wife.

Die Ehefrau.

A married woman, esp. in relation to her husband.

lady: May I introduce this lady to you?
She always behaved like a perfect lady.

Collocations: Ladies and Gentlemen! a perfect lady; a ladies' man (i.e. he gets on well with the ladies).

Ein gewählter Ausdruck für Frau; eine Dame (entsprechend *gentleman*); eine Frau gehobener oder vornehmer sozialer Herkunft.

A courteous term for woman (corresponding to gentleman); a woman of high social standing or refinement of education or behaviour. Also polite and old-fashioned form of wife.

madam: What can I do for you, madam?

Eine höfliche Form der Anrede für jede Frau.

A polite form of address to any woman.

Exercise 49 (A) Fill in a suitable term of the above group.
1. (Shop assistant:) That one certainly suits you, . . .
2. What beautiful manners! You can see she's a . . .
3. Many . . . took part in the demonstration.
4. He loved his . . . dearly.
5. Dear . . . We received your letter . . . . . .
6. Does this belong to you, . . .
7. My mother always warned me to beware of . . .'s wiles.
8. . . . have been struggling for equality for centuries.

9. *She*'s no . . .! (But, presumably, she certainly *is* a woman!)
10. "Where is the shoe department, please?"–"Over here, . . ."
11. Husband and . . . had long been estranged.
12. . . . is a mysterious species.
13. A man should listen to his . . .'s advice–and then do what *he* wants.
14. Some . . . have a way with them.
15. Which of you . . . was first in the queue?
16. My . . . cooks the meals and I wash up.
17. She is a very attractive . . .
18. Here's your breakfast, . . .
19. Has any . . . lost this article?
20. (Auctioneer:) Sold, to the . . . on my right.
21. At what stage does a girl become a . . .?
22. Until recently a . . . was not legally equal to her husband.
23. . . . Luck was not on my side last night, and I lost heavily.
24. We shall send you a receipt, . . .
25. She looked like a . . ., but she swore like a fishwife.
26. "I now pronounce you man and . . ." (end of marriage service)
27. Dear Sir or . . ., We should like to call your attention to . . . . . .
28. "Will you be my . . .?"

50
frei
free, liberal, vacant, disengaged, spare

free: After three months of imprisonment he is free again.
The bathroom is free (or vacant).
Collocations: of my own free will; a free moment; free time; a free hand-out; a free sample (for advertising purposes); free of charge; free of tax (or duty free); to give s.o. a free hand; to make free (i.e. to take liberties); a free-thinker (i.e. atheist); a free agent (i.e. independent).
Frei sein von Einengung, Bindung, Zwang oder Behinderung, Bewegungsfreiheit genießen; nicht mit Kosten verbunden.
Not subject to constraint or confinement; to enjoy liberty/freedom of action; provided without payment. (N.: *freedom*)

liberal: I approve of his liberal views.
Don't be so liberal/free with money, or people will take advantage of you.
Collocations: a liberal thinker; a liberal education/interpretation; a liberal helping (of food, etc.)/supply; liberal (or free) with one's money; the liberal arts/professions; liberal-minded; of liberal proportions (i.e. big, fat).
Frei von Engherzigkeit, Voreingenommenheit; freimütig; tolerant, großzügig; freigebig.

to be free from narrowmindedness, prejudice; to be tolerant, favourable to change or reform; to be generous; plentiful. (N.: *liberality*)

vacant: The post of managing director is still vacant.

There are still two rooms vacant at the hotel.

Can you see any vacant space in the car park?

Collocations: a vacant chair / apartment / house / plot / site; a vacant professorship; a vacant expression / smile.

Frei im Sinne von keinen Besitzer, Inhaber haben; unbesetzt sein; leer.

Not having an occupant, tenant, owner; empty. (N.: *vacancy*)

disengaged: I'll be disengaged this afternoon.

Keep yourself disengaged for the next few days.

Collocations: to disengage a gear (of a car).

Mit Bezug auf Personen: unbeschäftigt sein; mit Bezug auf Dinge: nicht benutzt werden (Telefon etc.). *Disengaged* gehört zuweilen einer gehobenen Stilebene an.

With reference to persons: to be free from engagement; disentangled; disconnection (in some senses). It can be used as a formal term. (V.: *to disengage*)

spare: I've had no spare time to attend to my hobbies for ages.

Collocations: spare hours/moment / money; no time / not a moment to spare; spare room / tyre / parts.

Frei im Sinne von zusätzlich; zur freien Verwendung, in Reserve haben.

Being surplus, in excess of what is required, kept in reserve for use.

Note:

Can I have a day off tomorrow?

May I have this afternoon off?

Exercise 50 (A) Fill in a suitable term of the above group.

1. The chair in History has been . . . for some time.
2. A certain amount of goods are allowed in, duty . . .
3. You can do it exactly as you like; you have a completely . . . hand.
4. The front room was completely . . .
5. You can sleep in the . . . room tonight.
6. He has a very . . . attitude and is opposed to all censorship.
7. I keep phoning him, but he's never . . .
8. Sorry, madam, not one of our rooms is . . .
9. My children have all had a . . . education.
10. I have hardly any . . . time these days.
11. They're giving away . . . samples to advertise the product.
12. The Arts faculty is so called because it provides courses in the . . . arts.
13. It was difficult to find a . . . building site.
14. I reported to the police of my own . . . will.
15. Quick! Phone the doctor. There's not a moment to . . .
16. His . . . views did not extend to foreigners.
17. "I've torn my stockings."–"Here's a . . . pair you can have."

18. Is this deck-chair . . .?
19. "What do you do in your . . . time?"–"*What* . . . time?"
20. I looked through his office window to see if he was . . .

Exercise 50 (B)

1. (Notice outside factory:) No . . .
2. When are you likely to be . . . this week?
3. He stopped pedalling and . . .-wheeled down the hill.
4. They are most . . . with their gifts.
5. We have a . . . for a junior clerk.
6. He's terribly busy; grab him as soon as he's . . .
7. I greeted him warmly, but he gazed at me with a . . . stare.
8. (Young lady, to boy friend:) "Now then, young man, don't make so . . ."
9. The landlady always keeps one room . . . for me.
10. I'd like to come with you, but I'm afraid I'm not a . . . agent.

51
fremd
strange, foreign, alien

strange: I am strange (or: a stranger) here, and I don't know my way around.

Collocations: a strange face / voice / remark / feeling; to be a stranger; don't be strange (i.e. keep in contact, don't lose touch).

Fremd, unbekannt; merkwürdig, seltsam.

Hitherto unknown, unfamiliar; odd, unusual, peculiar. Can suggest mystery, romance. (N.: *stranger*; V.: *to estrange*)

foreign: He has always been interested in foreign languages.

What he has said was quite foreign to our discussion.

Collocations: a foreign country / word / language / tongue; foreign trade / affairs; Foreign Office; a foreign body (=Fremdkörper); to be foreign to.

Ausländisch, auswärtig, Auslands . . .; nicht gehörig oder passend zu.

Not belonging to, or associated with, one's own country; not connected with, or not a natural part of, the thing under consideration. (N.: *foreigner*)

alien: Such an attitude is alien to me.

He was an alien when he came, and he remained an alien all his life.

Collocations: alien soil / culture; an alien creed; alien to our way of life; friendly / enemy aliens (during a war); to alienate sympathy.

Wesensfremd, zuwider (unsympathisch). Ein nicht naturalisierter Bewohner eines Landes (als juristischer Ausdruck).

Different in character or nature; adverse, opposed to (possibly even repugnant). A non-naturalized foreigner (the technical or legal expression). So *alien* can be an official term or an emotive term. (N.: *alien*; V.: *to alienate*)

Exercise 51 (A) Fill in a suitable term of the above group.

1. "There's Jones, over there."–"That's . . . , I thought he was in Paris."
2. He is the Minister for . . . Affairs.
3. It's . . . how fate takes a hand in one's life sometimes.
4. During a war there is a distinction between friendly and enemy . . .
5. The tourist industry is always trying to attract . . .
6. I had a . . . feeling that I had been there before.
7. "Where is the High Street, please?"–"Sorry, I'm a . . . here myself."
8. At ports of entry, . . . have their passports inspected separately.
9. A . . .-looking man is waiting outside for you.
10. I saw . . . faces all around me. (i.e. faces that I did not know)
11. We must reject such an . . . creed.
12. They looked at me . . . as though weighing me up.
13. I've never been to a . . . country in my life.
14. I have a number of . . . dictionaries in my possession.

Exercise 51 (B)

1. The . . . Act lays down that long-term visitors or foreign workers must report regularly to the police.
2. Jealousy is something quite . . . to my nature.
3. They had become . . . through some misunderstandings.
4. It's . . . to think that when one is abroad, one is a . . .
5. You . . .ed public sympathy by your actions.
6. I could see in the microscope that a . . . body had got into the mixture.
7. The natives get on O.K. with . . . , if they have money to spend.
8. It is . . . to my nature to bear a grudge.
9. Truth is . . . than fiction.
10. You'd have thought I was speaking a . . . language, the way she was looking at me.
11. I felt that I was treading on . . . soil.
12. I was a . . . in a . . . land, and you befriended me.
13. Their whole attitude of life was . . . to me.
14. Such goings-on are . . . to your way of life.

52
führen, leiten
to lead, to guide, to conduct, to direct

to lead: The blind woman had a dog to lead her.
Where does this road lead to?
What leads you to believe that I'm not telling the truth?
Collocations: to lead s.o. by the hand; to lead a political party; to lead the way; to lead a happy/a dog's life; to lead s.o. a dog's life; to lead

(s.o.) astray; to follow a (or s.o.'s) lead; a leading article (i.e. a leader in a paper); to take the lead; a leading question.

Führen im Sinne von vorausgehen; anführen, leiten, (in eine bestimmte Richtung) lenken. Im gegenständlichen und übertragenen Sinne gebraucht.

(In literal and figurative sense) to go in advance and show the way (and possibly to control others in doing so). *To lead* often suggests initiative so as to induce others to act in some desired way; to be the first to do, or go. (N.: *lead*; *leader*)

to guide: He guided (or conducted) the old lady across the road.
The guide showed us round the museum.

Collocations: to guide a traveller; to act as a guide; a guided missile; guide lines.

To guide verbindet sich gewöhnlich mit dem Gedanken des von einer Person oder Sache geleisteten Beistandes auf dem Wege zu einem Ziel, so daß eine Verirrung ausgeschlossen wird.

Usually implies (continuous) help, assistance (offered by a person or thing) on one's way so as to avoid going astray. (N.: *guide*; *guidance*)

to conduct: The delegation was conducted to the President.

Collocations: to conduct a policy / a law-suit / a business; to conduct a campaign / a war / an orchestra; a good (or bad) conductor (e.g. metal or wood).

Führen im Sinne von (höflich, zuweilen mit gewissem Zeremoniell) geleiten, gewöhnlich auf Gleich- oder Höhergestellte bezogen. (Allerdings auch *to conduct a prisoner.*) Ein Unternehmen, Geschäft etc. in Gang halten, leiten; (im physik. Sinne) leiten.

Conduct (when applied to another person) suggests the polite escort (sometimes with a degree of ceremony) from one place to another. *Conduct* also means be in command of; to manage or carry on some activity; to transmit (in physics); also *to conduct a prisoner.*

to direct: Who is directing the construction of that bridge?
Can you direct me to the central station, please?

Collocations: to direct the affairs (of some institution); to direct an operation; a government direction / directive.

Durch Sachkenntnis, Ratschlag leiten; auf dem zweckmäßigen Kurs zu einem Ziele halten. *Direct* impliziert gewöhnlich die Überlegenheit des Leitenden und kann den Sinn von Befehlen und Anweisungen geben annehmen. Mit *direct* verbindet sich nicht konkrete, körperliche Begleitung, im Gegensatz zu *conduct.* Auch im Sinne von 'den Weg weisen' gebraucht.

To guide with advice, competence; to regulate the course of some activity. *Direct* usually indicates superiority of the "director". It can suggest command or an order. Additionally one can *direct* a person in response to a request for information in local geography.
Note: when one directs, one does not go with the "directee". (N.: *direction*; *director*; *directive*)

Exercise 52 (A) Fill in a suitable term of the above group.

1. Our . . . spoke several languages.
2. You . . . and I shall follow.
3. Where will all this atomic science . . . to, I wonder.
4. They . . .ed a campaign of vilification against us.
5. He can . . . you on your journey.
6. The policeman was . . . the traffic.
7. (Commentator, at horse race:) The favourite has taken the . . .
8. Where can I engage a . . . to accompany me through the mountains?
9. Electricity is . . . through a wire cable.
10. You can trust her. She will not . . . you astray.
11. Dr. Spock was a sure . . . to the bringing up of children.
12. He . . .ed the whole operation from his wheel-chair.
13. Iron is a good . . . of heat.
14. He was my . . . philosopher, and friend.
15. . . . missiles have been developed since the war.
16. Please, . . . me to your master.
17. . . .-dogs make life more tolerable for the blind.
18. The . . . raised the baton, and the orchestra was silent.
19. Please . . . our business in an orderly manner, or get out.
20. The (official) town . . . (book) costs 20 p.

Exercise 52 (B)

1. The . . . of a film is the equivalent of the producer of a play.
2. It's an interesting theory, but it isn't a reliable . . . to action.
3. She . . . him a proper dance, but he enjoyed her provocative ways.
4. Let me . . . you through life.
5. The detective followed the . . . his informant had given him.
6. He . . .ed the ceremony with grace, skill and tact.
7. His . . . of the war was brilliant.
8. Could you . . . me to the Theatre Royal?
9. There doesn't seem to be any clear . . . in this establishment.
10. His wife . . . him a dog's life, so he divorced her.

53
ganz
whole, entire, all, total

whole: The whole country was up in revolt.

Swallow this pill down whole.

Collocations: the whole truth/time/year/family/apple; the whole lot; whole numbers (i.e. not fractions); a whole set (of stamps, books, etc.); also fig. to swallow s.th. whole (i.e. to believe every word without question.)

Ganz, gesamt, vollständig, ungeteilt.

Whole suggests that nothing has been left out; complete. (N.: *whole*)

entire: You have my entire support for your undertaking.
The whole thing was an entire waste of time.

Collocations: entire freedom of choice; entire liberty of conscience; the entire contents.

Entire kann im gleichen Sinne wie *whole* verwendet werden, ist jedoch emphatischer und hebt die völlige Unversehrtheit, Ganzheit hervor; uneingeschränkt.

Entire may have the same meaning as whole, but it is more emphatic. It stresses the idea of intactness, completeness, thoroughness. (Antonym: *partial*) (N.: *entirety*)

all: All (of) my money went on travelling and books.
All the world's a stage, and all the men and women merely players. (Shakespeare)

Collocations: all the country / world; all the time / way; all the year round; all day long; all the morning; all in all; a know-all (i.e. s.o. who thinks he knows everything).

All kann sowohl die Bedeutung von *whole* als auch von *entire* und *total* annehmen. Meist folgt auf *all* der bestimmte Artikel oder ein Possessivpronomen.

All can assume the meanings of *whole, entire,* and *total.* It is usually followed by the definite article or by a possessive pronoun.

total: The total expenditure exceeded the total revenue.
The total casualties were 5,000.

Collocations: the total sum/amount/number; a total failure/loss; total blindness/ignorance; to be totally wrong.

Die Gesamtmenge oder Summe; gänzlich, völlig (oft mit Bezug auf negative Feststellungen).

Total suggests that everything has been included and added up. It may also mean absolute, utter. (N.: *totality*; *total*; V.: *to total*)

Exercise 53 (A) Fill in a suitable term of the above group.

1. . . . the children crowded into the room.
2. I was with him the . . . (of the) time.
3. The . . . number of cars on the road is 3 million.
4. The nut came out of its shell, absolutely . . .
5. "... through the night." (Welsh hymn)
6. Are you . . . certain that you have the facts?
7. The . . . sum collected was £ 1,000.
8. He thinks he knows it . . . He's a bit of a know-. . .
9. I must read the . . . (of the) book, before I can judge.
10. She kept up her running commentary, the . . . time.
11. I speak for the . . . nation.
12. . . . in . . . , we've had an excellent day.
13. I've added it all up. Here's the . . .
14. He emptied the . . . contents onto the table.
15. All she does is powder her nose, . . . day long.

16. That's a . . . false idea.
17. I agree with you . . .
18. There's no one I love more, in the . . . world.
19. Work out the sum to the nearest . . . number.
20. "I swear to tell the truth, the . . . truth, and nothing but the truth." (oath in a law court, before giving evidence)

Exercise 53 (B)

1. Surely you didn't swallow that nonsense . . .!
2. I accept your scheme in its . . .
3. The . . . congregation rose to their feet.
4. The car had to be written off, it was a . . . wreck.
5. We removed the boat . . . from its moorings.
6. He felt himself all over, to see if he was still . . .
7. Does *your* . . . tally with *his*?
8. I'm sure he is guilty. I . . . agree.
9. I'm . . . too partial to a drop of Scotch.
10. He lifted the . . . weight onto his shoulders.

54
Gefühl
feeling, sensation, sense, emotion, sentiment

feeling: I have no feeling in my right hand.
I have a (funny) feeling that we have been deceived.
The general feeling was in favour of a compromise.

Collocations: to have a feeling of pain / fear / sorrow / warmth / happiness / insecurity/drowsiness, etc.; to have a funny feeling; to have deep feelings; with deep feelings; to hide one's feelings; to hurt s.o.'s feelings; to judge a situation by one's feelings; to let one's feelings get the better of one; to be guided by feelings rather than facts; to play on s.o.'s feelings; no hard feelings (i.e. We have no need to be enemies even if we have had a disagreement.).

Der allgemeine Ausdruck für körperliches oder geistig-seelisches Gefühl. *Feeling* bezieht sich i. allg. nicht auf sensorische Reize. Es wird oft im gleichen Sinne wie *emotion* verwendet.

The general term suggesting either a physical or mental experience. *Feeling* does not usually refer to sensory impulses and it often suggests the same as *emotion.*

sensation: Going up in a lift produces an odd sensation in the stomach.
In my dream I had a sensation of flying.

Collocations: to have a sensation of thirst or hunger (but to feel hungry / cold/hot, etc.); to have a sensation of nausea / sickness / giddiness / dizziness / cold / heat, etc.; an odd sensation.

Die vermittels der Sinnesorgane gemachte Wahrnehmung; die Empfindung, die man auf Grund eines äußeren, objektiven Reizes hat; die Sinnesempfindung. *Sensation* kann sich auch auf eine feinere, nicht näher bestimmbare Empfindung beziehen (z. B. *to have a sensation of weariness*). Diese muß jedoch auf einen körperlichen Reiz zurückgehen.

An impression on the mind or brain which is due to some objective, external stimulus; a perception through the sense organs. *Sensation* can also suggest that the *feeling* is imaginary, or at least difficult either to pinpoint or describe and thus it may connote something more ethereal than mere feeling.

sense: He had a sense of failure.
What is lacking is a sense of duty.
She has no sense of right and wrong.

Collocations: to have a sense of wrong / security / safety / wonder; to have a sense of duty / responsibility / justice / humour, etc.; the five senses; sensual perception.

Der (möglicherweise subjektive) Eindruck, das Gefühl oder Bewußtsein von etwas, das nicht selten nur in der Vorstellung existiert. Der Sinn, das Verständnis oder Gefühl für etwas.

An awareness, perception, consciousness, or impression of something. The stimulus is usually of a less objective nature than with sensation and the reaction more an individual, subjective one. A special capacity for understanding, recognition, estimation, or appreciation of something (V.: *to sense*)

emotion: You shouldn't let your emotions rule your life.
The election campaign stirred (up) strong political emotions.

Collocations: to tremble with emotion; to hide one's emotions; filled with emotion; emotional entanglement (e.g. love affairs); emotional outburst; overemotional; carried away with emotion.

Gefühlsaufwallung, (Gefühls)Regung; Erregung, (Gemüts)Bewegung, Emotion.

A feeling which implies excitement or agitation; a strong feeling. (Adj.: *emotional*)

sentiment: Public sentiment was opposed to the measure.
My sentiment towards such yes-men is one of contempt.
Sentiment is stronger than reason.

Collocations: to be actuated or animated by noble sentiments; to appeal to sentiment; the sentiment of pride / patriotism; sentimental mood; public sentiment.

Vom seelisch-intellektuellen Bereich her bestimmte Empfindung (oder Meinung); geistig-seelische Haltung; die Gesamtheit der eigenen Empfindungen; Feingefühl.

A mixture of thought and feeling. A mental attitude to or opinion of something; the sum of feelings on something; one's feelings collectively. An inclination to be influenced by emotion rather than reason; a refined mental feeling.

Exercise 54 (A) Fill in a suitable term of the above group.

1. We can only perceive through our five . . .
1 a. But some people claim to have a sixth . . .
2. Now you've hurt her . . .
3. Hot and cold . . . alternated throughout my body.
4. . . . outbursts like that do you no good.
5. I felt a funny . . . down my spine.
6. Looking into the sun produces an unpleasant . . . in the eyes.
7. I'm feeling in a . . . mood.
8. I harbour no hard . . . against you.
9. Their deep . . . could not be expressed in words.
10. A pleasant . . . is produced by stroking the skin.
11. He lost his . . . of smell in an accident.
12. How can you treat him so? Have you no human . . .?
13. They know how to play on patriotic . . .
14. His weakness produced . . . of giddiness.
15. In order to get the secret out of him, she played on his. . .
16. Fancy doing a thing like that! Where's your common . . .?
17. He gazed at her in deep . . .
18. A . . . of warmth crept over me, when I saw how much they enjoyed it.
19. I have 'pins and needles' in my leg. What a nasty . . .
20. His heart overflowed with (a) deep . . .

Exercise 54 (B)

1. . . . is one thing; business another.
2. An artist is someone with a heightened . . . of perception.
3. Her . . . were written clearly on her face.
4. I . . . something was wrong, as soon as I entered the room.
5. Try to be calm and logical, and not so over-. . .
6. I felt a . . . of nausea coming over me.
7. Heroes are not always actuated by noble . . .
8. I know you are angry, so don't try to hide your . . .
9. I have the . . . of being watched.
10. I have made my . . . perfectly clear.

55
Gegenstand
subject, topic, theme, matter, object

subject: The subject of the composition was, "The telly is a terrible waste of time".

Collocations: a specific subject; to broach / change / drop the subject; to lecture / talk / write on a (given) subject; to stick to / to keep to / to change the subject; the subject of a painting, etc.; the subject of rumour/ tittle-tattle / suspicion / conversation.

Gegenstand, Thema im weitesten Sinne gebraucht. Eine Person kann *subject* einer Diskussion oder Unterhaltung sein aber nicht *topic*. Thema als Sujet eines Kunstwerkes.

Subject is the broadest term for whatever is discussed orally or in written form. A person can be the *subject* of a discussion but not a *topic*. It also refers to what any work of art is about.

topic: Can you think of an interesting topic I could talk on?

Collocations: a topic of conversation, a topic for discussion; a topic of interest; a lively/interesting topic.

Der für mündliche oder schriftliche Erörterung angegebene Gegenstand. Das ausformulierte Thema.

The statement of what is to be discussed (orally or in written form). A *topic* is usually explicit, intentional, whereas a *subject* may also be implied.

theme: The theme of the play was somewhat abstruse.
His theme was lengthy, and he loved to embroider it.

Collocations: to embroider/develop a theme; the theme of a novel/treatise; to harp on a theme (colloq.).

Vorzugsweise mit Bezug auf Literatur und Kunst gebraucht. Außerdem im Sinne von Leitgedanke, durchgehendes Grundthema verwendet.

Preferably in reference to works of literature and art. *Theme* also suggests constant recurrence throughout a work, novel, thesis, etc. A *theme* runs through a book, treatise, symphony and unifies perhaps emotionally.

matter (or subject matter): Before choosing my theme I must first become more familiar with the whole matter.

Collocations: a matter under consideration/discussion; to deal with the matter; to raise the matter; a matter of some/of no importance.

Gegenstand =Materie, Stoff für eine mündliche oder schriftliche Darlegung; ein Problem, eine Frage, die zu untersuchen sind. *Matter* ruft in höherem Maße die Vorstellung von Quantität hervor als *subject* oder *topic*.

Material or substance for oral or written discourse; a question to be considered. *Matter* suggests greater quantity than *subject* or *topic*, which often can be expressed in one word, whereas matter means something like 'all the material'.

object: What's that strange object over there?
I've made ancient history the object of my studies.

Collocations: an object of thought/meditation/curiosity/affection/disgust; an object of one's attention/gaze; an object lesson (=Anschauungsunterricht).

Der konkrete Gegenstand. Der Gegenstand, auf den sich eine Untersuchung, Betrachtung etc. richtet, besonders wenn dessen Identität unbekannt ist.

A thing that is visible and tangible. Something to which one's thoughts or attention is directed, especially when its identity is unknown or the speaker wishes it to remain unknown (for a time).

Exercise 55 (A) Fill in a suitable term of the above list.

1. What a fantastic . . . for a novel, or a treatise on human nature.
2. The . . . of my attention was unaware that I was watching him.
3. There's that . . . again–it's fascinating.
4. That is a . . . of little or no importance.
5. His demeanour was an . . . lesson in calmness under stress.
6. That . . . is not likely to create much interest.
7. You have quite a lot of . . . to choose from.
8. You seemed to be engrossed in your conversation. Who was the . . .?
9. She pounced on the . . . of her wrath, and lashed him with her tongue.
10. We chose a neutral . . . to last us through dinner.
11. He tried to raise the . . . at the last meeting.
12. "How did that . . . go?"–"I'll whistle it for you."
13. The . . . of my thesis cannot be compressed into a few pages.
14. We kept off any . . . that might lead to a quarrel.
15. Whenever he can't answer, he changes the . . .
16. Love is a never-ending . . .
17. They hardly spoke to us. We were the . . . of much suspicion.
18. Tell the students I have the . . . under consideration.
19. The . . . was repeated again and again.
20. The fire at the town hall was the sole . . . of conversation.

Exercise 55 (B)

1. Keep to the . . . and don't wander away from it.
2. Let's deal with one . . . at a time.
3. That was a strange . . . she chose to write on.
4. Whether or not we should accept the offer, proved a lively . . .
5. I want to see the professor about the . . . of my thesis. (i.e. not its content–as in No. 13 ex. 55 (A)–but the whole question of my writing one)
6. The basic . . . of all Hollywood films: Boy meets girl, boy loses girl, boy gets girl.
7. "The . . . of my affection can change my complexion from white to rosy red." (from pop song of the 30's)
8. He was lecturing on the . . . of women's rights.
9. What . . . will you choose for your annual address?
10. These are the . . . down for discussion.

56

gehen

to go, to walk, to step, to stride, to stalk

to go: It's getting on for 11 o'clock. I must go now.
This road goes to High Town. My watch isn't going. This book does not go into my bag. Four goes into 12 three times.

Collocations: to go on holiday; to go to work; to go on foot; to go to great lengths (i.e. to make great or exaggerated efforts); to go along with (i.e. to agree with); to have a go (i.e. to make an effort/attempt; to use some instrument, toy, etc., usually s.o. else's); a going concern (i.e. business, etc. already prospering).

To go bedeutet sich (fort)bewegen, sich in Bewegung befinden (siehe Gruppe 42). Es ist nicht einfach gleichzusetzen mit dem deutschen 'gehen' =laufen.

To go is the general term for to move or to be in motion, and, in contrast to 'gehen', may be used for travelling by any means.

to walk: Shall we walk or go by bus?
My feet have got sore from all that walking.

Collocations: to go for a walk, to have or take a walk; to walk in one's sleep; a sleep walker; a road walk.

Zu Fuß gehen; spazierengehen.

To go on foot. (N.: *walk*; *walker*)

to step: He stepped back (or forward) one pace.
He stepped across the road.
Step this way, please.
He stepped out into the road and was knocked down by a car.

Collocations: to keep/change step; to step out; footsteps; to make a false step (fig.); a step in the right direction (fig.); to take steps to . . . (i.e. to take measures).

Einen Schritt tun oder einige Schritte machen.

To move one foot, or one foot after the other. To walk, esp. for a few steps=paces. (N.: *step*)

to stride: With one stride he was across the brook.

Collocations: to take s.th. in one's stride (i.e. to deal with a situation or problem calmly and without needing to make a special effort; colloq.); with giant strides; making great strides (fig.).

Mit großen, langen Schritten gehen, energisch ausschreiten.

To walk with big steps and with energy or speed.

to stalk: He stalks around his tiny garden as if it was (or were) a park.
The old ex-colonel stalks along as though he is still at the head of his troops.

Collocations: to stalk along/off (in a temper/in high dudgeon/in a huff); to stalk one's prey.

Mit (langsamen und) steifen Schritten einherstolzieren; sich anpirschen.

To walk with (slow) stiff (and possibly) haughty strides; to move quietly and cautiously to get near something.

Exercise 56 (A) Fill in a suitable term of the above group.

1. How far are you prepared to . . . , to stop him making a fool of himself?
2. I just don't feel like . . . I'm too tired.

3. The economy is advancing with great . . .
4. Ten miles! That's a long way to . . .
5. He . . . onto the stage and faced the audience.
6. Are we . . . the right way?
7. "How did you get there?"–"I . . . part of the way and ran the rest."
8. May I . . . to the picnic, too?
9. Our daughter could . . . when she was one year old.
10. One false . . . and you'll be over the cliff.
11. Sleep-. . . can be very dangerous.
12. Just . . . aside and let the others have a chance.
13. "This watch has stopped."–"That's funny, it was . . . five minutes ago."
14. I love to . . . along the top of the cliffs, breathing in deeply."
15. I . . . to school in London.
16. (Sergeant:) "Keep in . . . there, Jones! You're out of . . ."
17. "How is the apprentice doing?"–"Making great . . ."
18. I could hear foot . . . following me in the darkness.
19. We . . . through the hills silently, side by side.
20. . . . is good exercise for the figure.

Exercise 56 (B)

1. First he slithered, then he crawled, then he stood up and walked, and finally he positively . . . down the path.
2. (Little boy:) "Can I have a . . . on your bicycle?"
3. "Was it difficult?"–"Oh, no. I just took it in my . . ."
4. He reached her in three . . .
5. Defeated in argument, he . . . off in high dudgeon.
6. Come on, now, . . . it out! (i.e. walk faster)
7. He . . . forward and took charge of the situation.
8. We shall have to take . . . to prevent it happening again.
9. He . . . through the crowd of onlookers, angrily pushing them aside.
10. You'll have to take bigger . . . if we are to reach home by nightfall.

57
Geist
mind, spirit, genius, ghost

mind: The human mind is always striving to unveil the secrets of nature.
Newton was one of the greatest minds of his time.

Collocations: body and mind; mind and matter; to have a keen mind; to see s.th. in one's mind's eye; to bear s.th. in mind; to keep s.th. in mind; to make up one's mind; to change one's mind; to have great presence of mind; to be in a state (or frame) of mind; great minds; "Out of sight, out of mind."

Geist als Sitz des Denkens, Fühlens und Wollens. Auch im Sinne von Denker, Kopf (dann meist mit Adjektiv und im Plural).

Mind as the seat of thinking, feeling, and volition. If preceded by an adjective and used in plural, also in the sense of persons of great intellectual power.

spirit: To me it is the spirit of a constitution that matters rather than the letter.
I'll be present with you in spirit.
Collocations: with (or without) spirit; a kindred spirit; an evil spirit; the spirit of man; lacking in spirit; to keep up one's spirit; high-spirited; dispirited; to spirit somebody away.
Geist im Gegensatz zum Körper des Menschen; die geistige Haltung; auch im Sinne von Gespenst.
The immaterial part of man; the mental attitude underlying or being the basis of, some action or state of things. (*Spirit* is less physical than *mind*, which is fairly closely connected with brain.) *Spirit* is also used in the sense of spectre or ghost.

genius: He is a man of genius.
The genius of a nation is better shown in peace than in war.
The genius of the Renaissance differs greatly from that of the Middle Ages.
Collocations: the genius of a nation (or age); a child genius.
Geniale Begabung; Genie; Geist einer Epoche etc.; Schutzgeist.
A person having some extraordinary creative capacity of the mind or such capacity itself. The distinctive character of some epoch, nation, etc. The guardian spirit of a place, institution, or person.

ghost: Do you believe stories of ghosts that haunt churchyards and ancient buildings?
Collocations: ghost stories; the ghost of Hamlet's father; a place haunted by a ghost; not to have the ghost of a chance (i.e. no chance at all).
Geist im Sinne von Gespenst und in einigen Wendungen wie *to give up the ghost* (i.e. to die).
The soul of a dead person imagined as haunting living persons and in a few phrases like *to give up the ghost.*

Exercise 57 (A) Fill in a suitable term of the above group.

1. I could see him in my . . . eye, crawling through the mud.
2. Keep up your . . . , lads; help is on the way.
3. They trooped in, looking very di . . .
4. With great presence of . . . she snatched the dagger from his hand.
5. . . . stories are popular at Christmas time.
6. We can't all be . . . , but we can all develop ourselves to the full.
7. The human . . . is a powerful instrument.
8. (Defence lawyer:) "I ask the jury to consider the . . . rather than the letter of the law."
9. He returned from the ordeal, broken in . . . and body.
10. Medicine men tell their "patients" that they are inhabited by an evil . . .
11. . . . are born, not made, so they say.
12. Hamlet's father appeared to him as a . . .

13. Great . . . think alike. (saying)
14. He gave up the . . . before the race was over.
15. The Greeks had a motto: A healthy . . . in a healthy body.
16. They kept alive the . . . of revolt.
17. He was in a suicidal frame of . . .
18. He and I have long been kindred . . .
19. ". . . is the infinite capacity for taking pains."
20. The team were in high . . .; they had just won the cup final.

Exercise 57 (B)

1. . . . is all very well, but give me hard work and willingness to learn.
2. Try to bend your . . . to the problem.
3. Our . . . rose when we heard the news.
4. Come on, lad. Don't be afraid. Speak your . . .
5. He has the . . . for getting under everybody's feet.
6. The . . . gives way under such terrible stress.
7. You won't deflect her. She's got a . . . of her own.
8. I've a . . . to teach him a lesson he won't forget in a hurry.
9. The body had disappeared. Someone had . . . it away.
10. The . . . of man is expressed in great music and literature.

58
geistig
mental, intellectual

mental: His abilities are mental rather than physical.
A mental patient is one who is suffering from a mental disease.
Can you multiply 47 by 64, by mental arithmetic? (i. e. without using paper)

Collocations: to do mental arithmetic; a mental note; a mental hospital; mental power (=Geisteskraft); mental processes; a mental state (=Geisteszustand).

Von geistig-seelischer Beschaffenheit; durch geistige Kräfte bewirkt.

Pertaining to the mind; performed by the mind. (N.: *mentality*)

intellectual: The intellectual and the practical man can help each other.

Collocations: intellectual power (or prowess); intellectual pursuits.

Intellektuell, verstandesmäßig; die Denkkraft, Verstandeskraft, die höheren geistigen Kräfte betreffend. Oft drückt *intellectual* implizit einen Gegensatz zum Gefühlsmäßigen, Phantasievollen, zu den intuitiven geistigen Kräften aus.

Intellectual suggests reference to the higher powers of the mind. At the same time it may indicate some contrast to the intuitive, emotional properties of the mind. (N.: *intellect; intellectual;* V.: *to intellectualise*)

Exercise 58 (A) Fill in a suitable term of the above group.

1. What an . . . that man was!
2. Not all university graduates are . . .
3. ". . . trouble" sounds better than madness.
4. "A . . . hospital" is preferable to "the loony bin".
5. You must have a childish . . . to play tricks like that.
6. Matters of the . . . are not always best left to thinkers.
7. . . . arithmetic is not my strong point.
8. Her . . . capabilities were never in doubt.
9. We shan't quarrel about . . . niceties.
10. He made a . . . calculation before quoting me a price.
11. . . . are often failures as men of affairs.
12. I've made a . . . note to send her a birthday card.
13. Such phenomenal . . . power produced awed silence.
14. The . . . attitude may be far removed from practical reality.
15. Don't . . . your problems. Try to keep them down to earth.
16. It is difficult to trace the . . . processes by which you reached this conclusion.
17. The "Brain of Britain" contest requires the participants to demonstrate their . . . prowess.
18. The manual worker is often too tired for . . . pursuits.
19. Her . . . state will be greatly improved if she goes on holiday.
20. He is not easily influenced by sentiment; he is an . . .

59
Gelegenheit
opportunity, chance, facility, occasion

opportunity: When they offered her a holiday abroad, she grasped the opportunity with both hands.

Opportunity makes the thief.

Collocations: to have an opportunity of doing s.th. or to do s.th.; to miss (or lose) an opportunity; to seize (or take or grasp) an opportunity; to provide an opportunity.

Die sich bietende günstige Gelegenheit.

A favourable point of time for doing something; a concurrence of circumstances allowing the carrying out of something desired or intended. (N.: *opportunist*; Adj.: *opportune*)

chance: He was invited to become a director. The chance of a lifetime!

I'll give you another chance.

He never had a real chance of success.

Collocations: to give s.o. a chance; by pure chance; a lucky chance; the chance of a lifetime; to have a chance; a chance acquaintance; to have an eye on the main chance; to chance one's arm (i.e. to take a chance); to chance it.

Im Vergleich zu *opportunity* verbindet sich mit *chance* besonders der Gedanke des Zufälligen. Auch beinhaltet es zuweilen den Gedanken des Risikos. Oft im Sinne des deutschen 'Chance'.

Basically the same as *opportunity* but suggestive of its accidental nature; a favourable opportunity or possibility. *Chance* can also involve the idea of risk. (V.: *to chance;* Adj.: *chance; chancey*)

facility: There are excellent bathing facilities on the Baltic Sea. That college affords good facilities for studying foreign languages.

Gelegenheit im Sinne von Möglichkeiten, die sich auf Grund von vorhandenen Einrichtungen oder der besonderen Umstände ergeben. Meist im Plural verwendet.

An opportunity, often a material requisite, to make possible the performance of something. Mostly used in plural. (V.: *to facilitate*)

occasion: You can wear that dress on all occasions.
I had no occasion to visit him.

Collocations: on this occasion; to rise to the occasion; to be equal to the occasion.

Ein bestimmter Zeitpunkt oder eine bestimmte Situation, die eine besondere Gelegenheit zu etwas bieten. Auch im Sinne von Anlaß, Grund.

A definite situation or time which offers some special possibility. Also in the sense of reason or need. (V.: *to* occasion = to cause)

Exercise 59 (A) Fill in a suitable term of the above group.

1. (Convicted criminal, to judge:) "Give me another . . ., and I promise to go straight."
2. It was an . . . for wearing her finery.
3. We have just installed new washing . . . for our staff.
4. He was knocked down and killed instantly. Poor chap, he never had a . . . (i.e. it happened too quickly)
5. I've never had an . . . to learn tennis.
6. "Any . . . of a loan?"–"Not a . . .!"
7. Dining . . . at the works are hardly satisfactory.
8. On this . . . I chose to ignore the insult.
9. Give him the . . . to make good, and you won't regret it.
10. By a lucky . . . I found the note, lying where I had left it.
11. This centre provides . . . for rest and recreation.
12. Lost . . . are seldom repeated.
13. There are wonderful . . . for trade in the developing countries.
14. What are the swimming . . . like?
15. On the only . . . I had to speak to him, he was mortally offended by what I said.
16. Transport . . . in the new town are poor.
17. I made her birthday the . . . for repaying her for her many kindnesses.
18. "Do you know her well?"–"Oh no, she's just a . . . acquaintance."
19. Of all the . . . in my life, this was the most important. I hoped I would rise to it.
20. Cooking . . . are provided at all Youth Hostels.

Exercise 59 (B)

1. She'll never go under. She always has her eye on the main . . .
2. When . . . knocks at my door, I hope I shall be at home.
3. "I wouldn't marry you, if you were the last man on Earth!"–"H'm, . . . would be a fine thing."
4. You have no . . . to be rude to her.
5. The teaching is good, they say, but what other . . . do they have?
6. He is unreliable. He takes too many . . .
7. On the great . . . I fluffed my lines.
8. . . . for human intercourse were few and far between.
9. All his friends and family were there. It was a most happy . . .
10. In the army, we used to . . . our arm, and take a few days extra leave.

60
Geschäft
business, concern, transaction, bargain

business: They intend to wind up their separate businesses and become partners.

He has a prosperous business.

Business is slack.

Collocations: to open (or sell) a business; to be away on business; a business instinct; to do good business; to be in business; business acumen (i.e. skill); business is going to the dogs; business is looking up; business as usual; business-hours.

Geschäft = Geschäftsunternehmen; Handelstätigkeit; auch umgangssprachlich für Sache, Angelegenheit; Kram.

A commercial enterprise; activity concerned with this; (in informal speech) also in the sense of: affair, matter, event. (Adj.: businesslike)

concern: His shop was a flourishing concern.

The newly established concern made huge profits last year.

Collocations: a flourishing (or going) concern.

(Gewöhnlich) Große Firma, Handelshaus. (Dem deutschen Konzern entspricht gewöhnlich *trust*. *Concern* in diesem Sinne gebraucht, ist unbestimmter.)

A commercial or manufacturing firm, usually large. It is also used as a vaguer term, often to cover uncertainty, about the nature of the business, or unwillingness to disclose it.

transaction: I have just carried out a most profitable transaction.

The firm is mixed up in shady transactions.

Collocations: stock-exchange transactions (Börsengeschäfte); the transactions of a firm; under-cover or illegal financial transactions; to carry out or conclude a transaction; to transact business.

Geschäftsabschluß, Transaktion, die einzelne geschäftliche Unternehmung.

A single piece of business done. (V.: *to transact*)

bargain: I bought this watch for £ 2; it was a real bargain.

Collocations: to strike/make/stick to/keep to a (or the) bargain; to drive a hard bargain (i.e. to get an agreement very much in one's own favour); to bargain for (i.e. to expect a particular result or effect); into the bargain (i.e. 'in addition', 'as well'—appears at the end of sentence).

Ein günstiger Kauf; eine beiderseitig vorteilhafte Einigung, Übereinkunft

An advantageous purchase; an agreement mutually acceptable to both parties (usually small, individual). (V.: *to bargain*)

Exercise 60 (A) Fill in a suitable term of the above group.

1. I always charge my brother full price in my shop. After all . . . is . . .
2. The house was a . . . at £ 25,000.
3. The whole . . . was completed in two hours.
4. He was a shareholder in a very big . . . that went bankrupt.
5. I'm not helping you with your plans any further. The whole . . . stinks.
6. They say that in the East they love a . . .
7. Risky . . . are not in my line.
8. A . . . of that kind requires a great deal of thought.
9. "Who do you work for?"—"No one. I have my own . . ."
10. "How's . . .?"—"Very slack, I'm afraid."
11. International . . . divide the market between them.
12. He goes to . . . every morning at 9 o'clock.
13. They have some wonderful . . . in the sales.
14. They were selling the goods off at . . . prices.
15. He'll be a millionaire before he is twenty-one. He has remarkable . . . acumen.
16. All his illegal . . . came to light.
17. "What does he do for a living?"—"He's in . . ."
18. He was managing director of a large new . . .
19. He has a tailoring . . .
20. Some shops have fixed prices, but in others you can . . .

Exercise 60 (B)

1. I bought the . . . as a going . . .
2. I refuse to be a party to under-cover . . .
3. He wouldn't buy it till I had reduced the price. He drives a hard . . .
4. It makes him very angry when you try to . . . with him.
5. He owns an up-and-coming . . . in the provinces.
6. . . . on the Stock Exchange are conducted by brokers.
7. "Let's strike a . . .; I'll keep your secret if you'll keep mine." "It's a . . .!"
8. They were shut last week for repairs. But now it's . . . as usual.
9. When I invited him for a week, I hadn't . . . for his wife coming as well.
10. When I make a . . . I always stick to it.

61
geschichtlich
historical, historic

historical: I prefer historical novels to any others.

Collocations: historical evidence / analysis / studies / novels / atlases.

Historisch = sich auf die Geschichte beziehend; Geschichts ...

Relating to history.

historic: The historic friendship between our two peoples should be preserved.

Collocations: a historic spot / place / building / occasion; an event of historic importance.

Historisch = geschichtlich bedeutend, berühmt, von großer geschichtlicher Wirkung.

Important in history.

Note:

historic = that has *made* history; historical = that is *concerned* with history.

Exercise 61 (A) Fill in suitable terms of the above group.

1. You are standing on a ... spot; where Robert Bruce was killed.
2. The signing of the treaty was an event of ... importance.
3. My ... studies are not yet completed.
4. ... times often seem more interesting than our own.
5. Abraham Lincoln's ... speech was delivered at Gettysburg.
6. ... analysis is essential if we are to understand the present.
7. This castle is steeped in history; I love anything ...
8. This ... event will never be forgotten.
9. The legendary King Arthur is supposed to be based on a real ... character.
10. If there was no actual, ... Robin Hood, then there should have been.
11. Oliver Twist is a ... novel.
12. It was a ... moment, when the Parisians stormed the Bastille.
13. This ... battlefield has been drenched with the blood of our ancestors.
14. Some ... characters are fascinating.
15. What a ... final, when the young inexperienced challenger defeated the champion!
16. "Do you like ... novels?"–"Yes, better than hysterical ones!"
17. On that ... occasion we drank each other's health in champagne.
18. Is there any ... evidence to support your theory?

62
Gesellschaft
society, company, party

society: No human society can exist without law and order.[1]
They enjoy each other's society (or company).[2]
He is a fellow of the Royal Society.[3]
She mixes in (high) society.[4]

[1]Das Gesamtsystem der menschlichen Gesellschaft oder eine spezielle Variante desselben; [2]die Gegenwart anderer Menschen, der Umgang mit ihnen; [3]eine einem bestimmten Zweck dienende Organisation; [4]die sogenannte bessere Gesellschaft, die oberen Klassen.

[1]The community of human beings generally or a special system of such community; [2]companionship, intercourse; [3]an association serving a special purpose; [4]the upper classes. (Adj.: *social*)

company: I don't like being alone; couldn't you keep me company?
I had a letter from the Insurance Company this morning.

Collocations: to be in good (or bad) company; to be in s.o.'s company; to keep a person company; to keep company with; company premises; a limited company (i.e. limited liability).

Gesellschaft im Sinne von Begleitung, Umgang, Verkehr mit Menschen; (Handels)Gesellschaft, Aktien-, Versicherungsgesellschaft.

Persons who have come together for entertainment; companionship. A group of persons joined temporarily or permanently for common action (mainly for business purposes). (Adj.: *company*)

party: I was invited to a dinner party last night.

Collocations: a tea-party, garden-party; to attend / give / throw / hold a party; an all-night / a house-warming party; a bottle party (i.e. everyone has to bring a bottle of "booze"); to be party to s.th.

Geselliges Beisammensein, eine Party.

A group of persons joining temporarily for social enjoyment. (Adj.: *party*)

Exercise 62 (A) Fill in a suitable term of the above group.

1. I enjoy good . . .
2. . . . always has to protect itself against anti-social elements.
3. The family unit is one of the foundations of human . . .
4. Please come to my birthday . . . tomorrow.
5. The whole . . . rode out to meet her.
6. He joined a theatrical . . . at the age of fourteen.
7. We went to a house-warming . . . last week.
8. They sent out a search . . . for the missing boy.
9. She is stepping up into (high) . . .
10. Let's give a . . . to celebrate her return.
11. Anthropologists study primitive . . .

12. The directors of a limited . . . are not personally responsible, in law, for its debts.
13. The entire . . . rose when he entered the room.
14. That sort of thing cannot be done in the best . . .
15. My wife and I were invited to the mayor's garden . . .
16. I don't allow them to behave like that in *my* . . .
17. She indicated quite clearly that she did not want my . . .
18. I shan't go to their card . . . any more, they cheat.
19. I refuse to be . . . to the decision.
20. The opera . . . visited our town twice a year.
21. It was a glorious . . . We all finished up drunk.
22. I'm surprised to find you in such low . . .
23. The National . . . for the Prevention of Cruelty to Children, and the Royal . . . for the Prevention of Cruelty to Animals do splendid work.
24. It was a cheerful . . . that turned up at the police station to claim the reward.

63
gesetzlich, rechtmäßig
lawful, legal, legitimate, rightful

lawful: The ruling sovereign of a state need not be its lawful ruler.

Collocations: a lawful act / request / demand / marriage / sovereign; lawful property; one's lawful, wedded wife / husband.

Bezeichnet die Übereinstimmung mit einem Gesetz irgendwelcher Art (jurist. Gesetz, Naturgesetz etc.)

Suggests that something is in accordance with the law, divine, natural, etc. or that it is generally held to be permissible.

legal: Bull-baiting and cock-fighting are no longer legal in Britain.

Collocations: a legal document; to take legal action; a legal process; to have recourse to legal action; one's legal due; to consult one's legal adviser.

Bezeichnet die ausdrückliche Anerkennung eines Tatbestandes durch den Buchstaben des Gesetzes, durch das Gesetzbuch.

Suggests express recognition of something by the terms of the law of the statute book. That which can only be finally determined by a court of law. (N.: *legality;* V.: *to legalise;* Adj.: *illegal*)

legitimate: Is it legitimate for a doctor to withhold the truth from a patient?

Collocations: a legitimate heir; a legitimate successor to the throne; a legitimate excuse / right; legitimate absence; an illegitimate child.

Legitim; berechtigt. Einen rechtmäßigen Anspruch auf etwas haben (besonders gegenüber den Ansprüchen anderer Personen); sich in Übereinstimmung mit anerkannten Grundsätzen, Anschauungen der Logik, Tradition etc. befinden.

To have a legal right to the possession of something (esp. against some opposing claim); to be recognised by established principle, custom, logic, tradition, etc. Also a right conferred by birth. (N.: *legitimacy;* Adj.: *illegitimate*)

rightful: He claimed his rightful place at the head of the table.
Both boys pretended that the biro was theirs, but, actually, Mary was the rightful owner.

Collocations: the rightful owner of s.th.; one's rightful share / claim / due.

Rightful bezeichnet gewöhnlich einen moralischen und damit einen gerechten Anspruch.

Rightful suggests a moral or just claim. (N.: *rightfulness*)

Exercise 63 (A) Fill in a suitable term of the above group.

1. It is not a . . . document without both signatures.
2. Do you claim this is your . . . property?
3. He's not the . . . heir to the throne. He's a usurper.
4. Do you take this woman to be your . . . wedded wife? (marriage service)
5. The . . . process is long-winded and costly.
6. It seemed a . . . request, and I granted it.
7. Have you considered taking . . . action against him?
8. You can't cast aspersions on my parentage—I'm . . .
9. I think it's quite . . . to charge for an extra job.
10. Parliament is accepted as . . . ruler of the land.
11. I have been assured by my lawyer that your actions were quite . . .
12. They are the . . . owners of the house.
13. "Sorry I'm late. I missed the bus."—"That's not a . . . excuse."
14. I have a . . . claim to a share in the proceeds.
15. He may be . . . free and innocent, but morally he is damned for ever.
16. I had a note from her parents. Her absence was . . .
17. To the devout Jew it is not . . . to work on the Sabbath.
18. He may be small and weak, but he has the . . . authority.
19. It was his . . . property. He had earned it by the sweat of his brow.
20. If you can establish your . . . right to it, no one can deny that it is . . . yours.

Exercise 63 (B)

1. The inheritance is . . . his.
2. You may dislike what I have done, but it was perfectly . . .
3. This new law will . . . certain forms of gambling.
4. I don't like Variety; I prefer the . . . stage.
5. It is not . . . for Roman Catholic priests to marry.
6. He was not given his . . . due.
7. I don't regard your conclusion as a . . . deduction from the facts.
8. They all sound convincing, but who is the . . . claimant.

9. The . . . of the contract can only be tested in a court of law.
10. There is a . . . hope that peace can be restored in the area in spite of the present situation.

64

gesund

healthy, sound, wholesome, sane

healthy: Breathing in healthy air is what matters most to me on holiday.

Collocations: a healthy person / climate / life / condition; healthy ideas; a healthy appetite; strong and healthy; a healthy bank balance; an unhealthy situation.

Körperlich gesund (nicht krank); zuweilen auch der Gesundheit dienlich. Auch im übertragenen Sinne verwendet.

Physically *healthy* (of the human body); sometimes also in the sense of contributive to health. It is also used figuratively. (N.: *health*)

sound: Sound sleep is essential for one's health.
He has a sound judgement.

Collocations: a sound heart; sound in wind and limb; a sound mind / economy / idea / fruit; sound views / arguments.

Bezeichnet einen noch vollkommeneren Grad von körperlicher Gesundheit als *healthy*; gesund ohne Anzeichen von Minderung. Wird auch im übertragenen Sinne gebraucht.

Suggests flawless health in every respect. *Sound* is also used in figurative sense. (N.: *soundness*).

wholesome: Rye bread is wholesome.

Collocations: wholesome food; wholesome respect.

Der körperlichen oder geistigen Gesundheit förderlich (vor allem in bezug auf die Ernährung angewendet); heilsam.

Wholesome suggests something that helps to preserve or restore bodily or mental health; not adulterated; good for you. (N.: *wholesomeness*)

sane: He is not mad at all, he is as sane as you and me.
His views are thoroughly sane.

Collocations: sane advice; a sane person / course (of action) / attitude.

Geistig gesund; über gesundes Denk- und Urteilsvermögen verfügend.

Mentally sound (the opposite of mad); to show sound judgement; level-headed, keeping on an even keel. (N.: *sanity*)

Exercise 64 (A) Fill in a suitable term of the above group.
1. There was a . . . glow on her cheeks.
2. Fruit and vegetables are . . . and nourishing fare.
3. The countryman leads a . . . life than the city-dweller.
4. A . . . diet is a good foundation for health.

5. My medical test showed that I was . . . in wind and limb.
6. He speaks like a . . . man, but acts like a lunatic.
7. It is . . . to take exercise night and morning.
8. White bread is not . . . because it is adulterated.
9. I should go away for a while. The situation doesn't look too . . .
10. Let's follow his . . . and level-headed advice.
11. Brighton has a . . . climate.
12. The firm is perfectly . . ., and in no danger of going bankrupt.
13. Her whole attitude was well-balanced and . . .
14. "Come over to my place for a drink."–"What a . . . suggestion!"
15. This is her first illness. She's always been a . . . girl.
16. You showed . . . judgement by coming straight to me.
17. With their rosy cheeks, they looked the picture of . . .
18. I've discussed it with her, and I don't think her views are very . . .
19. The Greek ideal was: a . . . mind in a . . . body.
20. A modest . . . meal is better than a lavish and un . . . one.

Exercise 64 (B)

1. His judgement is usually . . . He takes such a . . . view of life.
2. Is it really . . . to go all that way, without a penny in your pocket?
3. His eyes were so wild that they feared for his . . .
4. They have a . . . respect for the law.
5. He told me that all my organs were thoroughly . . .
6. He explained that it was the only . . . course to adopt.
7. Do you regard it a very . . . scheme?
8. I began to suspect the . . . of his mind.
9. The countryman eats and lives more . . . than the townsman.
10. These cheap apples are not very . . .

65
gewinnen
to win, to gain

to win: He has won £ 10,000 in the lottery.

Collocations: to win a game / a competition / a race / a fortune / a prize / a war / a battle / a case; to win love; to win at cards / gambling; to win fairly / by cheating; to win on points / by x goals; a winning smile. You can't win (i.e. circumstances are against you).

Auf Grund zufälliger Umstände oder den Erfolg begünstigender Eigenschaften ein Ziel erreichen. Einen Wettbewerb gewinnen.

To get something desired esp. through favourable circumstances or advantageous qualities inherent in the person who wins. *To win* a competition.

to gain: I coughed and blew my nose to gain time.

Collocations: to gain the upper hand; to gain land from the sea; to gain time/ground; to gain on s.o. (i.e. catch him up); a clock may be gaining (time).

Etwas durch besondere Anstrengungen, Bemühungen gewinnen. Auch im Sinne von Fortschritte machen (bei intransitiver Verwendung). Häufig sind *gain* und *win* austauschbar.

To get something valuable through struggle. Sometimes *gain* suggests just improvement, something extra, a profit, or to make progress. Often *gain* is interchangeable with *win*.

Exercise 65 (A) Fill in a suitable term of the above group.

1. He . . . a meagre living from the soil.
2. Hooray! My horse has . . .
3. . . . or lose, always have a smile on your face.
4. Looking over my shoulder, I saw that he was . . . on me.
5. He . . . that 100-metre sprint with seconds to spare.
6. If you agree with him, he thinks you're soft. If you don't, he sulks. You just can't . . .
7. Can you adjust my watch for me? It keeps . . .
8. After a tremendous struggle, he . . . the upper hand.
9. I'm lucky at cards. I always . . .
10. In the fight I saw last night the champion . . . on points.
11. "She . . . that match easily."–"Yes, but only by cheating."
12. I don't do it for personal . . ., but just to help others.
13. They . . . the election by a large majority.
14. We . . . nothing by taking that short cut.
15. Faint heart never . . . fair lady. (saying)
16. She . . . all hearts by her charm and generosity.
17. It was worth arguing; you . . . your point.
18. First he was naughty, then he gave his mother a . . . smile.

66
Glück
happiness, fortune, luck

happiness: Successful work brings happiness.

Collocations: a happy co-incidence/chance; a happy phrase (i.e. one suitable for the occasion); happy-go-lucky; slap/goal-happy.

Seelisches Glück.

The pleasurable feeling of contentment of the mind; what all human life is supposed to be striving for. (Adj.: *happy*)

fortune: Fortune favoured him at his first attempt.
He had the good (or bad) fortune to win (or lose) all matches.
Every man is the architect of his own fortune.

Collocations: fickle fortune; to tell fortunes.

Das zufällige, vom Walten des (unergründlichen) Schicksals bestimmte Glück. (Auch im Sinne von Vermögen, Reichtum gebraucht.)

The good or bad chance (considered as some sort of blind force) on which success or failure depend. (Used also in the sense of *wealth*).

luck: We've missed the last bus. Bad luck!
I wish you good luck!

Collocations: to have (good) luck; to have bad luck; a stroke of luck (=Glücksfall); a lucky streak (=Glückssträhne); beginner's luck; as luck would have it; hard luck; Lady Luck; more by luck than judgement. just my/your luck (i.e. bad luck); to be lucky.

Im wesentlichen gleiche Bedeutung wie *fortune,* doch ohne dessen spezielle Assoziation mit dem (launischen) Walten der „Glücksgöttin". *Luck* ist somit ein schlichterer Ausdruck als *fortune* und bezieht sich lediglich auf die Zufälligkeit des Geschehens. Es wird häufig in bezug auf Glücksspiele, Wetten etc. angewendet.

Basically the same as *fortune* but without the degree of dignity which the latter suggests, because of its mythological origin. *Luck* is more colloquial than *fortune* and gives emphasis to the connotation of *chance.* It is often connected with gambling, betting, etc. (Adj.: *lucky*)

Exercise 66 (A) Fill in a suitable term of the above group.

1. Money does not always bring . . .
2. "My horse lost by a head."–"Oh, hard . . ., old man."
3. I caught the train by the skin of my teeth. That was a stroke of . . .
4. I do not seek fickle . . .'s fame.
5. I won £ 10 the first time I played cards. It was beginner's . . .
6. I saw you with a beautiful girl last night, you . . . chap.
7. . . . was written all over his beaming face.
8. His wife's . . . was his main concern.
9. As . . . would have it, I arrived a moment before she did. (may be advantageous or disadvantageous.)
10. They had been . . . married for a number of years.
11. I had the good . . . to marry the most excellent of wives.
12. The centre-forward was goal- . . . that afternoon. He scored six goals.
13. Lady . . . was not on my side tonight. I lost every penny.
14. . . . shared is . . . doubled.
15. My mother wished me good . . . when I went for the interview.
16. A gypsy told me my . . . at the fair.
17. The child's . . . at receiving the gift was as great as mine at giving it.
18. A wife and child are a hostage to . . .

Exercise 66 (B)

1. What ill . . . brings you hither on such a night?
2. The . . .s of the chase brought me home empty-handed.
3. "Aren't we all in search of . . .?
   But to each one it means a different thing.

To some it's wealth, to some it's health, to some it's love." (pop song)

4. More by . . . than judgement, my shot hit him right in the back of the neck.
5. May Heaven grant thee good . . . in thy endeavours.
6. He was slap-. . . with success, and behaved almost as though he were drunk.
7. . . . smiled on him all his life.
8. I wish you all the . . . in the world, in your married life.
9. ". . . is a perfume which you cannot spread on others without receiving a little on yourself."
10. Seek your . . . in the wide open spaces, young man.

67
Grenze
frontier, boundary, border, limit, bounds

frontier: When political tension grew, more troops were sent to the frontier.

Collocations: on the frontier; frontier town; frontier guard; a frontiersman; the frontiers of science, etc.

Die politische Grenze zu einem anderen Land; auch übertragene Bedeutung.

The extreme part of a country which is next to or fronts on another country. It is used in a political sense and also figuratively. Frontier can have a more *emotional* feel about it, e.g. in: the frontiers of human endeavour; a frontiersman, i.e. one who has pioneered the West (U.S.).

boundary: There is a wall along the boundary of the estate.

Collocations: natural/artificial boundary; boundary line.

Die exakte Scheide- oder Grenzlinie im geographischen Sinne. *Boundary* bezieht sich gewöhnlich auf kleinere Gebiete als Länder, also Distrikte, Gemeinden, Grundstücke etc.

The exact geogràphical dividing line. It is usually referred to territories smaller than countries, e.g., districts, counties, towns, estates, etc.

border: The Cheviot Hills are on the border between England and Scotland.
There has been fierce fighting on the border between the two countries.

Collocations: the border of a field / forest / garden; border-district; border clashes; border land; to border on (the ridiculous, etc.).

Das Gebiet beiderseits des Grenzverlaufes. *Border* kann aber auch im Sinne von *boundary* verwendet werden und im übertragenen Sinn.

The territory along the boundary, but also in the sense of *boundary*, and in a figurative sense. (V.: *to border on*).

limit: There is a limit to human endurance.
He was fined for exceeding the speed limit.

Collocations: the age limit; limited liability; to go to the limit(s); that's the limit! (exclamation of annoyance).

Die oberste, äußerste Grenze. Meist in übertragener Bedeutung verwendet.

The furthest point or line of something. Mostly in a figurative sense. (V.: *to limit;* Adj.: *limited*)

bounds: There are no bounds to his knowledge.

Collocations: the bounds of space and time; the bounds of a school/an estate; beyond all bounds; knows no bounds; out of bounds (=kein Zutritt [Am. *off limits*]).

Sehr häufig im übertragenen Sinn verwendet in der Bedeutung von Schranke, Grenze und stets im Plural. Auch im Sinne von Grenzbereich.

Frequently used figuratively suggesting the limiting line of something, and always used in plural. Sometimes also to denote the territory enclosed by such a line. (Adj.: *bounded*)

Exercise 67 (A) Insert a suitable term of the above group.

1. . . . clashes between England and Scotland were frequent in the old days.
2. You must . . . your smoking to five cigarettes per day.
3. "How will you mark the . . .?"–"With a ditch."
4. What is the age . . . for recruitment to the army?
5. We shall guard our . . . to the death.
6. . . . raids increased, as each side tried to revenge itself on the other.
7. The . . . of knowledge are always receding into the distance.
8. His conduct . . . on the ridiculous.
9. The Belgian . . . with France lies to her west and south.
10. His outlook is extremely . . .
11. This is outrageous! It goes beyond the . . . of decency.
12. What are the . . . of this constituency?
13. Life on the . . . has its compensations.
14. The . . . was sealed off to prevent his escape (across it).
15. Anything found within the . . . of my farm belongs to me.
16. His impudence knows no . . .
17. They will go to the very . . . to get what they want.
18. A thick white line indicates the . . . of a cricket pitch.
19. They were smuggled across the . . . at night.
20. Small bushes . . .ed the forest.

Exercise 67 (B)

1. There were no . . . to her greed.
2. Troops! Stand ready! The enemy is approaching our . . .
3. A grass verge marked the . . . between strips, in open-field farming.
4. He broke the . . . of propriety by his actions.
5. They were held up at the . . . for hours.
6. The typical adventurous American of the 19th century was a . . .
7. I had to put up a fence to mark the . . . of my garden.
8. There seems to be no . . . to the expenditure they are willing to incur.

9. In 1860, part of the American . . . lay approximately along the present Western . . . of Minnesota and Iowa.
10. They have moved up three battalions to the . . .

68
groß
great, large, big, tall, grand

great: Goethe is one of the greatest lyric poets and Shakespeare one of the greatest dramatists in world literature.

Collocations: great success / popularity; a great achievement / occasion; great expectations; a great man; one of the "Greats"; a great many / deal of.

Great bezeichnet einen hohen Grad von etwas. In übertragener Bedeutung drückt *great* hervorragende Qualität und Bewunderung aus. *Great* ist etwas gewählter als *large* oder *big*.

Great suggests a high degree. Used in a figurative sense it expresses distinction and admiration. *Great* is slightly more literary than *large* or *big*. (N.: *greatness*)

large: He's got a large family.

Collocations: a large room / house / town / garden / field / wood; a large income/salary; a large number of; large powers (=große Vollmachten); a large producer (=Großerzeuger); a large undertaking / enterprise; by and large (=im großen ganzen); writ large (=deutlich, leicht erkennbar); to take the large view.

Large bezieht sich vorzugsweise auf Raum, Ausdehnung, Anzahl, Menge, Fassungsvermögen.

Large usually refers to space, extent, amount, quantity, capacity.

big: The elephant is one of the biggest animals.

Collocations: a big box / building / book / dog; a big voice; a big man (i.e. s.o. high up in a particular sphere; a professor, etc.); a big shot (=ein "großes Tier"); to talk big (=prahlen); a big business tycoon; a bighead [ˈbigəd] (=eingebildete Person); to be big (fig.) (=großzügig sein).

Big bezeichnet Masse, Volumen, Umfang, Gewicht. Darüber hinaus kann es auch, allerdings auf etwas niedrigerer stilistischer Ebene, im Sinne von *large* verwendet werden. *Big* streift zuweilen den Bereich des Slangs und ist emphatischer als *large*.

Big refers in the main to mass, bulk, volume, weight. It can also be used in the sense of *large*, but it is more colloquial and more emphatic than *large*. *Big* may sometimes sound a bit slangy.

tall: You are not tall enough to reach the top shelf without a ladder.

Collocations: a tall tree / chimney / column; to be x feet tall; a tall story (i.e. an unbelievable one).

Groß der Höhe nach (bei gleichzeitig relativ geringem Durchmesser); groß gewachsen.

High (and at the same time of relatively small diameter). Basically, it refers to human beings of above average height. (N.: *tallness*)

grand: From the top of the tower you have a grand view of the scenery. That's a grand idea! (i.e. splendid)

Collocations: to have a grand time; grand news; a grand feeling; grandmother, grandfather; Grand Old Man (of politics).

Grand hat die Bedeutung von großartig, grandios, wunderbar, prächtig. Umgangssprachlich auch 'erstklassig'.

Grand usually means splendid, magnificent, noble, imposing. In colloquial use: first-rate.

Exercise 68 (A) Insert a suitable term of the above group.

1. Who is the ... boy in the class?
2. There were ... numbers of birds on the shore.
3. Who's that little chap, banging the ... drum?
4. The meeting was held in a ... hall.
5. ... preparations were made before the ... man arrived.
6. I have some ... news for you; your wife has just given birth to a son.
7. To be short is naught. To be ... is all.
8. They counted his efforts a ... success.
9. Many ... artists did not achieve ... popularity in their lifetime.
10. A five-million-pound order! That's ... business.
11. The new tower blocks were ... and slender, and so were some of the young ladies who lived there.
12. We took a ... basket of fruit with us.
13. Egypt is a land of ... impressive monuments.
14. A big man is not always a ... man.
15. The ... hills shrank into mounds, as they receded into the distance.
16. It was a ..., roomy cupboard.
17. They're putting up a very ... hotel with a thousand rooms.
18. ... Scott! You're not going to town in *that* outfit?
19. As the plane rose, I had a ... feeling of exhilaration.
20. By and ..., I prefer the countryside to the seaside.

Exercise 68 (B)

1. In the old days the wealthy used to send their sons on the ... tour, taking in much of Europe and parts of Asia Minor, too.
2. They talk ..., but when it comes to the crunch they let you down.
3. Gladstone was known as the ... Old Man of Parliament.
4. Guilt was writ ... all over his face.
5. That was a ... scene in the opera, with all the cast on stage.
6. He's always boasting. He's nothing but a ...-head.

7. She dressed up in her finery for the . . . occasion.
8. . . . is thought to be one of the characteristics inherited through the genes.
9. We ate a very . . . meal before setting out.
10. I believe he is a . . . shot in the clothing trade.

69
Grund
reason, ground, cause, occasion

reason: The reason for his failure was lack of energy rather than intelligence.
What's the reason you are late?

Collocations: the reason why; to have (a) reason to do/for doing s.th.; not without reason; without rhyme or reason; a reasoned argument; to reason why.

Der (oft persönliche) erklärende oder rechtfertigende Grund für eine Handlung, Haltung oder einen Sachverhalt; die Begründung, der Beweggrund. Darüber hinaus auch der logische, verstandesmäßige Grund.

The (often personal) arguments explaining or justifying some action, behaviour or fact. Also the logical ground. (V.: *to reason*)

ground: The real grounds for his objection will no doubt emerge later.
There are not sufficient grounds for intervention.

Collocations: to do s.th. on political/religious/false grounds; to have (good) grounds to do s.th. or for doing s. th.; on the ground(s) that . . . . . .; grounds for complaint; there is/there are no ground(s) for . . . . . .

Ground wird oft in den gleichen Situationen verwendet wie *reason.* Darüber hinaus betont es jedoch mehr die objektive Sachlage, die Fakten, aus denen sich ein bestimmtes Resultat ergibt (wohingegen bei *reason* mehr Überlegungen, Motive im Mittelpunkt stehen). Auch im Sinne von Grundlage und als juristischer Ausdruck verwendet. Es wird häufig im Plural gebraucht.

Ground is often used in the same situations as *reason.* But in contradistinction to *reason, ground* suggests greater objectivity, the facts on which some action, behaviour, judgement rests rather than the motive or any subjective considerations. It is also the legal term. It is frequently used in plural.

cause: The cause of the fire was a short circuit.
Alcohol is often the cause of road accidents.
A man of your ability has no cause for anxiety.

Collocations: to complain without (any) cause; cause and effect; to have just cause; the root cause.

Cause bezeichnet die Umstände, Gründe, Kräfte, die möglicherweise über einen längeren Zeitraum wirken und mit gewisser Folgerichtigkeit zu einem bestimmten Resultat führen. Die Ursache. *Cause* findet sich auch in der gleichen Bedeutung wie *reason* und *ground.*

The force, circumstances (possibly acting over a long time) which by their very nature result in some effect. *Cause* is also used in the same sense as *reason* and *ground.* (Adj.: *causal*)

occasion: There was no occasion for me to speak to him.

The cause of a war usually lies deeper than its occasion.

There is no occasion to worry.

Collocations: to be occasioned by; to provide the occasion for.

Der (äußere) Anlaß; die Veranlassung.

The incidental cause of some action or result; an event, situation or person which supplies an opportunity for a cause to be set in motion. (V.: *to occasion*)

Exercise 69 (A) Insert a suitable term of the above group.

1. We felt most alarmed, and not without . . . as it turned out.
2. Your objections were quite . . . less.
3. You were rude to me without any apparent rhyme or . . . Why?
4. You have just . . . for your anger. But be patient.
5. I don't eat meat on Fridays, on religious . . .
6. "Why are you leaving town in such a hurry?"–"I have my . . ."
7. There are good . . . for believing his story.
8. Give me one good . . . why I should resign.
9. . . . and effect are the subject of scientific enquiry.
10. What is the . . . for this disgraceful behaviour?
11. She had given him . . . for hope.
12. The party provided the . . . for his merry behaviour.
13. The . . . for his complaint are undeniably true.
14. "I'm giving notice."–"Why? What are your . . . for wanting to leave us?"
15. There were good . . . for my anger.
16. His birthday was the . . . for avowals of love and affection.
17. "Poverty is the root . . . of mortality, in backward countries."–"Yes, but what is the root . . . of poverty?"
18. We have . . . to believe that he was abducted.
19. She is said to have left on . . . of ill-health.
20. The . . . of the explosion was carelessness.

Exercise 69 (B)

1. You had no . . . to be rude about it.
2. "Sorry I'm late. I missed the bus."–"That's an excuse, not a . . ."
3. This theft was only the . . ., not the real . . . for his dismissal.
4. There are . . . enough for his defensive posture.
5. Hay fever and sneezing have a . . . relationship.
6. His defeat at tennis was the . . . for childish fury.
7. Your . . . are excellent. But you won't convince him.
8. What . . . have you for accusing him like this?
9. Don't stay away from the meeting without good . . .
10. Our seasickness was . . . by a violent storm which rocked the boat.

70
Hafen
harbour, port, haven

harbour: The entrance to the harbour is protected by a fortress.

Collocations: a natural harbour; a harbour-basin; a harbour-pilot (Hafenlotse); Harwich Harbour.

Der natürliche oder künstlich angelegte Hafen als Anlegestelle oder Zuflucht für die Schiffe. Auch im übertragenen Sinn.

A place (natural or artificially constructed) where ships take shelter. Also used in a figurative sense. (V.: *to harbour*)

port: A great seaport had grown up on the estuary of the river.

Collocations: the port of New York/London; the port of destination (Bestimmungshafen); naval port; to enter/reach port; to leave port; a river port; a seaport; a port of call (=Anlaufhafen); a thriving port; foreign ports; home ports; port installations.

Der Hafen in seiner Funktion für Wirtschaft und Handel; auch im Sinne von Hafenstadt.

Port suggests a harbour with a view to its commercial functions. It also means a town and its harbour, and all docks, wharves, offices, etc.

haven: His home was a haven of peace.

Collocations: a haven of rest/peace; to find a haven.

Hafen =Zufluchtsort (auch im übertragenen Sinne). Meist literarisch gebraucht.

A *haven* is a place of safety or refuge, a sanctuary. Used almost exclusively for figurative, poetic and literary purposes.

Exercise 70 (A) Insert a suitable term of the above group.

1. The ... of London is one of the greatest river ... in the world.
2. Please set me ashore at the first ... of call.
3. They opened their grounds as a ... of rest for old cart-horses.
4. This is a ... for deep-sea fishing.
5. Portsmouth ... is an excellent one for naval vessels.
6. When we arrived in ..., we disembarked with all speed.
7. Bristol was once Britain's main ... for (the import of) tobacco.
8. They are building an artificial ... further up the coast.
9. Liverpool is a thriving ... It serves the Lancashire cotton industry.
10. The island was a ... for sea-birds of every kind.
11. Southampton ... is deep enough for ocean-going liners.
12. They put in to a small bay to seek a ... from the stormy weather.
13. The little bay formed a natural ... for fishing and rowing boats.
14. All the ... installations were damaged by the blast.
15. Her arms were a ... of rest and comfort for him.
16. Many a hunted slave found a ... in the home of an abolitionist.
17. "Purser, when do we reach our ... of destination?"

18. In seaside towns one often sees the notice: This way to the . . .
19. In the Middle Ages fugitives could find a . . . in the church.
20. How many docks are there in this . . .?
21. The fleet lay at anchor in the . . .
22. The small, disused hut was only a temporary . . . from his pursuers.

71
halten
to hold, to keep

to hold: The girl was holding a doll in her arm.

Hold (on) tight, or you will fall off the bus.

Do you think the box will hold?

Hold your tongue.

Collocations: to hold a meeting/conference; to hold some belief/view/opinion; to hold shares; to hold one's breath; to hold at bay; to hold still/tight; to hold hands; hold hard (or hold your horses i.e. wait a minute/not so fast); to hold out hopes.

Einen Gegenstand (mit der Hand, dem Arm) in einer bestimmten Lage halten; halten im Sinne von nicht entzweigehen; zurückhalten, unter Kontrolle halten. Auch in übertragener Bedeutung.

To support something, to keep something in a particular position (with one's hand or arm); to remain unbroken; to restrain, to keep under control. Also used figuratively. (N.: *hold*)

to keep: You can keep these photos. They keep a watch dog. This sausage will not keep. Where do you keep your money? Keep him in bed for a couple of days.

Collocations: to keep a secret/promise; to keep silent/quiet; to keep a shop; to keep the peace; to keep s.th. cool/dry/safe; to keep up a pretence; to keep s.o. (= to provide them with food, clothing, shelter or money); to keep one's temper; one's keep (i.e. sustenance).

Behalten, im Besitz von etwas sein oder bleiben; in einem bestimmten Zustand bleiben oder erhalten; sich an etwas halten.

To retain in one's possession, to continue to have or hold; to maintain something in some specified condition; to pay regard to, to stand by something, e.g., a promise. (N.: *keep*)

Exercise 71 (A) Insert a suitable term of the above group.
1. They . . . him so firmly that he could not escape.
2. The mixture will . . . for three days in a fridge.
3. . . . this safe for me until I come back.
4. He . . . them at bay for hours, until help came.
5. I was . . . three aces and three kings.
6. I refuse to . . . silent any longer. I shall speak out.

7. (Judge:) "You will be bound over to . . . peace for 12 months."
8. They . . . the little grocery shop at the corner.
9. They sat, . . . hands and gazing into each others eyes.
10. We had to . . . our three children until after they left university.
11. Will the . . . of passport No. 735889 please report to the desk.
12. The wrestler got his opponent in a strangle . . . from which he could not escape.
13. ". . . the home fires burning." (1st World War song)
14. She . . . five-hundred one-pound shares in the company.
15. (Bus conductor:) ". . . tight!"
16. She earned her . . . by . . . the house clean and tidy.
17. You can . . . your filthy money! I don't want it.
18. I . . . the view that he will try to break in tonight.
19. It was difficult to . . . up the pretence any longer.
20. I'm afraid I can't . . . out any hopes of an early settlement.
21. . . . my case for a moment, whilst I lock up.
22. The teacher . . . his boys in after school as a punishment.
23. He . . . out the hand of friendship. (Could be figuratively.)
24. In such weather it is impossible to . . . active.
25. She . . . up her incessant chatter all night.

72
heilen
to cure, to heal

to cure: Physicians have not yet found a reliable method of curing cancer.

Collocations: to cure a disease/fever/headache; to cure people; to cure s.o. (or oneself) of a bad habit/superstition/vanity.

Eine Krankheit heilen; von (charakterlichen) Schwächen befreien.

To free a person from illness or some weakness of the character or from some economic problems, etc. (Adj.: *curative*; N.: *cure*)

to heal: The wound did not heal properly since it had gone septic.
Time heals all grief (or all wounds.)

Collocations: to heal a breach/quarrel; faith-healing; faith-healer; healing hands.

Heilen (mit Bezug auf eine Wunde, Verletzung, Entzündung). *To heal* kann transitiv, intransitiv und in übertragener Bedeutung gebraucht werden.

To heal usually refers to wounds, sores, etc. It can be used transitively, intransitively, and in figurative meaning.

Exercise 72 (A) Insert a suitable term of the above group.
1. Prevention is better than . . . (saying)
2. The . . . is worse than the disease. (saying)

3. Physician, . . . thyself! (saying)
4. (Nurse:) "That wound seems to be . . . very nicely."
5. The doctor pronounced him completely . . .
6. Yes, I've got . . . flesh.
7. Let me . . . you of all suffering.
8. I can't . . . you, but I can ease the pain.
9. He was . . . of smoking.
10. We are searching for a . . . , and we think we're getting near to one.
11. Put this . . . balm on the sore spot.
12. This herb has . . . properties.
13. It took five years to . . . the breach between them.
14. That doctor is wonderful. He has . . . hands.
15. What is the . . . for chronic unemployment?
16. Leave it alone and let it . . . itself.
17. Time, the great . . ., had worked its balm.
18. He stutters terribly. I'll soon . . . him of that.
19. There was a faith-. . . from Deal,
    Who said that though no pain was real,
    "If I sit on a pin
    And it punctures my skin,
    I dislike what I *fancy* I feel!"
20. "They murmured, as they took their fees: 'There is no . . . for this disease.'" (comic poem)

73
Herde
herd, flock

herd: A herd of deer bounded across the road.

Collocations: a herd of cattle / horses / swine / deer / oxen / elephants / whales / seals / giraffe / buffalo; the herd instinct.

Herd wird in bezug auf größere Tiere verwendet. In übertragener Bedeutung hat *herd* abwertenden Sinn.

This term refers to larger animals. If used in a figurative sense, it expresses contempt, e.g., the (common) herd.

flock: The shepherd has to look after a flock of sheep.

Collocations: a flock of birds / geese / goats / sheep.

Flock bezieht sich vor allem auf Vögel, Schafe und andere kleinere Tiere.

Flock mostly refers to birds, sheep, and smaller animals. (Also in religion: the minister and his flock)

Note: There are also special words for different groups of animals, e.g. a pack of hounds; a swarm of flies / bees; a school or shoal of fish; a pride of lions; a brace or covey of partridge; a flight of (almost any) birds.

Exercise 73 (A) Insert a suitable term of the above group.
1. He had a fine . . . of dairy cattle.
2. The hillside was covered by . . . of sheep.
3. A country girl came by with a . . . of geese.
4. He has no mind of his own. He always follows the . . .
5. The . . . stampeded, with a thunder of beating hooves.
6. "Whilst shepherds watched their . . . by night." (a Christmas carol)
7. He is a snob. He refuses to mix with the common . . .
8. The Indian boy drove the . . . of buffalo(es) along the dusty highway.
9. A . . . of tiny birds winged their way westwards.
10. A huge black stallion was the leader of the . . .

74
herrschen, regieren
to govern, to rule, to reign

to govern: The country is governed by the Cabinet rather than by Parliament.

Collocations: to govern one's temper / a person's actions; the motives governing a decision; a preposition may govern a certain case.

Auf der Grundlage von Wissen und Macht die Regierungsgeschäfte eines Landes betreiben. Einfluß auf jemand oder eine Sache ausüben, beherrschen; einen Fall regieren (in der Grammatik).

To be in charge of the administration of a country on the basis of power and knowledge; to exercise critical influence on persons or things, or abstractions such as linguistic forms, etc.; to control. (N.: *government*; *governor*)

to rule: William the Conqueror ruled England with an iron hand.
Many wives rule their husbands.

Collocations: the ruling classes; to rule by consent; to rule with an iron hand; democratic / dictatorial rule.

To rule betont mehr die Anwendung von Macht oder Gewalt (ganz gleich ob legal oder nicht) zur Beherrschung eines Landes, die Festlegung der Gesetze, nach denen die Bürger sich zu richten haben. Im übertragenen Sinne: jemanden oder eine Sache in absoluter Weise beherrschen.

To rule suggests the use of power in the governing of a country (no matter whether legal or illegal). If used in a figurative sense, the term means to exercise decisive influence over persons or things. (N.: *rule*; *ruler*)

to reign: Queen Elizabeth I reigned from 1558–1603.
The king's reign lasted until his death.

Collocations: a reigning monarch; a reign of terror; a peaceful / tempestuous reign; to reign supreme; peace reigned.

Regieren im Sinne von König oder Königin sein, den Thron innehaben. (Der Gesichtspunkt der tatsächlichen Macht wird außer acht gelassen.)

Im übertragenen Sinne in der Bedeutung von 'vorherrschen' verwendet. *To reign* wird nur intransitiv gebraucht.

To be king or queen, to hold royal office (with or without actual power); in figurative use: to be prevalent, to hold sway. *To reign* is an intransitive verb. (N.: *reign*)

Exercise 74 (A) Insert a suitable term of the above group.

1. When Charles II . . . , he was known as the Merry Monarch.
2. A government should . . . , and not simply allow things to drift.
3. He acted as regent when the . . . monarch was ill.
4. The headmaster exercises a dictatorial . . . over the children and staff.
5. You must . . . your temper, or you will get into trouble.
6. It is dangerous to accept the . . . of a despot, just because he is efficient.
7. Once he is crowned, the king will . . . until he dies.
8. An anarchist is against all . . .
9. Queen Victoria's . . . is usually described as "glorious".
10. Her . . . was just, but stern and inflexible.
11. How long has this party been . . . the country?
12. A democracy is . . . by majority vote.
13. In ancient times the kings of England . . . without a parliament.
14. Macbeth launched a . . . of terror against his real and imagined foes.

Exercise 74 (B)

1. The judge . . . that the evidence was inadmissible.
2. When the bombing started, panic . . . in the streets.
3. Low prices . . . on the Stock Exchange today.
4. The moon and the stars . . . in a cloudless sky.
5. She . . . over her kitchen like a queen.
6. After the battle the victor . . . supreme.
7. Be . . . by me, and you'll never regret it.
8. The island was . . . by a revolutionary council.
9. It is better to . . . by example than compulsion.
10. "Woe to the land where a usurper . . ." (i.e. where a usurper is on the throne)

75
jeder
every, each, any, either

every: He gets up at 5 o'clock every morning.
Every man is the architect of his fortune.

Collocations: every time; every chance; each and every one; every (single) one; every man for himself; every other day (=jeden zweiten Tag).

Jeder im Sinne von alle, jeder ganz allgemein. *Every* bezieht sich i. allg. auf eine größere Anzahl von Personen oder Dingen und wird häufig in Verallgemeinerungen gebraucht.

Every suggests universality. It is used in the sense of *all.*

each: Those oranges are 5p. each.

Each of you is wanted by the police.

Collocations: to like / hate, etc., each other.

Each hat eine stärkere vereinzelnde Bedeutung als *every*; jeder einzelne für sich genommen. *Each* bezieht sich auf eine kleine Anzahl.

Each means every one taken separately. It is the idea of separateness which distinguishes it from *every. Each* applies to small numbers.

any: You can come and go at any time.

Collocations: in any case; any time / place / suggestions, etc.; any amount (of) (=jede Menge); any fool can . . . ; any . . . you like.

Any bedeutet in bejahenden Sätzen jeder beliebige, ganz gleich welcher.

In affirmative sentences *any* means no matter which or whichever, i.e. no distinctions are made, or there are no hindrances.

either: We can go by either road.

Collocations: on either side (i.e. on both sides); at either end (i.e. at both ends).

Jedes von zwei Dingen (auch auf Personen bezüglich). Nicht selten wird *either* bei weniger strengem Gebrauch auch auf mehr als zwei Personen oder Dinge bezogen.

Each of two; often used, loosely, of more than two.

Exercise 75 (A) Insert a suitable term of the above group.

1. From . . . according to his ability, to . . . according to his need.
2. . . . child who gets full marks will receive a prize.
3. There's a phone call . . . minute of the day.
4. We do the washing . . . other day.
5. . . . one of you is precious to me.
6. "When shall I call?"–". . . time you like."
7. "Which would you like?"–"Oh, . . . will do."
8. "Who are you inviting?"–"Oh, . . . one can come."
9. He examined . . . petal minutely, for he was an expert botanist.
10. I've given you . . . opportunity to succeed.
11. In some shops you may pay with . . . currency you like.
12. "Mummy, who can I ask to my party?"–". . . little girl you like."
13. . . . woman he knew pitied him.
14. . . . little ornament in the room reminds me of her.
15. Now then, children, be nice to . . . other.
16. His strength ebbed, with . . . step that he took.
17. He took . . . of her hands in his.
18. We go camping . . . week-end.
19. "How much are they?"–"Five pounds . . ."
20. There are . . . amount of people trying to get hold of a ticket.

Exercise 75 (B)

1. "On . . . side the river lie
   Long fields of barley and of rye . . . . . ." (Tennyson)
2. . . . man for himself, and the Devil take the hindmost. (Scottish saying)
3. "Look, what I've done. Aren't I clever?"—". . . fool could have done that."
4. I couldn't make up my mind if . . . were right, or both were wrong.
5. "There's a fool born . . . minute." (saying)
6. "Do you always have nightmares after eating cheese?"—"Yes, . . . time."
7. George I and his son loathed . . . other cordially.
8. I don't care for . . . of the twins, myself.
9. . . . customer received a personal gift.
10. He didn't award a penalty to . . . side the whole afternoon.

76
Kanal
channel, canal

channel: The English Channel is narrowest between Dover and Calais.
We were informed through official channels.

Collocations: the channels of world trade; through diplomatic channels; a Channel swimmer; to swim the Channel.

Eine breite Meeresenge (z. B. zwischen einem Kontinent und einer Insel), eine Wasserstraße, der natürliche Verbindungsweg zwischen zwei Meeren; die Fahrrinne (im Fluß); ein natürlicher oder künstlicher Wasserlauf; eine Rinne, ein Kanal. Auch oft im übertragenen Sinn verwendet.

A wide strait (separating e.g., a continent from an island) or a navigable route joining two seas; the deeper part of a river; a natural or artificial waterway; a narrow groove. Also used in a figurative sense suggesting a means of conveying or transmitting something. (V.: *to channel*)

canal: By a network of canals ships can reach towns even in the central parts of the country.

Collocations: The Panama Canal; the Suez Canal; the Manchester Ship Canal; the Caledonian Canal (Scotland).

Der (i. allg. künstlich angelegte) Kanal für die Schiffahrt, Bewässerung, Entwässerung u. ä. (Auch gelegentlich der schmale natürliche Wasserweg, der tief ins Inland hineinreicht.)

Usually an artificial waterway for navigation, irrigation, drainage, or the like. (Sometimes, a narrow, natural watercourse which reaches far inland.) (V.: *to canalise*)

Exercise 76 (A) Insert a suitable term of the above group.

1. James Brindley was the great . . . builder of the age.
2. A whole network of . . . covered the country.
3. Please . . . your requests through the order department.
4. Brighton is on the . . . coast.

5. The Bridgewater ... was built to transport coal from Worsley to Manchester.
6. Horse-drawn barges ply the ... and waterways.
7. It is less than two hours across the ... from Dover to Calais.
8. The proposed ... Tunnel is often referred to as the "Chunnel".
9. ... were superseded by railways as a popular form of goods transport.
10. Swimming the ... was a popular sport in the 30's.
11. Many ... are being reopened for leisure purposes.
12. I obtained my information through the usual ...
13. Bristol ... lies between "Wessex" and Wales.
14. During the floods, a deep ... of water flowed between the houses.
15. The Caledonian ... cuts off the Highlands from the rest of Britain.
16. It is dangerous to navigate unknown ...
17. The disused ... have silted up.
18. Locks have been built along ... to raise barges to higher levels.
19. Narrow ... were carved into the wood.
20. There was a ... "mania" at the end of the 18th century.

77
klein
small, little, short

small: The chaffinch is a small bird.

Collocations: a small income / salary; a small farmer / shopkeeper; a small holding; small change; small-scale; small-minded; small wonder (i.e. it isn't surprising); to feel / look small (=sich schämen).

Klein im Vergleich zu anderen Größen(ordnungen), von geringen Ausmaßen. Auch im übertragenen Sinn verwendet (von geringem Wert u. ä.).

Small means not large in comparison with other persons, things or some other amount. If used figuratively *small* suggests something of minor importance or value.

little: She is a nice, little girl.

Collocations: a little too fat, etc.; of little importance; little (i.e. everyday) things; a little man (i.e. in business or the ordinary man in the street); a little favour.

In der Bedeutung von klein hat *little* emotionalen Gehalt (im Gegensatz zu *small*). Es wird in bezug auf Menge, Dauer, Anzahl oder Grad auch im Sinne von geringfügig, wenig, unwichtig, unbedeutend, ein klein wenig gebraucht.

Little also means not large, but, unlike *small*, it carries an emotional element. Thus it may mean endearingly small. It is also used in the sense of unimportant, insignificant referring to quantity, duration, number, or degree.

short: Uncle is a short man.

Klein von Wuchs (meist mit Bezug auf Menschen).

Of small stature, not tall (usually with reference to human beings).

Exercise 77 (A) Insert a suitable term of the above group.

1. I can't afford to buy in large quantities, I'm only a . . . man.
2. Please accept this . . . gift as a . . . token of our gratitude.
3. It is difficult to make ends meet on a . . . income.
4. A tiny . . . boy stepped forward and welcomed us.
5. I could hear the . . . coins jingling in his pocket.
6. She told him off in public and made him feel very . . .
7. "Bless 'em all, bless 'em all,
   The long and the . . . and the tall." (army song)
8. Speak up! I'm afraid I'm a . . . hard of hearing.
9. They were aghast at the situation. And . . . wonder!
10. He ran a very successful . . . holding.
11. The brewer was . . . but very fat.
12. Would you do me a . . . favour?
13. She smiled a pathetic . . . smile.
14. He was two inches too . . . for the police force.
15. We should control our own . . . desires, in the common good.
16. A mini car is hardly a . . .-scale Rolls Royce.
17. My father was a . . . shopkeeper at the corner of the street.
18. The . . . man suffers, whatever the economic climate.

78
klug
intelligent, clever, sensible, wise

intelligent: John is a very intelligent student.

That goalkeeper shows intelligent anticipation.

Collocations: an intelligent guess; an intelligence test; intelligent anticipation; a lively intelligence; intelligent perception; one's intelligent quotient.

Intelligent bezeichnet die geistige Qualität, die zum Verständnis mehr oder weniger komplizierter Zusammenhänge notwendig ist. Klug, von bemerkenswerter Denkkraft.

Able to use mental power for understanding new or difficult phenomena or problems, and coping with them. Of remarkable mental capacity. (N.: *intelligence*)

clever: The clever child wastes no time in his studies.

The chess player made a very clever move.

She is clever at painting/at arithmetic, etc.

Collocations: a clever invention/device/trick; a clever remark (=geistreiche Bemerkung); too clever by half (far too clever); damn clever, these . . . [sl.]; to be clever with his hands.

Clever kann in ähnlicher Bedeutung gebraucht werden wie intelligent, betont jedoch mehr die Fähigkeit zu raschem, geschicktem und einfallsreichem Denken und Handeln als zu tiefer gehender Gründlichkeit. (Es wird auch im Sinne von 'gerissen' verwendet.)

Mentally bright, similar to intelligent. But *clever* suggests quickness rather than depth of understanding. A person may be clever but shallow. Thus it may have a pejorative nuance. *Clever* also suggests ingenuity and natural skill. (N.: *cleverness*)

sensible: It isn't sensible to drink too much whisky.

Collocations: sensible precautions; it wasn't sensible (of you) to . . . ; is it sensible to . . .?

Klug im Sinne von vernünftig, einsichtvoll, verständig, vom gesunden Menschenverstand geleitet. *Sensible* bezeichnet eine schlichtere, gewissermaßen naturnähere Qualität als die übrigen Ausdrücke.

To be guided by common sense and natural reasonableness. Much more earthy and simple than *intelligent*, *clever*, or *wise*.
Note that *very* is often used with *sensible*. (N.: *sensibleness*)

wise: You were wise not to accept that offer.

Collocations: a wise decision; a wise policy; wise guidance / leadership; as wise as Solomon; a wise old owl; to learn / gain wisdom.

Die Fähigkeit, Personen, Tatbestände, Situationen etc. auf Grund von Wissen und langer Erfahrung klar beurteilen oder einschätzen zu können, so daß die richtigen Schlußfolgerungen (gegebenenfalls auch für das praktische Handeln) daraus gezogen werden können.

Having the capacity of assessing persons, things, or situations properly on the basis of knowledge and experience so as to discern what is right or true. Deepthinking and knowledgeable, usually only achieved by long experience.
(N.: *wisdom*)

Exercise 78 (A) Insert a suitable term of the above group.

1. Fancy doing a stupid thing like that! Where's your . . .?
2. I'm afraid I'm not very . . . at maths.
3. It wasn't very . . . of you to go out in the rain without a hat.
4. He was steeped in the . . . of the ancients.
5. You've misjudged the whole issue. And I thought you were . . .
6. I can sew, but I'm not very . . . at designing and cutting.
7. Human . . . makes man a superior being to all other creatures.
8. When you are a bit older, you'll learn . . . , my boy.
9. The Government has pursued a . . . policy.
10. Is it . . . to expose your deficiencies like that in public?
11. She's a . . . old owl. Nobody can fool her.
12. She was a lively . . . girl and learnt the trade quickly.
13. The . . . parent knows when to use the carrot, and when the stick.

14. Now be . . . , little girl, and go to bed when mummy tells you.
15. She's . . . at making excuses.
16. The old man gave . . . guidance to his grandchildren.
17. . . . tests were an integral part of the British educational system. But the whole concept of . . . as a fixed quotient, has been seriously challenged.
18. She's not beautiful or witty, but she's a nice . . . girl and should make you a good wife.
19. It is . . . to be careful when you are new to the game.
20. Be . . . and work it all out very carefully before making a decision.

Exercise 78 (B)

1. It was very . . . of you to land that job, against such stiff competition.
2. I don't know the answer but I'm prepared to make an . . . guess.
3. They're too . . . by half. They'll come to a bad end.
4. I'm not over-anxious but I like to take . . . precautions.
5. You thought the better of it. Very . . . , too.
6. "I came top of the class in maths, science, English and French."–"Oh, you . . . girl!" (Could be sarcastic.)
7. By . . . perception he was able to work out the problem in his mind.
8. He is a no-nonsense, . . . lad, and will go far.
9. Don't try to be . . . with me, young man.
10. "What beautiful carving!"–"Yes, he's very . . . with his hands."

79
kochen
to boil, to cook

to boil: Water boils at 212 degrees Fahrenheit.

Kochen im Sinne von sieden, etwas in siedender Flüssigkeit kochen. Auch bildlich gebraucht.

Of a liquid: to be brought to boiling point by heat; to be immersed in continuously boiling water.
Note: Kaffee/Tee kochen = to *make* coffee/tea.

to cook: He usually cooks his own meals.

Durch Kochen zubereiten.

To make food more edible, digestible, tasty by subjecting it to heat. (N.: *a cook*)

Exercise 79 (A) Insert a suitable term of the above group.

1. Empty the contents into one pint of water, bring it slowly to the . . ., and let it simmer for five minutes. (instructions on a packet of dried soup)
2. She makes my blood . . . , when she talks like that.
3. "Too many . . . spoil the broth."
4. I like my eggs . . . five minutes.
5. My mother is a wonderful . . .
6. French . . . is absolutely delicious.

7. I like . . . , but I don't like the preparations that have to precede it.
8. She constantly provoked him, just to keep the pot a . . .
9. I'll . . . the meal, and you can do the washing up.
10. Has the kettle . . . yet? I'm dying for a cup of tea.
11. The soup . . . over, and the gas-stove was ruined.
12. When we first got married, my wife couldn't . . . and admitted it. Now, she's not so modest.
13. When liquid reaches . . . point, you can turn off the gas, but when father reaches . . . point, there's no such remedy.
14. I like my tea to be . . . hot. I can't stand lukewarm drinks.
15. (Diner, to waiter:) "Please compliment the . . . on a delicious meal."
16. . . . is an art and a science rolled into one.
17. The storm raged, lashing the river to fury, and the water . . .
18. I like my potatoes well-. . .

80
kommen
to come, to get

to come: Come back as soon as possible.
How did you come by this priceless stamp?
Collocations: to come late/early/on time; to come down out of the clouds; to come to a conclusion/to an idea.
Kommen im Sinne von herkommen, näher kommen (vom Sprecher aus gesehen). Darüber hinaus in vielen übertragenen Bedeutungen.
Seen from the standpoint of the person speaking: to approach; to arrive. *Come* is often used in a figurative sense.

to get: When I got to Penzance, I immediately boarded the boat for St. Mary's.
Collocations: to get somewhere (or nowhere); to get somewhere on time; to get as far as . . .
Kommen im Sinne von hinkommen, ankommen, sich zu einem Ort hinbegeben.
To arrive at some place (mostly away from the person speaking).

Exercise 80 (A) Insert a suitable term of the above group.
1. Mary, stop dreaming! I'm talking to you. . . . down out of the clouds.
2. . . . here immediately and explain yourself.
3. Now . . . to mummy, darling, and let mummy brush your hair.
4. When I . . . to New York, I had a walk round the town first.
5. She always . . . down late to breakfast.
6. "Hallo! Fancy meeting you. When did you . . . here?"–"Oh, about an hour ago."
7. "Do you know the place well?"–"Oh, yes, I always . . . here for my holidays."

8. They . . . to the village twelve years ago, and settled down to village life.
9. I . . . as far as the door, and then I stopped.
10. "Hallo! Fancy meeting you. How did you . . .?"–"I . . . by bus."
11. They . . . to London in time for supper.
12. I've . . . to the conclusion that I need a holiday.
13. You must hurry if you want to . . . to the station on time.
14. I hope you . . . home safely.
15. Would you like to . . . to my party?
16. ". . . live with me and be my love." (C. Marlowe)
17. How do I . . . to the town-hall?
18. They . . . into difficulties.
19. Do you think that will ever . . . back into fashion again?
20. "Oh, you'll never . . . to Heaven.
In an old Ford car,
'Cos an old Ford car,
Can't . . . that far." (comic song)

81
Kraft, Stärke, Macht
power, force, strength, vigour

power: Electric power is of vital importance for any industry.

Collocations: the power of an engine; horse-power; water-power; power-station; steam-power; a source of power; the lust for power; the powers that be (i.e. those in charge); to seize / gain power; to hold power; to get into power; power-mad; high-powered; will-power; power of the mind (i.e. mental ability); the super powers (i.e. states, nations).

Das generelle Vermögen, die Fähigkeit, eine bestimmte Kraft wirksam werden zu lassen. Häufig als technischer Ausdruck im Sinne von Antriebskraft, mechanische Kraft, Energie u. ä. gebraucht.

Power implies the capacity to bring about some effect. It is also used in mechanics and government. (V.: *to power*; Adj.: *powerful*)

force: The force of the explosion ripped the roofs off the houses.

Collocations: to be unable to do s.th. owing to the force of circumstances/ destiny; to open a door / safe etc. by force; to remain in force (of a law); to come into force (e.g. with regard to regulations); to use force; a force for good (or of good); a force for evil; to join forces; superior force; the armed forces; social forces (less precise than classes).

Die tatsächlich zur Anwendung kommende, die wirkende, frei werdende Kraft. *Force* wird auch in der Wissenschaft verwendet, z. B. in der Physik.

The actual exercise of power, power in action. *Force* is also a scientific term used e.g. in physics.

strength: He showed his strength of character by refusing the tempting offer. They say that a horse doesn't know its own strength.

Collocations: physical strength; the strength of a horse; the tensile strength of a rope; strength of will / judgement / mind / character; the strength of coffee / tea / an acid; the blasting strength of an explosive; on the strength of (i.e. basing oneself on).

Die (innewohnende) Stärke, Widerstandskraft oder Festigkeit, mit Bezug auf Personen und Dinge. Auch die zahlenmäßige Stärke (von Truppen etc.).

The quality of being strong of a person or thing so that the capacity of enduring, showing energy, resisting pressure can be manifested. *Strength* is also applied to numerical force. (Adj.: *strong*)

vigour: He tackled his job with great vigour.

Collocations: the vigour of s.o.'s argument; the vigour of an attack; vim and vigour.

Tatkraft, vorwärtsdrängende Energie, Durchschlagskraft.

Vigour is a combination of strength and energy. It suggests being full of animation or impetus, and liveliness of mind. (V.: *to invigorate*; Adj.: *vigorous*)

Exercise 81 (A) Insert a suitable term of the above group.

1. He has tremendous will-... You won't compel him to do something against his will.
2. He has enough ... to lift 3 cwt.
3. We have done very well in business since we joined ...
4. He has the ... of a horse.
5. "... to the people" is a revolutionary slogan.
6. After his illness he was quickly gathering ...
7. When did the present government get into ...?
8. The toy boat was ...ed by an electric motor.
9. I cannot rely on the ... of my memory.
10. God, give me ...! (exclamation of impatience, when irritated)
11. There are many sources of ...: coal, oil, atomic fission.
12. The Indian fakir demonstrated the ... of the mind over the body.
13. He still retained his youthful ..., right into old age.
14. We must yield to superior ...
15. The ... of destiny are often blamed for man's stupidity.
16. He was a ... for good in the neighbourhood.
17. "The pen is mightier than the sword" means that the written word has more ... effect than armies.
18. The lorry went out of control, and I was ...less to stop it.
19. The deputy minister made a ... speech in support of the government's policy.
20. I have a ... suspicion that he is lying.

Exercise 81 (B)

1. His ...ed laugh deceived nobody.

2. She stirred the mixture . . . until it frothed.
3. These regulations remain in . . . until they are cancelled.
4. Shakespeare's poetry reflects the . . . of the Elizabethan Age.
5. Saints are often credited with the . . . of curing people of illnesses.
6. They acknowledged the . . . of my argument.
7. The author's prose is full of energy and . . .
8. Bring him here by persuasion or by . . .
9. I've not the least doubt that his . . . of will will overcome the difficulties he is faced with.
10. He strode . . . down the cobbled road.

82
krank
ill, sick

ill: He has been ill now for three weeks.

Collocations: to fall ill; to feel ill; to be taken ill; dangerously ill.

Im Sinne von krank wird *ill* nur prädikativ gebraucht.

In the sense of 'unwell' *ill* is used only predicatively. (N.: *illness*)

sick: Mr. Binks is a sick man. He should retire on a pension.

Collocations: sick benefit; sick diet; on sick-leave; to be written off sick; to go/report sick; to be off sick; to be seasick; to be homesick; to tend the sick.

Note:

to be sick = sich erbrechen; it makes me sick = mir wird übel davon; to be sick of s.th. = etwas über haben.

Bei attributivem Gebrauch wird *sick* im britischen Englisch im Sinne von krank oder siech verwendet. (Im amerikanischen Englisch auch bei prädikativer Verwendung). Als Teil des Prädikats bedeutet *sick* 'übel, zum Erbrechen neigend'. In übertragener Bedeutung: unter einem Gefühl leidend; einer Sache überdrüssig, etwas leid sein.

If used attributively, *sick* means (in British English) *ill* or *ailing.* (In American usage *sick* has this meaning also if used as part of the predicate.) (N.: *sickness*)

Exercise 82 (A) Insert a suitable term of the above group.
1. After that large dinner, I feel positively . . .
2. The doctor told me I was in for a long . . .
3. "Where have you been lately?"–"I've been off . . . for a few days."
4. He was taken . . . at midnight and driven to the hospital in an ambulance.
5. I am not so . . . that I can't continue with my work.
6. You'd better report . . . straight away.
7. I'm . . . and tired of all this talk.
8. I'm afraid your father is dangerously . . .
9. He was violently . . . , and vomited all over the carpet.

10. He's been a . . . man for some time, and isn't likely to last long.
11. He is seriously . . . with pneumonia.
12. Turkey used to be called "The . . . Man of Europe".
13. On our last holiday our son was constantly sea . . .
14. I don't want to see her again; I'm . . . of the sight of her.
15. Are they really . . . , or are they just malingering?
16. Her . . . was difficult to diagnose.
17. After ten years abroad, she's naturally a little home . . .
18. If you're . . . , see a doctor, don't just mope around the house.

83
Kritik
criticism, critique, review

criticism: Your criticism of my book was very helpful.
One should be able to stand criticism.

Collocations: to make a criticism (Kritik üben); open to criticism; constructive/destructive criticism; self-criticism; a theatre/cinema critic; to accept criticism; to put up with criticism.

Kritische Äußerung oder auch Untersuchung.

A critical remark or a favourable or unfavourable judgement, an appraisal. Note: a critic = ein Kritiker

critique: The professor's critique of the classical authors was widely studied by all intellectuals and readers of the quality press.

Eine umfassende kritische Einschätzung. Gewählter Ausdruck von geringerem Anwendungsbereich als *criticism.* Bezieht sich vor allem auf Philosophie und Politik.

A careful critical assessment. *Critique* is a somewhat affected term of waning use. It tends to refer to politics and philosophy.

review: Book reviews often reveal more of the reviewer than of the author.

Collocations: a book review; a poetry review; a favourable (or an unfavourable) review; a lengthy/short review.

Eine Rezension, kritische Besprechung eines Buches, Theaterstückes etc.

This term is used for slighter articles on individual books, etc.; a critical survey or summary of something written. (V.: *to review*)

Exercise 83 (A) Insert a suitable term of the above group.
1. I never believe what the . . . say; I prefer to read the book myself.
2. Good . . . always educates the reading public.
3. They gave the young journalist a last chance, . . .ing books. He had failed at everything else.
4. Her few words, though well chosen, were hardly a serious . . . of the subject.

5. Drug-taking by the young may be regarded as a practical, if misguided, ... of modern society.
6. The work under ..., this week, is the author's second novel.
7. My dear chap, if you want to be a public figure, you'll have to put up with ...
8. All the ... of his book were favourable.
9. Kant wrote a book entitled: "The ... of pure reason."
10. Short ... of current literature are published every day.
11. Genuine self-... is a very valuable experience.
12. This book constitutes a well-grounded ... of modern painting. And all ... voiced so far does not detract from its merits.
13. I welcome constructive ...
14. There is a longer ... of a selected work in the week-end edition.
15. He obtained a divorce because his wife was always ... him in public.
16. The ... should be regarded as a friend by the serious author.

84
Land
land, country

land: They fought by sea and by land.[1]
After a three days' voyage we came in sight of land again.[1]
These lands belong to the Duke of Windsor.[2]
The settlers turned the woods into arable land.[3]
He lives in a land of dreams.[4]

Collocations: to go (or travel) by land (also: over land); to be on dry land once more; one's native land; a landowner; land reform; fertile/arable land; landed gentry.

[1]Das Festland (im Gegensatz zur See); [2]der Landbesitz, Ländereien; [3]der Boden (hinsichtlich seiner Qualität, Nutzung); [4]ein bestimmtes durch natürliche oder politische Grenzen abgestecktes Gebiet (besonders im gehobenen Stil).

[1]The solid surface of the globe (as distinguished from the parts covered by water); [2]landed property; [3]solid ground (esp. referring to its quality, use); [4]a district or area designated by natural or political boundaries (in literary or poetic style).

country: Russia is the largest country in the world.[1]
I would not mind living in the country.[2]
Between Blair Atholl and Inverness I passed through a wild stretch of country.[3]

Collocations: town and country; country air; a country-house; country life; flat/swampy, etc. country; out in the country; in the (heart of the) country; a walk in the country; country of origin; industrial/

developing country; to leave the country; to go into the country; town and country planning; country dancing.

[1]Das Land als politischer Begriff, Staat, Vaterland; [2]Land, Provinz als Gegensatz zur Stadt; [3]Terrain, Gegend.

[1]The territory occupied by a particular nation, a State; the land of one's birth; [2]a rural district (as distinguished from town or city); [3]a stretch of land, region.

Exercise 84 (A) Insert a suitable term of the above group.

1. Did you travel by air or over . . .?
2. We made the . . . journey across Africa from east to west.
3. What . . . do you come from?
4. It was wonderful to be on dry . . . once more.
5. On an official form: Please state your . . . of origin.
6. Out in the . . . , the air is purer.
7. I'm a . . . boy, born and bred.
8. The fertile crescent is an area of . . . in the Middle East.
9. The old lady lived in a . . . cottage.
10. . . . dancing used to be popular in schools.
11. They toured the . . . from end to end.
12. "Back to the . . ." was a slogan to encourage the revival of agriculture.
13. I was delighted to be back in my native . . .
14. We rode for miles over hilly . . .
15. (Look-out, on board ship:) ". . . ahoy!"
16. Life in the . . . can be very dull.
17. Having been defeated on a motion of censure, the Government resigned and went to the . . .
18. . . . End really is at the south-west end of England.

85
Landschaft
landscape, scenery

landscape: From the top of the hill we saw a beautiful landscape.

Collocations: a mountainous / romantic / breathtaking / flat landscape; a seascape; a landscape painter.

Die Gesamterscheinungsform eines meist größeren Landschaftsausschnittes von einem bestimmten Blickpunkt aus.

The *overall* picture of (mostly) an extensive area of country as seen from a single point of view.

scenery: Saxon Switzerland is rich in imposing scenery.

Collocations: a piece of mountain scenery (eine Berglandschaft); picturesque scenery; to study the scenery.

Das sich dem Betrachter bietende Landschaftsbild in seinen Einzelheiten (Berge, Felsen, Seen, Bäume etc.).

Scenery suggests the scenic *details* presented by some district.

Exercise 85 (A) Insert a suitable term of the above group.

1. Downland . . . are full of gentle undulations.
2. We were surrounded by beautiful . . .
3. Let's go, I don't like the . . . around me.
4. . . . are always tempting to paint or photograph.
5. Come with me, and I will show you some of the loveliest . . . in the world.
6. The . . . in East Anglia is flat and uninteresting.
7. I prefer mountain . . .
8. Observe the lush . . . in this tropical wonderland.
9. (Travel bureau advertisement:) We have . . . to suit all tastes.
10. Almost anywhere in the Lake District one is presented with romantic . . .
11. The inviting . . . seemed to beckon us forward.
12. On rounding the corner of a hill, we were confronted with a breathtaking . . .
13. Bring out the picnic basket, I didn't come here to study the . . .
14. We passed through miles of splendid . . .
15. The . . . looked quite different in the half light.
16. The . . . consisted of baked grass and scrubland.
17. We bought the house on the strength of the . . .
18. Turner was a great . . . painter, who usually included sunsets in the view.

86
legen, setzen, stellen
to put, to place, to lay

to put: Put the book on the shelf when you have done with it.

Collocations: put coal on the fire / salt in the soup / the books back in their place, etc.; put the children to bed; put the blame on s.o.; put the clock back, etc.

Setzen, stellen, legen ganz allgemein; häufig in übertragener Bedeutung.

To move something to a place other than where it is, with no special reference to method and frequently in a figurative sense.

to place: Take the vase and place it carefully on the mantelpiece.
Aren't those two paintings placed too closely together?
He placed his hand on the Bible and took an oath that he was telling the truth.

Collocations: to place things in their right order; to place confidence in s.o.

To place ist ein vergleichsweise gewählter Ausdruck und zielt auf Genauigkeit der Bewegung oder Plazierung ab. Etwas mit gewisser Sorgfalt an eine bestimmte Stelle legen oder bringen.

To place is a more formal word than *to put.* It suggests precision of movement or location, care and exactness.

to lay: The mayor laid the foundation stone of the monument.
He laid his finger on his lips.

Collocations: to lay rails / a cable / a carpet / mines, etc.; to lay the table / an egg.

Etwas zum Liegen, in horizontale Lage bringen.

To place something in some particular, usually lying position.

Exercise 86 (A) Insert a suitable term of the above group.

1. He . . . the pipe carefully on the shelf behind the vase.
2. "Where shall I . . . this ball?"–"You can . . . it anywhere you like."
3. I . . . my hand into my pocket and took out a coin.
4. She . . . the book in its proper place on the bookshelf.
5. . . . bricks is a skilled job.
6. Now, just . . . your hand on this surface. What do you feel?
7. . . . your hand on the banisters to steady yourself.
8. The patient was . . . on a stretcher.
9. You . . . the child to bed, and I'll . . . the kettle on.
10. He . . . his clothes underneath a large stone, before he went swimming.
11. "What are you doing with that knife?"–"I was . . . it back in your drawer."
12. (To dog, who has picked up a stone:)" . . . it down, boy. . . . it down."
13. . . . yourself in *my* place, old man. What would you have done?
14. The table is . . . How about bringing in the tea?
15. An ostrich . . . enormous eggs.
16. The woman . . . the vase where it showed off to advantage.
17. "I've . . . the sack of coal in the coal-house."–"Oh, please, . . . some lumps on the fire."
18. (Undertaker:) "Where is the body?"–"We've . . . him out in the bedroom."
19. Have you . . . any sugar in my tea?
20. The nurse . . . a jug of water on the table beside my bed.
21. After I had . . . a silver coin in his hand, he became much friendlier.
22. He . . . the blade on the top shelf where his child could not get it.
23. I'm afraid you've . . . the cutlery out incorrectly.
24. The mayor . . . the foundation stone of our school.
25. I must tell you that I . . . complete trust in him.

87
leihen
to lend, to borrow, to loan

to lend: Would you lend me your pen, please?
"Friends, Romans, countrymen, lend me your ears!" (Shakespeare)
Collocations: to lend a hand / an ear (i.e. to listen); a lending library (as against a reference library); a money lender.
Verleihen, jemandem etwas leihen; also im Sinne von 'geben'.
To give something for temporary use with the understanding that it shall be returned. *Lend* implies a slight nuance towards a personal arrangement.

to borrow: May I borrow this book from you?
Collocations: to borrow from another writer; in borrowed plumes; borrowed time.
Etwas entleihen, ausborgen; also im Sinne von 'nehmen'.
To take something for temporary use on the premise that it shall be returned afterwards. It is also used as a euphemism for 'to steal'.–In English, *lend* and *borrow* are antonyms.

to loan: The bank loaned the firm £ 2000.
Collocations: to negotiate / to float a loan; interest on a loan; loan conditions; a Government loan; a loan from the IMF.
Vor allem im amerikanischen Englisch für *to lend*; aber auch im britischen Englisch, vorzugsweise im Geschäftsleben verwendet.
To loan stands for *to lend* in American English. It is also used in British English and tends to be used more for business and large deals. (N.: *loan*)

Exercise 87 (A) Insert a suitable term of the above group.
1. "May I . . . a match?"–"I'll give you one. Don't bother to return it."
2. . . . me a handkerchief, please. I've left mine at home.
3. I refuse to . . . you any more money. You owe too much already.
4. A . . . from a moneylender is an expensive luxury.
5. This house was . . . to me by my friend whilst he was abroad.
6. I seldom . . . books from the library.
7. If you . . . something, always be sure to give it back.
8. We have a . . . library in every town.
9. The finance minister took six months to negotiate the . . .
10. Building societies are money-. . . organisations. They accept the property you are buying as collateral.
11. His shelves are full of books, . . . from his friends.
12. The Bank of England floated a . . .
13. Since his operation, he's been living on . . . time.
14. They will . . . you money at a high rate of interest.

15. Look at her, all dressed up in . . . plumes!
16. What were the conditions under which the bank . . . you the money?
17. Large sums of money are . . . to entrepreneurs, regarded as good risks.
18. It's a question of "to be or not to be", to . . . an expression from Shakespeare.
19. I can't lift this on my own. Would you . . . me a hand?
20. Distance . . . enchantment to the view. (saying)
21. (Soldier, in barrack room:) "Who's '. . .' my shoe polish?"
22. He says that he only . . . her the boat, but she claims he sold it to her.
23. Ask your father if he will . . . me his mower.
24. Good payers can always . . . a second time.

88
machen
to make, to do

to make: "What are you making?"–"Some pies."
They make cars at that factory.
Don't make such a noise!

Collocations: to make tea / coffee / a fire; to make a mistake / a mess of s.th.; to make money / a speech / a remark / an impression / an offer; to make trouble / history / haste / enquiries / efforts; to make a journey / room for / friends, etc.

Machen im Sinne von herstellen, hervorbringen.

The fundamental meaning of *make* is to produce or construct.

to do: "What are you doing?"–"I'm looking for my purse."
Do your homework first, then you can go out.
Do as I do. (=Mache es so wie ich).

Collocations: to do repairs; to do one's best / worst; to do business / trade with; to do good; to do one's hair; to do exercises / a translation.

Machen im Sinne von durchführen, verrichten. Die Grundbedeutungen von *do* und *make* sind bei idiomatischem Gebrauch der beiden Verben kein sicherer Anhaltspunkt mehr. Daher müssen solche Wendungen gesondert memoriert werden.

The basic meaning of *to do* is to carry out, to perform.–However, *make* and *do* often deviate from their fundamental meanings if used idiomatically. Such idiomatic uses can only be mastered by experience.

Exercise 88 (A) Insert a suitable term of the above group.
1. He . . . a lot of money on the Stock Exchange.
2. "Will you help me?"–"I'll . . . the best I can."
3. What did you . . . last night?
4. I provide the material and she . . . the dresses.
5. They . . . a terrible fuss when they found out.

6. . . . way for His Most Illustrious Highness.
7. I have a woman in to . . . the housework.
8. Hallo! What are *you* . . . in this part of the world?
9. He . . . some remark that I couldn't quite catch.
10. It is wonderful to watch Chaplin . . . his stuff.
11. They . . . strenuous efforts to keep up with us.
12. Do you know how to . . . a fire?
13. They are . . . a lot of business with us.
14. The president . . . an excellent speech last night.
15. . . . it better next time.

89
Mann
man, male, husband

man: Men and women do not always get the same pay for the same work.

Collocations: a man of property / of standing / of the world / of his word/ about the house; a one-man delegation; the man in the street.

Der Mann im Gegensatz zur Frau.

A grown-up male (as opposed to a grown-up female).

male: Among the patients there are 36 males.

Collocations: fully grown males; adult males.

Gewählterer Ausdruck als *man*.

Much more formal term for a male person than *man*.

husband: Mrs. Smith's husband is a joiner.

Der Ehemann, Gatte.

Husband indicates the relationship of a married man to his wife.

Exercise 89 (A) Insert a suitable term of the above group.
1. The central character of The Forsyte Saga was described as a . . . of property.
2. He's a perfect . . ., kind and considerate at all times.
3. "Do you take this . . . to be your lawful, wedded . . .?" (wedding service)
4. You may be a . . ., but it's your turn to do the washing-up.
5. I've known her for some time, but I've never met her . . .
6. I'm surprised that a . . . of the world, like you, should be so easily deceived.
7. I went, as a one-. . . delegation, to No. 10 Downing St.
8. My parents were delighted that their first child was a . . .
9. She got on better with those colleagues who were . . .
10. My sister's . . . is my brother-in-law.
11. The . . . in the street wants peace.

12. She's terribly domineering; I shouldn't like to be her . . .
13. I can't tell if that nurse is a . . . or a female. They wear the same uniform.
14. She's gone through three . . . already, and now she's looking for a fourth.
15. Good heavens, . . ., where did you get that black eye?
16. A nod's as good as a wink to a blind . . . (saying)
17. Queen Victoria's . . ., Prince Albert, was known as the Prince Consort.
18. She didn't marry for love, but to have a . . . about the house.
19. You can rely on him. He's a . . . of his word.
20. It is said that tribes were originally formed to control the belligerence of the grown . . .
21. My ex-. . . re-married soon after our divorce.
22. . . . who stay late at the office come under wifely suspicion.
23. ". . . of England, heirs to glory." (P. B. Shelley, Mask of Anarchy)
24. There are more . . . born than females. But far more . . . have been killed off by wars.

90
Maschine
machine, engine

machine: We've bought an electric sewing machine.

Collocations: washing / sewing / calculating machine; machine tools; an infernal machine; the machine age; the state machine / machine-made; to set a machine in motion; simple / complicated machinery; the party machine.

Eine durch fremde Kraft angetriebene Maschine; zuweilen auch für bestimmte Fahrzeuge gebraucht (Autos, Flugzeuge u. ä.).

A mechanical device used to perform some work, but not moving on its own power. *Machine* suggests intricate construction, but *engine* suggests force, power, e.g. an aeroplane is often called a machine, but an engine supplies it with power. Thus *a machine* may be set in motion by *an engine.*

engine: The internal-combustion engine was invented in the late 19th century.

Collocations: a steam engine; a (railway) engine; an engine driver; a (motor) car engine; the internal-combustion engine; a ship's / an aeroplane engine.

Die aus eigener Kraft arbeitende Maschine, der Motor; auch Lokomotive.

Any mechanism designed to convert energy into mechanical work.

Exercise 90 (A) Insert a suitable term of the above group.
1. The electric . . . is now being developed and modernised.
2. In my youth every little boy wanted to be an . . . driver.
3. The . . . age began with the Industrial Revolution.
4. With a screeching of brakes, he brought his . . . to a standstill.

5. My car always develops . . . trouble when I am miles from nowhere.
6. When the enemy planes were sighted, there was a rush for the . . .
7. Reaping-and-binding . . . were first used in the 19th century.
8. We heard the . . . throbbing, deep down in the ship.
9. There is no danger that men will be dominated by . . .
10. The Police Force, Army and Navy are part of the state . . .
11. You don't often see a steam . . . pulling a train.
12. The terrorists planted an infernal . . . in the president's car.
13. Our washing . . . saves my wife endless work.
14. Who invented the steam . . .?

91
Mittel
means, remedy, medium

means: The ever increasing speed of our means of transport is developing into a serious danger to modern man.
He is a man of means.
Collocations: a means to an end; to find ways and means; beyond one's means; means of production; a means of communication; by means of.
Das Mittel zur Erreichung eines Zieles; finanzielle Mittel.
An instrument, agent, etc. which helps to reach some end; also in the sense of income, revenue. *Means* tends to be more abstract than *medium*.

remedy: She knows a remedy for almost every ailment.
Collocations: a drastic/effective remedy; a remedy for all ills; a legal/political remedy; remedial treatment; to remedy an evil.
Mittel im Sinne von Heilmittel, Gegenmittel; auch bildlich gebraucht.
Something which cures a disease. Also in the sense of setting right something bad and in a figurative sense.

medium: Astronauts can send messages from the Moon to the Earth in a matter of seconds through the medium of wireless.
Collocations: a medium of exchange; a chemical medium; a medium of expression; a propaganda medium; a spiritualist medium; the mass media.
Mittel im Sinne von Medium, vermittelnder Stoff oder vermittelnde Person, Träger. *Medium* ist ein gewählterer Ausdruck als *means*.
A transmitting substance or vehicle, an agency through which anything is done. *Medium* is more elegant than *means*. (Pl.: *media*)

Exercise 91 (A) Insert a suitable term of the above group.
1. Aspirins are the usual mild . . . for headaches.
2. I can't afford that; it's far beyond my . . .
3. Air is the . . . for transmitting sound waves.

4. Television has added another . . . for the spreading of information.
5. Private ownership of the . . . of production and distribution usually ensures high efficiency.
6. Their crude flattery is just a . . . to an end.
7. A stimulating argument is the best . . . for boredom.
8. A newspaper is also a . . . of propaganda.
9. The . . . is worse than the disease.
10. Some people say that the end justifies the . . .
11. Money is a . . . of exchange.
12. Ways and . . . were found for raising the money.
13. He has a . . . for all ills.
14. Money doesn't worry him. He's a man of almost unlimited . . .
15. Language, as a . . . for transmitting ideas, has helped to make us human.
16. The . . . sat in a darkened room and called upon the spirits to appear.
17. The telephone, radio and TV are all . . . of communication.
18. What is the . . . for the country's economic problems?
19. I refuse to disclose the . . . by which I obtained access to his office.
20. It is quite beyond my . . . to go on holiday just now.

Exercise 91 (B)

1. Epstein favoured bronze as a . . . for his sculptures.
2. If you feel insulted, there is always the legal . . .
3. One couldn't see how the shelves were held up. They had no visible . . . of support.
4. The U.N. exists as a . . . for accord among nations.
5. Backward children need special . . . treatment.
6. During the Hungry Thirties the . . . Test was hated by the unemployed.
7. He acted as a . . . in our negotiations with the other side.
8. Man's inquisitiveness has always been a . . . of change.
9. She has to live on her brother's charity, as she has little . . . of her own.
10. After I had . . . the fault, we continued serenely on our way.

92
Null
nought, zero, nil

nought: Seven five nought is 750.

Collocations: to bring to nought (i.e. to frustrate s.o.'s plans); to set at nought; to come to nought; noughts and crosses (a game).

Die Ziffer Null und im Sinne von 'nichts'. (Auch die Schreibung *naught* ist üblich.)

The figure 0 and in the sense of 'nothing'. (also spelt *naught.*)

zero: When the temperature falls to zero, water turns into ice.

Collocations: below/above zero; right down to zero; zero hour.

Null besonders in bezug auf Meßinstrumente. *Zero* wird vor allem im amerikanischen Englisch für *nought* gebraucht.

Preferably used with reference to the starting-point in scales. American usage for *nought*.

nil: Our team won by five goals to nil (five nil).

Collocations: nil report (= Fehlanzeige); nil returns; of nil importance.

Null = nichts; die erzielte Punktzahl null.

Nil = nothing; a score of nothing.

Exercise 92 (A) Insert a suitable term of the above group.

1. He can rise from . . . to boiling point in next to no time, when he's angry.
2. He had travelled 300 miles through dangerous country–and all for . . .
3. It is usually below . . . in North Siberia.
4. The match was a draw: . . ., . . .
5. Starting from . . ., we measured three-and-a-half centimetres.
6. A million is written with six . . .
7. It is a matter of absolutely . . . importance to me.
8. A washing-machine doesn't exactly reduce a woman's work to . . .
9. By morning our spirits had sunk to . . .
10. When I saw her face, my hopes fell to . . .
11. We went into the whole scheme minutely, but the upshot was . . .
12. She complained that her husband continually set her at . . .
13. Please complete and return the enclosed questionnaire. . . . returns are also required.
14. Her intervention brought all his plans to . . .
15. You are . . . but a dreamer. All your schemes will come to . . .
16. We shouted and whistled, but the effect was . . .

93
Politik
politics, policy

politics: We are all greatly interested in politics.

Collocations: national / local / party / power politics; to take part in politics; politics of the right (or the left).

Politik in der Bedeutung von Staatsführung und Kunst oder Wissenschaft der Staatsführung; das politische Leben, die politische Tätigkeit.

The science or art of government; matters related to, or connected with this. (N.: *politician;* Adj.: *political*)

policy: I agree with the government's policy. (i.e. with the plan they are following)

Collocations: government(al) policy; a firm's policy; commercial policy; economic / educational policy; a policy of peace; peaceful policy; to pursue / work out / revise / explain a policy; a policy-making body; home / domestic / foreign policy; a wise / successful/fatal policy; a policy statement / document; a crisis of policy.

Die praktisch verfolgte politische Linie und in der allgemeineren Bedeutung von Methode, Taktik, Verfahren.

A practical course of action pursued or a plan of action to be pursued.

Exercise 93 (A) Insert a suitable term of the above group.

1. Some men and women go in for . . . as a profession.
2. Power . . . are only possible for powerful nations.
3. Honesty is the best . . . (saying)
4. We must pursue a firm . . . or no one will take us seriously.
5. He is a student of . . . and he attends Parliament every day.
6. I must warn you that your present . . . will lead you nowhere.
7. There is broad agreement on foreign . . . between the two main parties.
8. He likes to argue about . . ., but not seriously; he's only playing . . .
9. The firm's . . . was to employ mainly young men.
10. His . . . was to admit all and seek forgiveness–an unusual . . .
11. . . . should be seen as both an art and a science.
12. If you want a political career, that is, if you want to stay in . . ., you've got to have a thick skin.
13. It was the . . . of the last government to encourage comprehensive schools.
14. Interest in . . . is at its height during a general election.
15. What is the best . . . for peace?
16. My mother's . . . was to buy cheap but cook well.
17. One of the new government's . . . is to cut public spending.
18. It is a peculiar, even a dangerous . . ., but it seems to work.

94
Rand
margin, edge, verge, rim, brim, brink

margin: Fold a margin 1 in. wide down the edge of your paper.

Collocations: the margin of a page; at the margin; a margin of error / profit; to write something in the margin.

Der klar abgegrenzte Rand von bestimmter Breite, der Randstreifen, Seitenrand.

The limited strip bordering some area; narrow area to the left of the line usually drawn down the left-hand side of a page in a school exercise book. (Adj.: *marginal*)

edge: The edge of the knife has been damaged.
I cut my finger on the sharp edge of a blade.

Collocations: a book with gilt edges; the edge of a box / table / page / forest / lake / river / precipice / cliff / knife; to set one's teeth on edge; to take the edge off.

Der äußerste, scharfe Rand einer Fläche, die Kante.

The sharp line which marks the extremity of some surface. (V.: *to edge*)

verge: The country was on the verge of another economic crisis.
There was a narrow grass verge beside the road.

Collocations: to be on the verge of a war / of tears / of a nervous breakdown; to be on the verge = to be about to do s.th.

Die Grenzlinie, hinter der irgend etwas anderes beginnt (meist in übertragener Bedeutung verwendet); zuweilen auch im Sinne von schmaler Grenzstreifen.

The extreme limiting line beyond which something new begins; sometimes in the sense of a narrow strip limiting some area. *Verge* is mostly used in figurative meaning. (V.: *to verge on*)

rim: The rim of the wheel has broken.

Collocations: the rim of a pair of spectacles / of a cup / of a bucket; red-rimmed eyes; rimless glasses; gold / steel / tortoise shell rimmed glasses.

Der äußere Rand eines runden Gegenstandes.

The outer edge of a circular object.

brim: The glass was filled to the brim.

Collocations: full to the brim; the brim of a bowl / basin; the brim of a hat; to rise to the brim.

Der obere innere Rand eines hohlen Gegenstandes oder Gefäßes.

The inside of the rim, at the top of some vessel or hollow object. (V.: *to brim over*)

brink: The boy stood shivering on the brink of the river.

Collocations: on the brink of a cliff / abyss / precipice / the grave / eternity / destruction / ruin / absurdity; the river's brink (abrupter than edge or verge).

Der Rand an einem steilen Abhang (auch im übertragenen Sinne).

The verge beyond which something steep begins (often used figuratively).

Exercise 94 (A) Insert a suitable term of the above group.

1. The moon had a . . . of cloud around it.
2. Fill my mug to the . . . I'm thirsty.
3. The teacher wrote his corrections in the . . .
4. The . . . in some library books contain scribbled comments.
5. There was lip-stick around the . . . of the tea-cup.
6. He felt the . . . of the paper to see how sharp it was.
7. His business is on the . . . of bankruptcy, and he's on the . . . of suicide.
8. On the . . . of the grave he repented.
9. His jacket sleeves were frayed at the . . .
10. With all this unnerving uncertainty, he's on the . . . of collapse.
11. I placed the bucket upside down and rested it on its . . .
12. Just before the crash I felt I was on the . . . of eternity.
13. A fly was crawling along the . . . of the window-sill.
14. He peered at me through his gold-. . . spectacles.

15. . . . less glasses were all the rage at one time.
16. Draw a one-inch . . . on the left-hand side of the page.
17. After a morning in the pub, he was full to the . . .
18. Plans should always allow for a . . . of error.
19. The grass . . . had been trampled on by careless sightseers.
20. The city is on the . . . of destruction.

Exercise 94 (B)

1. It was mildly funny to start with, but now it's . . . on the ridiculous.
2. The field became wet and swampy at its . . .
3. My brother had hesitated long before getting married; now he was teetering on the . . .
4. Manslaughter sometimes . . . on murder.
5. . . . manship is a new and dangerous form of diplomacy.
6. Her eyes were red-. . . through lack of sleep.
7. Mariners used to be afraid of falling off the . . . of the world.
8. The sheep were stampeded over the . . . of a cliff.
9. The glass was cracked at the . . .
10. The child was . . . ful of happiness, watching the clowns at the circus.

95
reif
ripe, mature

ripe: The apples in our garden are not ripe yet.

Collocations: ripe corn / cheese / grapes; a ripe harvest; to live to a ripe old age; to be ripe for discussion / decision / action; fully ripe; overripe; a ripe beauty.

Allgemeiner Ausdruck für reif; im eigentlichen und übertragenen Sinne gebraucht.

The general term for having completed growth so as to be ready for reaping or eating; arrived at the highest or a high point of development. (N.: *ripeness;* V.: *to ripen*)

mature: After mature deliberation he drew up a new plan.

Collocations: a mature plan; a mature person; mature wine; to be mature for one's age; mature judgement / wisdom; mature tobacco / wood.

Reif im Sinne von voll entwickelt, ausgereift. *Mature* wird häufig im übertragenen Sinne gebraucht. *Mature,* auf Personen angewendet, ist positiver als das etwas neutralere *ripe.*

Fully grown or developed; to be at the height of one's mental or physical development. *Mature* is often used in figurative meaning and it is somewhat more dignified than *ripe,* which is more neutral. (N.: *maturity;* V.: *to mature*)

Exercise 95 (A) Insert a suitable term of the above group.

1. The corn is still green; it's not quite . . . for harvesting yet.
2. Methuselah lived to a . . . old age.
3. On . . . reflection I decided to reject the offer.
4. My tomatoes didn't begin to . . . until the end of August.
5. Children of warmer climates tend to . . . more rapidly.
6. Now remember–only pick the . . . ones.
7. We've been skirting round the topic for months, now it's . . . for discussion.
8. Some people . . . early; some never!
9. I never buy cheese when it is too . . .
10. "Shall we issue a public statement?"–"No, the time is not . . ."
11. We always leave it to his . . . judgement.
12. That lad has been playing me up all day, now he's . . . for punishment.
13. Our plans have . . ., and now the time is . . . to put them into practice.
14. Tobacco has to be thoroughly . . . before it can be smoked.
15. Sodom and Gomorrah were . . . for destruction.
16. Nell Gwynne's . . . beauty fascinated Charles II.
17. When an animal can produce young, it has reached . . .
18. This wine has . . . in the wood.

96
Reise
journey, voyage, trip, travel, tour

journey: It's a long journey from Scotland to Land's End.

Collocations: to go on a journey; to make a journey; a day's (two days') journey; a train/plane/car journey; a journey through life; a journey on foot.

Die Reise (meist Landreise) mit einem bestimmten Ziel.

Journey is the general word. It suggests going by any means of transport (but usually by land) to some definite destination. *To journey* suggests a certain effort. (V.: *to journey*)

voyage: The ship set out on a voyage to Cape Town.

Collocations: a voyage of discovery (need not be by sea; could refer to learning from a book); "Bon voyage!" "Not wanted on voyage" (i.e. luggage, so that it can be stowed away out of reach).

Eine meist lange Seereise. Auch im übertragenen Sinne gebraucht.

Usually a long journey by sea. Also used figuratively. (V.: *to voyage*)

trip: Over the weekend we made a trip into the country.

Collocations: a pleasure trip; a business trip; a day trip; a trip (in)to the country; a trip (up) to town.

Jede Art von (kurzer) Reise oder Ausflug.

Any kind of journey of short duration or excursion. (N.: *tripper*)

travel: Travel broadens the mind.

Collocations: to go on one's travels; travel agents; travellers' tales; a commercial traveller.

Travel, im Singular gebraucht, ist eine Verallgemeinerung und bedeutet soviel wie alle Reisen, die man unternehmen könnte, also das Reisen schlechthin. Im Plural wird *travel* für (meist) ausgedehnte, weite Reisen verwendet.

If used in singular *travel* is an abstraction of all the journeys one might make. It is a generalisation, in fact, a kind of collective noun. In plural *travel* means journeys to distant places. (V.: *to travel*)

tour: During my tour of England I visited many places of interest.

Collocations: a round tour; a day's / week's tour; a package tour.

Die Rundreise.

An extended journey, usually made for pleasure, visiting places of interest. (V.: *to tour*)

Exercise 96 (A) Insert a suitable term of the above group.

1. We made the long . . . to Australia, via Cape Horn and the Atlantic.
2. He makes the same . . . every day, from London to Brighton and back.
3. My companion suggested that we make a . . . of the Highlands.
4. Londoners often go on a day . . . to Brighton.
5. . . . broadens the mind.
6. A boatman was persuading the people to come for a pleasure . . .
7. How long does the . . . take by car?
8. "I'm a commercial . . ."–"Really, what do you . . . in?" (i.e. sell)
9. A Mediterranean . . . is good for the health.
10. The earth . . . round the sun.
11. The organisation of . . . has become big business.
12. When Chapman first read Homer, he also made a . . . of discovery.
13. "I've come to warn you."–"You could have saved yourself the . . ."
14. Our . . . across the lake was calm and peaceful.
15. She took a . . . to town to do some necessary shopping.
16. Snowdonia is hundreds of miles away–but it's worth the . . .
17. A . . . up the Elbe, on a steamer, is an enjoyable experience.
18. A ship's last . . . before being broken up is a sad occasion.
19. They went on a sentimental . . . back to their honeymoon resort.
20. . . . agents do a roaring trade in the holiday season.

Exercise 96 (B)

1. Package . . . are all the rage, as they are so much cheaper.
2. The best known of the famous . . . of discovery was made by Columbus.
3. It's the . . . who bring the money to the seaside.
4. He regaled his fellow . . . with witty stories for hours on end.
5. His business . . . became more frequent and his wife became more suspicious.
6. You can buy a book of tickets for twelve . . .
7. Foreign . . . is enjoyable, but rather expensive.

8. After years of . . ., he returned home tired and weary.
9. Rich young men in the 18th century used to go on the Grand . . .
10. A short . . . abroad is a pleasant break from the daily grind.

97
Rest
rest, remainder, remains, remnant, relic

rest: Pick out the good strawberries and throw the rest away.

Collocations: the whole of the rest / all the rest; the rest of the world / the day / the time / the crowd; the rest of us / of them; as for the rest.

Rest im Sinne von das übrige, die übrigen, die anderen.

Rest in the sense of 'the others' or what is left over.

remainder: Subtract 8 from 10 and the remainder is 2.

Der Rest vor allem in der Subtraktion und Division; im übrigen häufig in der gleichen Bedeutung wie *rest*, jedoch etwas gewählter.

The quantity that remains after subtraction or division. *Remainder* is also often interchangeable with *rest* although it is a somewhat more formal word.

remains: The remains of Troy were unearthed by the German archaeologist Heinrich Schliemann.

Collocations: the remains of a nation / castle / civilisation; prehistoric / Roman, etc. remains; the remains of a meal; the remains of a person (after death).

Die letzten Reste, Überreste; auch sterbliche Hülle.

What *remains* after disintegration, decline or consumption. (V.: to remain)

remnant: After the Battle at Waterloo the remnants of Napoleon's once powerful army were annihilated by the pursuing German, British, and Dutch troops.

Collocations: the remnants of former greatness; a sale of remnants (=Resteverkauf); the remnants of a meal.

Die kümmerlichen, dürftigen Reste, Überbleibsel.

A small part or quantity left over, fragments. Most commonly used about a length of material, left over from a roll.

relic: Folk dances are a relic of a by-gone age.

Collocations: a relic of the past; ancient relic(s); a relic of former glory.

(Oft besondere Wertschätzung genießende) Überreste aus der Vergangenheit; Andenken.

Something specially valued left over from times past, often kept as a memento.

Exercise 97 (A) Insert a suitable term of the above group.

1. Three goes exactly into fifty-one. There is no . . .
2. The . . . of the week was given over to preparing for the party.
3. Would you like this . . . at half price, madam?
4. That may be all very well for you. What about the . . . of us?
5. Roman . . . are to be found all over Britain.
6. I received a thousand pounds, in his will. The . . . of his property went to his children.
7. I owe you £ 5. Here's three, and I'll give you the . . . tomorrow.
8. I drew out most of my money, and only left a small . . . in the account.
9. Old ruins and . . . have little interest for her.
10. The . . . of the team applauded when he was named Player of the Match.
11. Thanks for the three eggs. Did you sell the . . .?
12. The Lake District is a . . . of the Ice Age.
13. I'm going to Brighton for my holiday. The . . . of the family can go where they like.
14. Her mortal . . . were placed in a coffin.
15. The shrine contained the . . . of a saint.
16. Two stones were perfect. The . . . were faulty.
17. I'll take the suitcase with me, and send the . . . on by rail.
18. Gathering together the . . . of his courage, he pushed open the door.
19. The . . . of the chicken were a few bones and feathers.
20. "When the . . . of the crowd go home, I always go home alone." (pop song)

Exercise 97 (B)

1. She was left without so much as a . . . of her former pride.
2. Lolling back in our seats, we contemplated the . . . of the feast.
3. We sent two platoons to HQ. The . . . stayed put where they were.
4. This old-fashioned watch and chain is a . . . of one I loved.
5. The . . . of resistance were slowly and methodically crushed.
6. Although it is a . . . of long-forgotten cottage life, it is still in use today.
7. Throw the . . . in the dust-bin.
8. Stonehenge is the most famous . . . of the Bronze-age Britons.
9. What . . . of his former affluence remained were insufficient to support his family.
10. He served a term in gaol, and for the . . . of his sentence he was on probation.

98
sagen
to say, to tell

to say: I couldn't hear what he said. I've nothing to say to you. He said that he was ill.

Collocations: they say (= man sagt); to have one's say (= mit gewissem Nachdruck seiner Meinung Ausdruck verleihen); I say! (an exclamation of alarm, surprise, etc.); well said! (an exclamation of approval of what someone has said); I cannot say (=Ich weiß es nicht. Ich kann es nicht sagen.); "Say it with flowers!" (florists' advertising slogan).

Sagen, reden, sprechen, sich äußern. Das indirekte Objekt wird stets mit *to* angeschlossen.

To utter, to speak, to declare. The indirect object is always preceded by *to*.

to tell: He told me his reasons. Tell me what he said. She told me the truth.

Collocations: to tell the old, old story (i.e. either propaganda or some deceitful approach, perhaps to a girl); there's no telling (=it is difficult to predict; I can't tell).

Erzählen, mitteilen, berichten. Das auf *tell* unmittelbar folgende indirekte Objekt wird ohne *to* angeschlossen.

To relate, to communicate; to give information, an account of something. The indirect object, if placed immediately after tell, is not introduced by *to*.
Note: Never use a *that*-sentence immediately after tell.

Exercise 98 (A) Insert a suitable term of the above group.

1. "I asked her to come to the dance with me."–"Oh yes, and what did she . . .?"
2. George Washington, they . . ., couldn't . . . a lie.
3. "Come home early tonight", . . . my mother.
4. ". . . us the secret of your success."–"There's really nothing to . . .".
5. They . . . that there's many a true word spoken in jest.
6. "What time does the train get in?"–"Sorry, I can't . . .".
7. Can you . . . me the time, please?
8. There's no . . . when he'll come home tonight.
9. She . . . "No", when she means "Yes".
10. "For he's a jolly good fellow, and so . . . all of us." (traditional doggerel, sung of a popular person in his presence.)

Exercise 98 (B)

1. There were . . .-tale blood marks on the sofa.
2. After the third lap the pace began to . . .
3. ". . . what you like, it was a mean trick."–"Perhaps it was, but when all's . . . and done, it harmed no one."
4. She was . . . her grandchild a story before she went to bed.
5. I must . . ., I think you're going a bit too far.
6. "Who scored that goal?"–"Truth to . . ., I wasn't watching."
7. She was determined to have her . . .–and have it she did!
8. The salesman started . . . the housewife the old, old story.
9. "Do you think he's angry?"–"I can't . . ."
10. She . . . I'm lazy–and I must . . . I agree with her!

99
Schaden
damage, injury, harm

damage: The earthquake caused much damage to buildings.
How much have we to pay for the damage?

Collocations: to do damage to; to pay damages (= Schadenersatz leisten); damage to s.o.'s reputation.

Die meist meßbare, konkrete materielle Beschädigung; der Verlust, die Einbuße.

The (usually) calculable direct impairment of usefulness or material value, the loss of it. (V.: *to damage*)

injury: The allegations did injury to his good reputation.

Collocations: to add insult to injury; to sustain injury; an injury to one's feelings.

Die Verletzung eines Rechtes; das begangene Unrecht; die Beeinträchtigung (des guten Rufes, eines Anspruchs); auch die körperliche Verletzung.

Injury signifies the violation of what is right, good, just, or useful. The term is also applied to bodily *injury* (with or without consequent pain). (V.: *to injure*; Adj.: *injurious*)

harm: Sooner or later smoking will do harm to your health.
Did the frost do any harm to the roses in your garden?
No harm was meant. (=Es war nicht böse gemeint.)
She is so late–I hope she has come to no harm.

Collocations: to do (bodily) harm to s.o.; to mean no harm; to come to harm; out of harm's way (=in Sicherheit); harm to one's self-confidence; to protect s.o. from harm.

Jede Art von materiellem, häufig aber auch ideellem, seelischem Schaden. Oft geht *harm* mit dem Gedanken an ein Übel, etwas Böses oder mit der Vorstellung von Kummer und Leid einher. (Gewöhnlich wird es ohne Artikel gebraucht.)

Any kind of physical or mental injury. *Harm* is more general than *damage* and *injury*. *Harm* often connotes a sense of evil or sorrow. (It is usually used without an article.) (V.: *to harm;* Adj.: *harmful*)

Exercise 99 (A) Insert a suitable term of the above group.

1. The . . . to the parcel was not very great, but it was annoying.
2. I only asked her how old she was. There's no . . . in that.
3. Head . . . are frequent and fatal when no seat belts are worn.
4. Propaganda of that sort does a lot of . . .
5. My car was badly . . . in the crash.
6. The judge awarded me £ 500 . . .
7. Opium is a drug which does considerable . . . to the whole system.
8. Bomb . . . was considerable during the war.

9. He knocked me down in his car and, to add insult to . . ., he sued me for obstruction.
10. The boy is having a . . . effect on the whole class.

Exercise 99 (B)

1. She fell fifteen feet, but suffered no . . .
2. . . . is not always accompanied by bleeding.
3. He wasn't crying because it hurt, but because his self-esteem was . . .
4. An . . . to one's pride may be harder to bear than physical . . .
5. *Me*, attack her? I wouldn't . . . a hair of her head!
6. An apology will hardly undo the . . . you have done.
7. "But I've got a hat already, thank you."–"Oh, there's no . . . in having two."
8. She stayed out all night, but she came to no . . .
9. 19th century trade union motto:
   "United we stand; divided we fall.
   An . . . to one is an . . . to all."
10. Put that poison on top of the cupboard, out of . . . way.

100
schälen
to peel, to pare, to skin

to peel: Shall I peel you an orange (or: an orange for you)?
The skin of my arms is peeling off.

Collocations: to peel potatoes/onions/a hard-boiled egg; to peel the bark off a tree.

Schälen, vor allem durch Abstreifen der Schale oder Haut, also vorzugsweise, ohne schneiden zu müssen. Darüber hinaus jedoch auch nicht selten im Sinne von *pare*.

To remove the skin of some fruit (or tree), esp. if it can be stripped off without using a knife.
Note: But peel is quite often used of the same action with a knife.

to pare: You'd better pare that apple before eating it.

Collocations: to pare one's nails; to pare fruit/an apple; to pare down expenses/costs/unnecessary items, etc.

Schälen in der Bedeutung von die Schale wegschneiden; auch im Sinne von stutzen, beschneiden und in übertragener Bedeutung. (In der Umgangssprache relativ selten gebraucht; es gehört vorzugsweise der Fachsprache an.)

To remove the outer covering of some fruit by cutting it away; to trim; also used figuratively. (To *pare* is mainly used in specialised speech.)

to skin: The hunter skinned the fox.

Collocations: to skin (esp. thick-skinned) fruit, e.g. banana-skin, but apple peel); to skin an animal; a lion- / tiger- / leopard-skin rug.

Allgemeiner Ausdruck für schälen (besonders Früchte mit dicker Schale), abschürfen, (ab)häuten.

The general term for removing the skin of a fruit or animal.

Exercise 100 (A) Insert a suitable term of the above group.

1. He was . . . down a stick to give it a pointed end.
2. Even a monkey usually . . . a banana before eating it.
3. I had to steam the label off the glass; it wouldn't . . . off.
4. That was a good shot. Now let's get the beast . . .
5. Tins of . . . tomatoes are now on the market.
6. What a beautiful tiger-. . . rug!
7. It is better to let a chiropodist . . . your toe-nails.
8. My mother was . . . potatoes in the kitchen.
9. Why is it always regarded as so funny, when someone slips up on a banana-. . .?
10. After our holiday my forehead was . . .
11. If you keep . . . it down too long you'll have nothing left.
12. Always . . . apricots before cooking them.
13. I had difficulty in . . . the paper off the tin to open it.
14. We have to . . . down our costs so that we can sell more cheaply.
15. Killing baby seals to . . . them for the fur trade seems cruel to some.
16. The gold-leaf was . . . off the lettering.
17. The elephants had . . . the bark off every tree.
18. She'll . . . you alive, if you tell them her age.

101
schätzen
to estimate, to appraise, to value, to esteem, to appreciate

to estimate: The distance was estimated at 2500 miles.

Collocations: to estimate the weight / size / length / cost of / damage to s.th.; (at) a conservative estimate (i.e. a careful, smallest possible one); at an estimate; as an estimate.

Veranschlagen, schätzen auf, d. h. einen Annäherungswert geben.

To ascertain (on the basis of personal judgement) the value, weight, etc. of something. (Some guesswork is implied.) (N.: *estimate*; Adj.: *estimated*)

to appraise: The value of the diamond was appraised at £ 200.

Collocations: the appraised value (= Schätzwert); to run an appraising eye over s.th. (or s.o.).

Den Geldwert einer Sache exakt abschätzen. Nicht selten auch in bezug auf allgemeinere Werte. *Appraise* gehört der gehobenen Stilebene an.

To fix the exact monetary worth of something. But often used of less tangible values. *Appraise* has a certain elegance and is, consequently, fairly rare except in literary or refined speech. *Appraise* is most used about diamonds, gold, jewellery, and for insurance purposes. (N.: *appraisal*)

to value: This bracelet has been valued at £ 350.
What I value most is good health and personal independence.
Wertschätzen ganz allgemein. Den Geldwert von etwas abschätzen (*to value s. th. at a certain price*). Mit *to value* verbindet sich dabei ein ausgeprägt subjektives Element.
In the sense of to rate at a certain price; to consider as of certain importance or desirability. (N.: *value;* Adj.: *valuable; invaluable = beyond value, extremely valuable*)

to esteem: I esteem him highly as a painter.
Collocations: to hold in high esteem; to esteem s.th. a favour / honour / privilege.
Hochschätzen, hochachten.
To think highly of someone. *Esteem* combines high respect with a feeling of warmth and affection. (N.: *esteem*; Adj.: *esteemed*)

to appreciate: Tell her how much I appreciate her offer to help me.
Auf Grund kritischer Einsicht den vollen Wert einer Sache erfassen, (oft) mit dem Gefühl der Dankbarkeit.
To realise the worth of something through keen insight and understanding and also to be grateful for it. (N.: *appreciation;* Adj.; *appreciable*; *appreciative*)

Exercise 101 (A) Insert a suitable term of the above group.

1. What do you . . . the total cost will be?
2. I am in no position to . . . his true worth.
3. I would . . . it if you would stop contradicting me in public.
4. I should . . . that you won't get it done under £ 2500.
5. No one was more highly . . . in his day than Sir Francis Drake.
6. He may be an expert, but I don't think he has . . . the value accurately.
7. We . . . all you have done for us.
8. You must . . . which course will be most profitable to you.
9. Jewellery . . . at a million pounds was stolen last night.
10. Could you . . . the full extent of his indebtedness?
11. Please send us an . . . for painting the house.
12. People are beginning to . . . the value of plain, wholesome food.
13. They . . . that a man will be on Mars by the middle of the next century.
14. She . . . my friendship more than personal gain.
15. I just could not . . . the damage he had done.
16. Those who are high in public . . . must constantly earn it.
17. Property . . . at £ 10,000 sold at considerably less than that.
18. Don't move if you . . . your life.
19. I'm a philistine. I simply can't . . . classical music.
20. Who can . . . the pleasure Shakespeare has given to millions?

Exercise 101 (B)

1. He cast an . . . eye over her as she passed.
2. Dear Sir, we are in receipt of your . . . order and wish to assure you . . . . . .
3. I . . . his service too much to refuse him a rise when he asks for one.
4. His advice was . . . (i.e. it was excellent advice)
5. The insurance assessor must . . . his firm's exact liability.
6. I would say, as an . . . , it will take three days to complete.
7. No one can really . . . good food until they've had to go hungry.
8. They . . . the property more highly than I did.
9. She cast a keen . . . glance at the dresses in the window.
10. We submitted it to him for his . . .

102
Schicksal
fate, destiny, fortune, lot

fate: Napoleon met his fate in Russia. Who knows what fate has in store for us. Fate decided otherwise. Fate is blind.

Collocations: to seal / meet / decide one's fate; the cruelty of fate; the hand / irony of fate; to be s.o.'s fate (i.e. future husband / wife); to be fated; what fate has in store.

Das dumpf waltende, rätselhafte, unaufhaltsam seinen Lauf nehmende Schicksal. *Fate* verbindet sich oft mit dem Begriff des Verhängnisvollen, sogar in Verbindung mit '*pleasant*', also '*not a pleasant fate*'; tödlich. (Krankheit).

The supreme irrational power unalterably determining events. *Fate* often carries the suggestion of ruin or destruction. It is often a 'doom' word. (Adj.: *fateful*; *fated*; *fatal*, i.e. leading to death)

destiny: He thought it was his destiny to free his people from slavery. He considered himself an instrument in the hands of destiny.

Die (erhabene) Macht, die die menschlichen Geschicke unverrückbar vorherbestimmt; das sich vollziehende persönliche Schicksal. *Destiny* ist mehr der literarischen, poetischen Stilebene zuzurechnen, obgleich es, wie auch *fate*, ebenso in weniger seriösem Sinne verwendet werden kann.

Destiny denotes the power predetermining events, an invincible necessity; what happens to a person as something predetermined. *Destiny* is more literary and poetic than *fate*, although both can be used more lightly. (The term *destiny* is less doom-laden than *fate*.) (Adj.: *destined*)

fortune: He had the good fortune to be endowed with an extraordinary talent for painting.
Fortune favours the brave.
Everybody is the architect of his own fortune.

Collocations: good / bad fortune; to tell fortunes; a fortune teller; to seek one's fortune; a soldier of fortune; 'Dame Fortune'.

Die als Glücksgöttin gedachte Schicksalsmacht. Das unbeständige, launische Schicksal; das zufällige Los, das einem beschieden ist.

The power of chance or luck (personified as a goddess). Good or bad luck that falls to somebody.

lot: Her lot has been a hard one.
I am content with my lot.

Collocations: to share s.o.'s lot; a hard lot; to be content with one's lot.

Lot hebt die Zufälligkeit des persönlichen Schicksals hervor.

What falls to one by fortune or chance. *Lot* is less literary and poetic than the other terms of this group.

Exercise 102 (A) Insert a suitable term of the above group.

1. It was my good . . . to have known him for many years.
2. Open the mail. Let's see what . . . has in store for us today.
3. Dick Whittington went to London to seek his . . .
4. Once she gets her eye on you, my lad, your . . . is sealed.
5. Mercenaries like to be thought of as soldiers of . . .
6. Napoleon was known as a man of . . .
7. . . . seldom gives you your chances again.
8. The crofters in the Scottish Highlands have a hard . . .
9. I met my . . . at a dinner party.
10. He won £ 10,000, bought a car, had a smash, was killed–the irony of . . .
11. Whither my . . . leads me, there shall I follow.
12. I was nearly in despair, when good . . . came my way.
13. He met his . . . (i.e. he died) when he was struck by a bullet.
14. Florence Nightingale's . . . was to succour the sick.
15. . . . favoured him at his first attempt. It was beginner's luck.
16. She saw the hand of . . . in every disaster.
17. Our . . . is better than that of the poor.
18. The opening four notes of Beethoven's Fifth Symphony are supposed to be . . . knocking at the door.
19. It has never been his . . . to suffer cold and hunger, as we have had to do.
20. It is man's . . . to suffer.

Exercise 102 (B)

1. "I am the master of my . . . ; I am the captain of my soul."
2. Some believe that men's . . . lie in the stars.
3. Don't worry about drowning at sea –you're . . . to be hanged.
4. Blind . . . had raised our hopes, then led us to disaster.
5. The man of initiative doesn't wait on . . .
6. It is the . . . of few to be absolutely satisfied with life.
7. People are usually discontented with their . . .
8. Don't try to avoid marriage; just accept your . . .
9. I could wish you no happier . . . than to raise a healthy family.
10. The gypsy told me my . . .

103
schlagen
to strike, to hit, to beat

to strike: The clock has just struck 11.
Why did you strike him in the face (or hit him in the face)?
Collocations: to strike a match / a gong; (an army is said) to strike at its opponents; to strike a blow; a striking personality; to strike the right note; on the stroke of midnight; (for a thought or idea) to strike one; to strike a coin (at a mint).
Schlagen im Sinne von einzelne Schläge führen. Etwas gewählter als die anderen Verben.
To deliver one or several single blows. More literary or poetic than the other terms. Used in more educated speech. (N.: *stroke*)

to hit: She hit him on the nose. (or: struck him ......)
He hit his head against the door. (or struck his head ......)
He began to hit out. (or strike out)
Collocations: to hit the target; to hit the nail on the head (i.e. guess exactly right); to hit on an idea; a hit (i.e. big success).
Einen einzelnen, genau gezielten Schlag versetzen. Im übrigen ist *hit* jedoch häufig mit *strike* austauschbar.
Usually to deal a single, strong blow, definitely directed. *To hit* is often interchangeable with *to strike*; if, however, the idea of impact is implied, *to hit* is to be preferred. (N.: *hit*)

to beat: Some parents beat their children when they are not good.
His heart is still beating.
Collocations: a beaten up egg (in milk); to beat s.o. black and blue; to beat s.o. up (=verprügeln); to beat a record; to beat a carpet; to beat one's breast (in anguish; as admission of sin); to have s.o. beat(en) (i.e. on the point of victory over him); can you beat that? (an exclamation of surprise or admiration); to beat the drum.
Wiederholt schlagen; prügeln. Auch bildlich verwendet.
To strike repeatedly, to give repeated blows. Also used figuratively. (N.: *beat*)

Exercise 103 (A) Insert a suitable term of the above group.
1. She . . . the previous record time of eleven seconds.
2. On the . . . of midnight Cinderella had to return.
3. He . . . the ball with all his might.
4. The rain was . . . against the window.
5. It's dark in here; let's . . . a match.
6. That song was a big . . . in the 60's.
7. No gold coins are being . . . at the Royal Mint.
8. . . . a drum gives one great satisfaction.

9. . . . up the eggs with a whisk, it's better than a fork for the purpose.
10. I'll . . . you so hard you won't stop bouncing.
11. Who will . . . the first blow?
12. We had them well-. . . before the final whistle.
13. He was . . . on the head with a stone.
14. Don't you dare . . . me!
15. . . . the gong to bring them in for dinner.
16. The conductor . . . time with his baton.
17. We . . . on the idea of forming a club.
18. He was badly . . . up by thugs on his way home.
19. Yes, that . . . the nail right on the head. That's what we'll do.
20. The British housewife traditionally . . . her husband with a rolling-pin, not a carpet . . . , when he comes home drunk.

Exercise 103 (B)

1. He scored a great . . . with the ladies.
2. Charles I's head was . . . off.
3. My father was badly . . . in the financial crash.
4. The Hollywood star had a . . . personality.
5. (Wife, dramatically:) "You coward! You . . . me! I shall go back to mother."
6. Doesn't his behaviour . . . you as strange?
7. We don't believe in . . . our children.
8. First our army surrounded them, then we . . .
9. I . . . the target with my first shot.
10. He . . . his head against the table as he fell.

104
schließen
to shut, to close, to lock

to shut: Shut the door, please, it's draughty.
It's no good shutting one's eyes to the facts.

Collocations: to shut one's eyes; to shut out the light; to shut up a shop; to shut one's eyes/ears/heart to s.th.; shut in (i.e. enclosed, surrounded); to shut one's mouth (but to close one's lips).

Schließen im Sinne von zumachen. Auch in übertragener Bedeutung gebraucht.

To put something in position so as to cover an aperture, stop an opening, etc. Also used figuratively. (Adj.: *shut*)

to close: The meeting closed with the singing of the national anthem.
I must close my letter now.

Collocations: to close a gap/a debate/an electric circuit; to close the ranks (=sich enger zusammenschließen); to close up (a hole, etc.), to close down; the closing bars (of a symphony, etc.); to close a market / a park (to the public) / a letter / an account / a chapter / a bargain.

To close kann als gewählterer Ausdruck für *to shut* und in übertragener Bedeutung gebraucht werden. Darüber hinaus hat es auch die Bedeutung von: beenden, zu Ende führen; schließen (mit Bezug auf Büros, Ämter etc.); sich zusammenschließen.

To close can be used as a more formal term for *to shut* and in the sense of to bring or come to an end; to bring together the parts of something; to unite; (with reference to offices, shops, etc.) to stop work or to stop being open to the public. *To close* may suggest a more gentle action than *to shut*. It is often used figuratively.

to lock: After shutting the door he locked it.

Collocations: to lock a door / a gate / one's fingers together; to lock up a house / a shop; to lock s.o. in an embrace; to lock s.o. in / out; a lock-up shop (i.e. where the owner does not live on the premises).

Etwas mit einem Schlüssel verschließen, abschließen. Auch im übertragenen Sinn: umschließen, umgeben; ineinanderschließen etc.

To fasten or secure something with a lock or key. Also figuratively for something very tightly held, prevented from moving, etc. (N.: *lock*)

Exercise 104 (A) Insert a suitable term of the above group.

1. He did not . . . his house up before he went away.
2. The case (i.e. legal case) was . . . , and I did not want to re-open it.
3. The child . . . his mouth tight and refused to eat.
4. He . . . his eyes to the petty thefts that were going on around him.
5. . . . the gate so that no stray animals can get in.
6. He . . . the window gently so as not to waken the baby.
7. When do the pubs . . . in this town?
8. He . . . the child in an impassioned embrace.
9. Don't . . . me out of your heart.
10. If you come home late, I'll . . . you out for the night.
11. The suspected criminals were . . . up in the local jail.
12. We . . . hands and heaved and pulled him out together.
13. They . . . down the business when they went bankrupt.
14. It is no use . . . the stable door after the horse has bolted. (saying)
15. For Goodness sake . . . up and listen to someone else for a change.
16. She . . . her jewel case every night.
17. The water . . . over him, and he was drowned.
18. Don't . . . the door. I haven't got a key.
19. The . . . bars of the symphony died away and there was a roar of applause.
20. It's 5.30. I'm . . . up shop for the night.
21. We can . . . up those mouse-holes with cement.
22. I'm . . . my account with that bank.

105
schnell
fast, swift, rapid, quick

fast: Winter was fast approaching.

Collocations: a fast train / car / plane / horse; a fast race / worker / walker; a fast woman (i.e. of loose morals).

Fast bezieht sich vorzugsweise auf sich schnell bewegende Gegenstände. Darüber hinaus wird es auch im Sinne von *rapid* und *quick* verwendet.

Fast usually applies to the speed of moving objects. It is often interchangeable with *rapid* or *quick*. (N.: *fastness*)

swift: The boat moved through the waves swiftly.
The starling is a swift bird.

Collocations: a swift glance; a swift runner.

Rasch dahineilend, flink, hurtig. *Swift* verbindet häufig die Vorstellung hoher Geschwindigkeit mit dem Begriff der Behendigkeit oder Leichtigkeit der Bewegung.

This term denotes great speed. At the same time it often connotes ease or facility of movement. *Swift* is a poetic word. (N.: *swiftness*)

rapid: The fire spread rapidly from house to house.
Your English has made rapid progress.

Collocations: a rapid river / gait / current / glance; in rapid succession; rapid fire (technical expression for army marksmen); the rapids (= Stromschnellen).

Rapid bezeichnet einen besonders hohen Grad von Geschwindigkeit (erstaunlich, reißend schnell) und bezieht sich mehr auf die Bewegung selbst als auf den sich bewegenden Gegenstand.

Rapid applies to great velocity and characterizes the movement itself rather than the moving object. (N.: *rapidity*)

quick: He gave a quick look round before he opened the door.
She is quick at arithmetic.
He spoke too quick(ly) for me to understand.
Be quick or we shall miss the bus.

Collocations: a quick reaction / answer / thinker; quick-witted (= schlagfertig, scharfsinnig); quick-tempered; a quick eye (= ein scharfes Auge); quick of apprehension; quick's the word!; be quick!; to be quick on one's feet (i.e. be nimble); to make a quick buck (sl.: dollar, i.e. a cheap trick to make money quickly and perhaps deceitfully).

Schnell, lebhaft, prompt im Handeln und in der Reaktion.

Quick usually refers to instantaneous, prompt action or reaction. (N.: *quickness*; V.: to *quicken*)

Exercise 105 (A) Insert a suitable term of the above group.

1. The train was a . . . one, and we got there in good time.

2. She strode along with a . . . gait.
3. Planes can now travel . . . than sound.
4. Thank you for your . . . response.
5. Don't go so . . . I can't keep up with you.
6. He was nimble and . . . on his feet.
7. We were hungry and consumed the huge meal . . .
8. The tide was coming in . . .
9. I heard three shots fired in . . . succession.
10. He took in the whole situation with one . . . glance.
11. You'll never get the better if *him.* He's too . . .-witted for you.
12. "I make it seven o'clock already."—"Your watch must be . . ."
13. She ran a . . . race for the first lap, but faded out in the end.
14. A . . . blow to the solar plexus put him down for the count.
15. Come on! . . .'s the word! I want to be out of here before they come.
16. We changed to a . . . horse for greater speed.
17. The river became more . . . as we approached the weir.
18. He spoke so . . . that we could hardly understand a word he said.
19. Do you think you could . . . your step a little?
20. The task was completed with remarkable . . .

Exercise 105 (B)

1. Our sledge-hammers made . . . work of the stone wall.
2. . . . swoops the swerving swallow.
3. Don't be so . . .-tempered; give me a chance to explain.
4. I undid the parcel . . . , as I was eager to examine the contents.
5. He was off, . . . as lightning, when he saw me coming.
6. The sleek, . . . craft raced past the buoy.
7. I tried to keep it a secret, but the news spread . . .
8. His condition worsened . . .
9. She made a . . . calculation and decided to buy it.
10. Time passed as . . . as a summer's night.

106
schön
beautiful, pretty, handsome, good-looking

beautiful: What a beautiful night! Just look at the stars.

Collocations: a beautiful face / picture / landscape / sunset / poem / body, etc.; a beautiful solution (to a problem); a beautiful catch / shot / trick (in sport).

Von idealer Schönheit, vollendet schön (nicht mit Bezug auf das männliche Gesicht). *Beautiful* kann auch auf Gedankliches bezogen werden (eine wundervolle Lösung für ein Problem u. ä.).

Beautiful implies ideal beauty, of classical proportions. It can also be used about ideas, especially logic (a beautiful solution to a problem).

pretty: I wouldn't call Jane beautiful, but she's certainly a pretty girl.

Collocations: a pretty face / little garden; a pretty sight (sometimes used to mean the opposite); a pretty kettle of fish (eine schöne Bescherung).

Hübsch. (Gelegentlich auch im negativen Sinne gebraucht.)

Quickly attractive in a simple way, and not necessarily longlasting or deep. Sometimes it is even used pejoratively or sarcastically.

handsome: Bob is a handsome boy.

Collocations: a handsome gift / allowance / gesture; to pay s.o. a handsome compliment; tall, dark, and handsome; to make a handsome apology.

Von angenehmer Erscheinung. *Handsome* kann auf Menschen (besonders Männer) und Dinge bezogen werden. (Neuerdings auch im Sinne von "Prima!" gebraucht.)

Well formed, of fine appearance. Handsome can be used with reference to persons (especially males) and things. ("*Handsome!*" is the latest form of "*Smashing!*")

good-looking: She made the acquaintance of a good-looking young man. (*handsome* possible)

Collocations: good looks.

Gut aussehend (von Personen und Dingen). Oft auf die Gesichtszüge eines Menschen bezogen. (Etwas weniger ausdrucksstark als *handsome* und *pretty.*)

A bit less expressive than *handsome* and *pretty* (often with reference to an attractive face). *Good-looking* can be applied to men, women, and things.

Exercise 106 (A) Insert a suitable term of the above group.

1. Helen of Troy was considered the most . . . woman in Ancient Times.
2. This is a very . . . part of the coast.
3. Her father makes her a . . . allowance.
4. Your garden is small, but it's very . . .
5. He is both charming and . . .–a formidable combination.
6. Each feature is near perfect. What a . . . woman!
7. She was wearing such a . . . little hat.
8. Would you rather have a . . . face and an ugly body, or vice versa?
9. Don't be so proud of your . . .
10. . . . people often take a good look at themselves in the mirror–when nobody else is looking.
11. He's a . . . boy, and will grow into a handsome man.
12. When young she was beautiful. At sixty she was still a . . . woman.
13. Young girls dream of tall, dark and . . . men.
14. Hollywood is full of . . . men.
15. A gold wrist-watch! What a . . . gift!
16. He had his mother's dark . . .
17. Who is that . . . girl over there?
18. The Greek ideal of . . . is still the accepted one in Europe.

19. They made a . . . pair, as they posed for the wedding photograph.
20. She was all done up in . . . little ribbons and bows.

Exercise 106 (B)

1. . . . is in the eye of the beholder. (saying)
2. He was the . . . of all those fine-looking men.
3. What's cooking, . . .? (a cheeky American approach to a girl)
4. Now we've missed the train. That's a . . . kettle of fish.
5. After they had finished with him, he wasn't a very . . . sight.
6. He has made a . . . apology and the matter is now closed.
7. A . . . Rolls Royce drew up at the kerb.
8. What a . . . trick! And he fell for it!
9. She's not just a . . . face. She's got brains too.
10. The chauffeur was wearing a . . . uniform.

107
sehen
to see, to look, to glance, to gaze

to see: We couldn't see anything for the fog.
I see (what you mean).

Collocations: to see the point (of a joke, etc.); to see the difficulty; let me see; we shall see; can't see for looking (i.e. misses things that can easily be seen); to see to it.

Sehen im Sinne von wahrnehmen, erblicken; auch einsehen, verstehen. *To see* kann auch ein unbewußtes Wahrnehmen bezeichnen.

To become conscious of an object with the eyes; also in the sense of to perceive something mentally, to understand.

to look: Look at those wonderful daffodils! There must be hundreds of thousands of them.
We may look without seeing, as in pitch-darkness, and we may see without looking, as in case of a flash of lightning. (Fernald)

Bewußt nach etwas hinschauen, etwas sehen wollen, hinsehen, gucken.

Consciously to fix the eye upon something or someone in order to see.

to glance: I was only able to glance at them, as they flashed along.

Einen flüchtigen Blick auf etwas werfen.

To give something or someone a quick, casual look.

to gaze: He gazed at her full of admiration.

Collocations: to gaze at someone in amazement / horror / disbelief, etc.

Aufmerksam betrachten; anstaunen; anstarren.

To look intently for some time including a certain dreamy quality.

Exercise 107 (A) Insert a suitable term of the above group.

1. Can you . . . the number on that bus?

2. Just . . . at the mess you've made!
3. The ticket collector . . . into our compartment, but did not enter.
4. We were . . . at the tigers in the zoo.
5. The fog was so thick, you couldn't . . . a hand in front of you.
6. I'm sorry we're late, but, you . . . , we missed the last bus.
7. . . . here, old chap, I want to ask you a favour.
8. They all . . . at him in horror.
9. We were ashamed, we couldn't . . . her in the face.
10. We're going to London to . . . the sights.
11. Can't you . . . what a fool you're making of yourself?
12. She . . . at him quickly and, as quickly . . . away again.
13. (Policeman:) "Now, . . . here, young man, you'll be getting into trouble if you're not careful."
14. She sat there as if stunned, . . .ing into nothingness.
15. What's the matter with you this morning? You can't see for . . .
16. They . . . at each other dreamily.
17. I just don't . . . the point in doing that. (i.e. the logic of or reason for it)
18. I've . . . many strange sights in my travels.
19. Don't . . . away when I'm speaking to you.
20. "You've won!" he cried. I . . . at him in disbelief.

Exercise 107 (B)

1. One merely has to . . . at him to . . . that he was sick.
2. Could you . . . your way clear to lending me a fiver?
3. They didn't even . . . at us. They just weren't interested.
4. Provincials wander round the metropolis and . . . at its marvels.
5. When you catch him . . . at you absent-mindedly, watch out.
6. Previously I had only . . . around the room, now I examined it minutely.
7. I leaned on the old gate and . . . up at the sky.
8. We . . . and . . . until our eyes ached.
9. We . . . at them in open-mouthed wonder.
10. He . . . at me slyly and winked.

108
sicher, gewiß
sure, certain

sure: Reading an English newspaper daily is a sure way to improve your knowledge of the language.

Don't be upset. I'm sure he didn't mean to insult you.

Collocations: a sure cure / method / hand / thing; sure enough; I am sure (that); to be sure of oneself / of something; to make sure; surefooted.

Sich persönlich einer Sache sicher sein, ohne unbedingten Anspruch auf objektive Gültigkeit des Urteils zu erheben. Bei attributivem Gebrauch bedeutet *sure* 'zuverlässig'.

To believe firmly, to have no doubts that something is the case. *Sure* implies a subjective judgement.

certain: I'm certain that I posted the letter on 18th January, 1984. To have all your teeth out is a certain cure for toothache. (Parnwell)

Certain bezeichnet absolute Gewißheit.

Certain expresses that one knows as a fact that something is the case, that there is no room left for the slightest doubt. (N.: *certainty*)

Exercise 108 (A) Insert a suitable term of the above group.

1. "Are you . . . you don't want any breakfast?"–"Quite . . . , thanks."
2. I beg you not to try it. It's . . . death.
3. He says he's quite . . . he can make it in time.
4. He cut through the tissue with a . . . hand.
5. "You get a rise every year, I suppose."–"Oh no, that's by no means . . ."
6. Make . . . there is no traffic coming, before you cross.
7. This horse is a . . . winner.
8. I knew she would come and . . . enough, there she was.
9. "Would you take this to the post for me?"–". . ."
10. He didn't look too . . . of himself, sitting there biting his nails.
11. That climber is as . . . footed as a mountain goat.
12. Some people are always . . . they are right.
13. I was . . . he would return, yet I kept looking at my watch.
14. He'll never get back alive, of that I'm . . .

109
sicher (vor Gefahr)
safe, secure

safe: It is not safe to touch that wire.
Here we are safe from any sudden attack.

Collocations: safe and sound; a safe bet; safely stowed away; a safe place / trip / journey; to drive safely; to play safe (i.e. to take no risks); it is safe to say that . . .

Safe bezieht sich auf überstandene oder nicht mehr bestehende Gefahren oder Notlage. Häufig wird es auch im Sinne von ungefährlich, zuverlässig gebraucht. *Safe* und *secure* sind oft austauschbar.

Safe may imply that a person or thing is out of danger, that risk no longer exists. *Safe* can also mean involving no risk of any mishap, error, etc. or dependable. (N.: *safety*)

secure: This prison is very secure. Escapes are almost unknown.
They tied up their captives securely with stout ropes.

Collocations: securely tied up.

Sich sicher fühlend vor künftigen Gefahren oder frei sein von jeder Gefahr oder Gefährdung; gut geschützt; sicher befestigt.

Secure means free from any danger or free from fear of danger; well-protected; firmly fixed. *Safe* and *secure* are often interchangeable.

Exercise 109 (A) Insert a suitable term of the above group.

1. The door was . . . fastened.
2. I was delighted to see her again, . . . and sound.
3. Look after her and keep her . . . from harm.
4. I only feel warm and . . . in bed.
5. It's a . . . bet that he'll come home as soon as he's spent his money.
6. It's . . . to say that there's more fish in the sea than ever came out of it.
7. How can one feel . . . in one's job when there are three million unemployed?
8. "O Molly dear, and did you hear what all the neighbours say
   About that hundred sovereigns you've got . . . stowed away?" (old song)
9. (Poster, in the road-safety campaign in an American town:) "Drive . . .– we love our children."
10. "Come on, let's chance it."–"No, let's play . . . and wait till tomorrow."
11. In his family circle he felt well-protected and . . .
12. The caves provided a . . . cache for their booty.
13. It is difficult to find a . . . investment in these troubled times.
14. Good-bye. Have a . . . journey!
15. He has no reason to feel . . . about the future.

110
Spiel
play, game, match

play: Early childhood is usually a time for play.
Everybody can do it. It's just child's play.
Collocations: free/fair/foul play; the play of light/of words; to be at play.
Spiel im Gegensatz zur Arbeit.
Any activity undertaken for amusement, recreation, sport, etc. (V.: *to play*; Adj.: *playful*)

game: Football is our favourite game.
How about playing a game of chess?
The game is up. (=Das Spiel ist verloren.)
Collocations: card games; to play a game of cards/of golf, etc.; to play games (=Gesellschaftsspiele machen); a game of chance (=Glücksspiel); Olympic Games; a rough/lost/dirty/dangerous/outdoor/indoor game; to play the game (i.e. to deal fairly with s.o.); your little game (i.e. secret, suspect scheme or activity).
Das festen Regeln folgende Spiel. Eine Partie (Schach etc.).
A *game* is usually governed by set rules; a recreational contest.

match: We won the match two nil.

Collocations: a boxing match; a cricket match; a football match (one can also say "a game of football", but it need not be a contest; "a football match", however, is); the match of the day / week / year / century; a thrilling match; a "needle match" (i.e. between two bitterly opposing people or sides).

Spiel im Sinne von Wettkampf.

A competition or contest of skill in which teams or persons are matched against each other. (V.: *to match*; Adj.: *matchless*)

Exercise 110 (A) Insert a suitable term of the above group.

1. It's a dangerous . . . to try and bluff him.
2. The . . . was played in heavy rain.
3. Rugby is a very rough . . .
4. . . . is as important for children as work is for adults.
5. Let's have fair . . . , now, and no cheating.
6. All right, I'll play the . . . according to *your* rules. (fig.)
7. I've seen through his dirty little . . .
8. The . . . went on, despite the injury.
9. All work and no . . . makes Jack a dull boy. (proverb)
10. The . . . of sunlight on the sea makes a wonderful picture.
11. The children were playing . . . in the playground.
12. After the . . . they remained bad friends.
13. A filmed ". . . of the Day" is shown every Saturday evening on TV.
14. We must allow sufficient free . . . for the wheel (to spin freely).
15. As soon as I saw blood, I suspected foul . . .
16. She's good at organising party . . .
17. She was as . . . as a kitten.
18. The referee cancelled the . . .
19. It was a thrilling and hard-fought . . . from beginning to end.
20. The ball was still in . . . when the referee blew the whistle.
21. I've never trusted him. But he's always played the . . . with me.
22. Table-football is a real . . . of skill.
23. The . . . ended in a draw. (or: It was a drawn . . .)
24. Let's stand here, unobserved, and watch them at . . .
25. When Spurs play the Arsenal it is always a needle . . .

111
Spitze, Gipfel
top, summit, peak, head

top: The icy wind made it impossible for me to reach the top of the mountain. (*Summit* and *peak* are also possible here.)
I think they'll win. They are at the top of their form just now.

Collocations: the top of a tree / house / hill / of the class; to come top of the class; at the top of one's profession / class, etc.; from top to toe (=vom Scheitel bis zur Sohle); top speed; to shout at the top of one's voice; to get to the top (also figuratively, i.e. in business, socially, etc.).

Top ist der allgemeinste Ausdruck dieser Gruppe. Der höchste Punkt oder Teil eines Gegenstandes; der Gipfel eines Berges; die Krone eines Baumes etc. *Top* wird auch im übertragenen Sinne verwendet, z. B. im Sinne von Spitzenposition, erste Stelle, höchster Grad.

Top is the most general term. It denotes the highest point or part of something. It is also used figuratively in the sense of the highest rank, position, degree, etc. (V.: *to top;* Adj.: *top*)

summit: The Great Powers agreed to hold a summit conference.

Collocations: a summit meeting / conference; the summit of ambition.

Der höchste Punkt oder Teil (besonders eines Berges). *Summit* ruft die Vorstellung von einem höheren Berg hervor, als dies bei *top* der Fall ist. Anderseits bezieht sich *summit* i. allg. auf eine weniger ausgeprägte Bergspitze als *peak*. Auch der Gipfel der Bestrebungen oder des Erreichten.

Summit ist ein gewählterer Ausdruck als *top*.

The highest point or part especially of a mountain. But it suggests a higher mountain than *top* and not so pointed a mountain as *peak*. It also means the highest point or level of attainment or aspiration. *Summit* is a more dignified term than *top*.

peak: Above the clouds just the peaks of the Alps were to be seen.

Collocations: to reach the peak; the peak of a career; a peak performance / product / period / condition; to be at one's peak; the Peak District (i.e. Derbyshire).

Die schroffe Spitze besonders eines steilen Berges, auch im übertragenen Sinne.

The pointed summit of a steep mountain, and in figurative meaning. (Adj.: *peaked*)

head: The Duke of Wellington was at the head of the British army in 1815.

Collocations: the head of a procession / school / business / list / class / column; the head of a rock / spear / arrow; the fountain-head (of all wisdom).

Der vorderste Teil von irgend etwas; die leitende Position.

The foremost or uppermost part of anything; the position of leadership. (V.: *to head*)

Exercise 111 (A) Insert a suitable term of the above group.

1. Love is the . . . of the emotions.
2. He went upstairs, right to the . . . of the house.
3. Her name was at the . . . of the list.
4. He was in . . . condition.
5. He's a little deaf; you must shout at the . . . of your voice.
6. The drum major was at the . . . of the procession.
7. He earns much more, now that he is at the . . . of his profession.
8. That was a . . . performance when he beat the record.

9. "Etna's smoking . . ." (Gray)
10. He seems to think he's the fountain- . . . of all wisdom.
11. Don't think of the . . . , as soon as you start climbing the mountain.
12. My ball has got stuck in the . . . of the tree.
13. They reached the . . . of Everest at dawn.
14. I was at the . . . of the column as we passed the gasworks.
15. One . . . stuck up from the range, above all the others.
16. I am applying for the job of . . . gardener.
17. Smoke was belching out of the . . . of the chimney.
18. We climbed up to the . . . of the mountain.
19. My son came . . . of the class in maths.
20. He is the . . . of the firm in this area.

Exercise 111 (B)

1. The traffic builds up to a . . . at 4.30 p.m.
2. An office desk and respectability were the . . . of his hopes.
3. It was a struggle to get to the . . . (i.e. commercially, professionally, etc.).
4. She was at her . . . last year; since then she's gone downhill.
5. We gazed at . . . upon . . . receding into the blue.
6. They haven't reached their . . . yet.
7. The spear-. . . quivered in the tree, three inches from my neck.
8. Do you see where the graph reaches the . . .?
9. He is very moody; sometimes up on the . . . , sometimes down in the depths.
10. He achieved the . . . of recognition later in life.

112
Spur
trace, track, trail, vestige

trace: The water contained traces of poison.
Excessive work has left its traces on his face.
The police could not find any trace of the stolen picture.

Collocations: to leave no trace behind; the traces of an ancient civilisation; a trace of evidence; to disappear without trace.

Der allgemeine Ausdruck für Spur, besonders im Sinne von Fußabdruck; (Über)Rest (einer Substanz); (An)Zeichen von etwas.

Trace is the general term. It applies to any kind of mark indicating that somebody or something has been present, that something has happened or has existed. (V.: *to trace*)

track: The police are on the track of the smugglers.
I could see the tracks of the sheep on the hillside.
The tracks led to the back door.

Collocations: to follow the beaten track (bildlich für: ausgetretene Wege gehen); to lose track of s.o. (jmd. aus den Augen verlieren); to be/to get on s.o.'s track; to leave tracks; to make tracks (i.e. to leave, esp. in a hurry [sl.]); to make tracks for (i.e. to start off in the direction of); to stop dead in one's tracks; to be on the track of (i.e. believe I/he etc. will find it soon).

Gewöhnlich eine Linie von Spuren, die Fährte; die von einem Fahrzeug hinterlassene Bahn.

A line of marks produced by the passing of a person, animal, or a vehicle. Also a well-trodden path. (V.: *to track*)

trail: We could follow the lion by the trail of blood from his wounds.
The jet-liner left a long black trail behind it.

Collocations: to follow the trail; to be on the trail; a trail of smoke; the trail of a meteor; the slimy trail of a slug.

Die langgezogene Spur, auch Schleifspur (vgl. *to trail* = schleppen, schleifen); die Fährte (wie *track*); der ausgetretene Pfad (besonders durch unwegsames Gelände).

A track produced by something that has moved or has been drawn over a surface (cf. V.: *to trail* = to draw or drag along behind); a scent (followed in hunting); a beaten path (especially through wild region).

vestige: In Saxon Switzerland you can find the vestiges of many a stronghold of medieval robber-knights.

Die letzte, schwache Spur, das schwache Anzeichen; die letzten Überreste, Zeugnisse der Vergangenheit.

A very slight trace; a surviving evidence of something. Also used figuratively. *Trace* tends to be more abstract than *vestige,* which, in concrete contexts, means a tiny bit of something, whereas *trace* may be, e.g. a smell, a disturbance of something from its normal position, etc. (i.e. not something you can touch).

Exercise 112 (A) Insert a suitable term of the above group.

1. He disappeared without . . .
2. Let's see where these . . . lead to.
3. We are examining the . . . of lost civilisations.
4. There's not a . . . of selfishness in my nature.
5. I searched with a magnifying glass, but could find no . . . of my lost letter.
6. A frightened skunk leaves a frightfully stinking . . . behind him.
7. The authorities are on the . . . of the wrongdoer.
8. They destroyed every . . . of the evidence.
9. There were no . . . of iron ore in the rock.
10. We followed the . . . until we came to a group of mud huts.
11. My son left a . . . of mud right through the house.
12. In the ashes I found the last . . . of the strong-box.
13. There was not a . . . of envy in his tone of voice.
14. A . . . of smoke was pouring from the building.
15. The . . . of a large quadruped were clearly evident.
16. There was a . . . of steam drifting from the funnel.
17. You haven't a . . . of evidence to support your contention.

18. You have no . . . of proof for your assertion.
19. Once *she* gets on his . . . , he'd better watch out.
20. Don't leave any . . . of your presence for the police to follow up.

Exercise 112 (B)

1. When we heard the scream, we stopped dead in our . . .
2. I'm tired. Let's make . . . for home.
3. The two dogs followed the . . . silently and purposefully.
4. He never follows the beaten . . .
5. There's not a . . . of truth in your accusation.
6. I've completely lost . . . of the argument.
7. His wife is hot on his . . .
8. They removed the last . . . of the splinter from my finger.
9. It is difficult to . . . a tiger to its lair.
10. Can you . . . the address for me?

113
Stellung (berufliche)
job, position, post, situation, place

job: He's fed up with his present job.
He is the right man for that job.

Collocations: to get a job; out of a job; to offer s.o. a job; the man for the job; a soft job (=eine leichte Beschäftigung); to have a hard job to do s.th. (=angestrengt mit etwas zu tun haben).

Job kann jede Art von beruflicher Stellung bezeichnen und bezieht sich darüber hinaus auch oft auf den Charakter der damit verbundenen Arbeit. *Job* ist ein vergleichsweise umgangssprachlicher Ausdruck.

Job can be used with reference to any kind of employment. At the same time this term stresses the work involved. It is a rather colloquial term.

position: She is in a high position of trust.
Bob has got a good position with an oil company.

Collocations: a man of position; a position of trust; a high position; a low position in society; people of position (i.e. of the middle or upper classes); to get/apply for the position of . . . . . .

Position bezieht sich auf den gesellschaftlichen Rang, besonders, aber nicht ausschließlich, auf eine gehobene oder hohe berufliche Stellung. Es kann auch mit Bezug auf eine nur vergleichsweise gehobene Stellung verwendet werden. *Position* ist ein gewählterer Ausdruck als die übrigen Synonyme dieser Gruppe.

Position implies reference to social status, i.e. it refers to a person's place in relation to others in society. So it can denote an (actually or comparatively) high or important rank in employment. It is a more dignified term than the others of this group. There may even be a certain old-fashioned snobbery about the term.

post: He has been offered a post in the Government.

Collocations: a post of responsibility; to obtain / hold, etc. the post of general manager / Secretary of State for war, etc.; to have a post as a cook, etc.; to be given a post as . . . . . .; a teaching post; to be appointed to a post (or position); to fill a post; to give up one's post.

Berufliche Stellung im Sinne von Amt, Posten. *Post* läßt an die Pflichten und die Verantwortung denken, die sich mit einem Amt verbinden. (Häufig für Stellung im Lehrberuf.)

Post implies the responsibility and duties associated with some office.

situation: The maid is looking for another situation.

Collocations: "Situations Wanted", "Situations Vacant" (in Zeitungen: Stellengesuche und Stellenangebote); a permanent situation (= Dauerstellung).

Vorzugsweise in bezug auf Zeitungsinserate verwendet. Darüber hinaus auch zur Bezeichnung einer beruflichen Stellung, vor allem untergeordneter Art (Hausangestellte u. ä.). Umgangssprachlich nicht mehr gebräuchlich.

Usually in newspapers as headings for notices of employment offered and asked for. It can also denote a place of employment, frequently of a subordinate kind, e.g. of domestics.

place: They owed their places (situations or jobs) to the head doorkeeper.

Collocations: to take a place; to keep one's place; a place at Court.

Place ist ein ganz allgemeiner Ausdruck für eine hohe oder auch niedrige Stellung. Es hat mehr umgangssprachlichen Charakter.

This term is a familiar word for both a public office (esp. a government appointment) and a menial employment. Its meaning is rather indefinite.

Exercise 113 (A) Insert a suitable term of the above group.

1. . . . are hard to get these days.
2. You had better look into the ". . .s Vacant" column.
3. Holding a leading . . . of that kind, he required much tact.
4. I've been after three . . . this week.
5. There is great competition for the higher . . . in industry.
6. You're just the man for the . . .
7. When she left, her . . . was taken by a younger woman.
8. There are thousands without a . . .
9. She lost her . . . as a housekeeper.
10. Good . . . are getting more difficult to obtain.
11. I offered him a . . . in my factory.
12. She held the . . . of Minister of Education.
13. This is only temporary. I'd like a more permanent . . .
14. Government . . . are not for sale, as they were in the olden days.
15. He took a . . . in a lawyer's office.
16. The . . . of manager is now vacant.
17. I shall advertise on the ". . . Wanted" page.
18. She has not yet obtained a . . . of special responsibility.

19. Our chauffeur has threatened to look for another . . .
20. I don't fancy the . . . of looking after an invalid.

Exercise 113 (B)

1. She has had a hard . . . to control her temper.
2. She obtained a . . . as governess in a wealthy family.
3. They all competed for a . . . at Court.
4. I have been in this . . . , at my present school, for seven years.
5. I wouldn't do your . . . for worlds.
6. He is a man of . . . , a man to be reckoned with.
7. Who holds the . . . of chairman of your company?
8. The . . . of chief clerk is a . . . requiring great experience.
9. I am seeking a . . . as lady's maid.
10. Shut your mouth if you want to keep your . . .

114

streng

severe, stern, strict

severe: He did not deserve such a severe punishment.
Some roofs were destroyed by severe storms.

Collocations: a severe judge / sentence / teacher / penalty / law / critic; a severe illness / headache / heart attack / pain / fever; a severe blow / winter / storm / cold; a severe look / face, etc.

Von extremer Strenge im Wesen, in der Qualität. Es kann sich auf Personen und deren Verhaltensweise (Äußerungen, Urteile, Handlungen), auf Aussehen, Witterung, Krankheiten u. ä. beziehen.

Severe suggests harshly extreme character, quality, rigorous standards, complete absence of mildness or indulgence.
(N.: *severity*)

stern: Mr. Rod is a stern teacher; he won't stand any nonsense.

Collocations: a stern look / countenance / voice; a stern judge / teacher / father / ruler; stern treatment; stern resolve (=unbeugsame Entschlossenheit); to rule with a stern hand.

Stern impliziert Starrheit, Abwesenheit von Beweglichkeit bzw. Flexibilität. Daher im Sinne von kompromißlos, unerbittlich oder gebieterisch streng. Zuweilen auch bezüglich der Erscheinung fast abstoßend und finster.

Stern suggests uncompromising, inflexible firmness, harshness and sometimes even forbidding aspect or nature.

strict: The teacher maintained (a) strict discipline.
If you want to avoid trouble, you should observe a strict diet.

Collocations: strict orders / obedience / injunctions / self-restraint; in strict confidence; strict observance (of any rules); strictly speaking (=genaugenommen).

Streng, peinlich genau sein in der Einhaltung von Grundsätzen, Regeln, Anordnungen etc.

Allowing no deviation from a principle, rule, order, etc.; exact.

Exercise 114 (A) Insert a suitable term of the above group.

1. It is a . . . rule, and I can allow no exceptions.
2. It was a . . . penalty for such a minor offence.
3. I'm under . . . orders to stay in bed.
4. I'm telling you in . . . confidence.
5. He was in bed with a . . . cold.
6. We are in for a . . . winter this year.
7. Be . . . but just and nobody will complain.
8. There was . . . observance of the rules of their order.
9. There was a . . . epidemic of 'flu' last year.
10. Necessity is a . . . master.
11. He is a . . . critic but a just one.
12. Don't be such a . . . and heartless critic.
13. I expect . . . obedience to my orders.
14. He sustained . . . injuries, from the . . . blow he received.
15. They kept . . . to their principles.
16. They impose . . . standards of behaviour.
17. . . . speaking, you shouldn't be here at all.
18. Keep a . . . watch on him.
19. Our teacher looks . . ., but he isn't.
20. Her father was . . . and unapproachable.

Exercise 114 (B)

1. "I never saw a man's face change from lively to . . . so suddenly in all my life." (J. K. Jerome "Three men in a boat")
2. The judge looked . . . and solemn.
3. She stood . . . awaiting me, at the top of the stairs.
4. Her kind action belied the . . . expression on her face.
5. The house looked . . . and forbidding.
6. . . . remedies may be as dangerous as the disease.
7. His . . . voice was an indication of what was to come.
8. . . . necessity made me a thief.
9. William the Conqueror ruled with a . . . hand.
10. It was my . . . resolve to see it through, come what may.

115

suchen

to look for, to seek, to search

to look for: What are you looking for?

I'm looking for my gloves.

Collocations: to look for work / safe investment / trouble / a wife; to look for a needle in a haystack; to look for the silver lining; to look for the name on the label; looked-for; unlooked-for.

Nach etwas suchen, das man haben möchte, verloren hat etc. *Look for* ist stilistisch neutral.

The ordinary term for to try to find something or someone.

to seek: I was seeking his aid.

He was seeking to convince me.

The Pilgrim Fathers sought new homes in America.

Collocations: to seek a remedy / a solution; to seek solace / sympathy; to find what one seeks; long-sought; much sought-after.

Nach etwas trachten, etwas zu erlangen suchen; etwas versuchen (=*to try*, aber schriftsprachlich, also gehobene Stilebene). Gelegentlich wird *seek* auch als gewählterer Ausdruck für *to look for* verwendet.

To seek is used in literary style in the sense of 'to try to obtain'; 'to ask for'; 'to attempt' or 'try'. Sometimes *seek* is used (but not in ordinary spoken English) as a more dignified or high-flown term for *to look for.*

to search: The customs officer did not search my luggage.

The police searched the house for weapons.

They tried to search out all the facts about the murder.

Collocations: to search vainly; a search warrant; searchlight; search-party.

Durchsuchen, durchstöbern; untersuchen, ausfindig machen, herausfinden.

To look through carefully, extensively (perhaps desperately) in trying to find; to find out by careful examination. To *search* is stronger than *to look for.*

Exercise 115 (A) Insert a suitable term of the above group.

1. . . . water in the desert is a hopeless task.
2. "What can I get you, sir?"–"I'm . . . a grey, nylon shirt, size 16."
3. She has been . . . a husband for years.
4. The . . . light shone out over the sea.
5. The medical profession has long been . . . a remedy for the common cold.
6. They . . . for hours without success.
7. Women go to the sales to . . . bargains.
8. The intruder . . . through the papers very thoroughly.
9. I'm . . . a present for my wife.
10. I've . . . the seven seas and not found happiness.

11. The Act enables the police to . . . without a warrant.
12. I was . . . a place to park my car.
13. She's a very much . . .-after young lady.
14. . . . work can be heartbreaking when unemployment is high.
15. I . . . through my pockets but could not find the key.
16. We organised a . . .-party for the missing boy.

Exercise 115 (B)

1. He found his long-. . . haven in the heart of the countryside.
2. I didn't know where to . . . first.
3. They . . . after (or for) treasure, but never found any.
4. She came home . . . sympathy.
5. If you are . . . trouble, young man, you've come to the right address.
6. They . . . to put a curb on my activities.
7. That was an un. . .-for compliment.
8. Trying to find anyone in this crowd is like . . . a needle in a haystack.
9. Philosophers are always . . . after the truth.
10. "We're out to . . . for gold tonight." (Alfred Noyes "The moon is up")

116
Tat
action, act, deed, feat, exploit

action: The time has come for action now.
He is a man of action.
Actions speak louder than words.

Collocations: to suit the actions to the words; a hasty / kind / instinctive / reflex action; to put s.th. into action (=etwas in die Tat umsetzen); to take action against (=vorgehen gegen).

Tat im Sinne von das Handeln, die Handlung, die Tätigkeit.

The process of acting. Thus *actions* are usually thought of as occupying some time and consisting of a complex of single steps.

act: The turning down of their offer was an unwise act on his part.
The rescue of the drowning boy was a brave act.
He was caught in the act.

Collocations: an act of kindness / cruelty / folly; a voluntary act; acts and thoughts; caught in the act.

Die einzelne, in einer gegebenen Situation vollbrachte Tat. Oft wird dabei *act* näher bestimmt (siehe obige Kollokationen). *Act* bezieht sich im Gegensatz zu *action* mehr auf das Ergebnis und nicht auf den Prozeß des Handelns. Dennoch sind zuweilen *act* und *action* austauschbar, z. B. *I judge him by his acts* (*or actions*).

Act usually refers to a thing done, to a single, individual, a momentary deed rather than to a more or less complex process. Sometimes, *act* is, however, interchangeable with *action.*

deed: We should try to do a good deed every day.
I take the will for the deed.
Great deeds of valour are described in Greek mythology.
Collocations: in word and deed; a heroic / good / bad deed.
Die große (mutige, gute, böse etc.) Tat. Auch die Tat im Gegensatz zu bloßen Worten.
Deed usually denotes any kind of conspicuous act, such as a good, bad, heroic deed. It is a poetic or literary term.

feat: The champion performed an astounding feat.
The feats of Hercules are legendary.
Collocations: an athletic feat; a feat of horsemanship.
Bravourstück, Kraftleistung, Kunststück.
A performance of something requiring extraordinary skill, physical strength or daring.

exploit: The fighter pilot got the highest military orders for his exploits.
The exploits of Don Quixote make entertaining reading.
Die strahlende Heldentat. Bei *exploit* kann die Vorstellung von Großtuerei, prahlerischer Schaustellung mitschwingen.
Exploit connotes brilliant achievement requiring especially bravery, boldness and ingenuity. But it may also suggest exhibitionism, ostentation.

Exercise 116 (A) Insert a suitable term of the above group.

1. His good . . . live after him.
2. His prompt . . . saved my life.
3. The thief was caught in the . . .
4. Every . . . evokes a reaction.
5. Climbing Mount Everest was a wonderful . . .
6. Napoleon and Caesar were men of . . .
7. It wasn't murder; it was an . . . of self-defence.
8. Crossing Niagara Falls on a tight-rope was a . . . requiring iron nerves.
9. I judge a man by his . . ., not by his words.
10. Explorers of the Amazon do not always live to tell of their . . .
11. He has proved himself both in word and . . .
12. Breaking his window was a senseless . . . of vengeance.
13. There are still many mountaineering . . . yet to be accomplished.
14. My son's . . . could fill a book–but who would want to read it?
15. Horatius performed a heroic . . .
16. The boxing fans were shouting for . . .
17. When the eye blinks, it is a reflex . . .
18. Your intercession on my behalf was an . . . of kindness I shall never forget.
19. What an . . . of courage to stand up to him in public!
20. "Suit the . . . to the words, the words to the . . ." (Shakespeare)

Exercise 116 (B)

1. Fasting for a week is a . . . of endurance.
2. We've heard enough of your . . .
3. Acrobats perform . . . of skill daily.
4. It was the . . . of a brave but foolish man.
5. He loved to recount his endless . . .–endlessly.
6. It was a brave . . . to snatch the child from the jaws of death.
7. "For such a gallant . . . of arms
   Was never seen before." (Lord Macaulay "Horatius")
8. Whoever did the . . . deserves our gratitude.
9. Lord Byron's famous . . . was to swim across the Hellespont.
10. It was a great . . . to persuade my aunt to *fly* here.

117

tragen

to carry, to bear, to wear

to carry: He carried a parcel under his arm.
He usually carries an umbrella in his hand.
He will never be a great singer since his voice does not carry.
The loan carries 3 % interest.

Collocations: to carry germs/responsibility.

Die Grundbedeutung ist 'tragen' =(von einem Ort zum andern) befördern.

The basic meaning is to convey from one place to another.
It is also used in a figurative sense.

to bear: Be careful, the ice may not bear your weight.
The roof was borne by a number of stone pillars.
This tree does not bear any fruit.
He bore his pains patiently.

Collocations: to bear arms; to bear a title/name; to bear witness; (a document may) bear a signature; to bear the cost/expense; to bear great sorrow; to bear interest/an inscription; an interest-bearing investment; to be more than one can bear.

Tragen im Sinne von das Gewicht aushalten (also etwas im Ruhezustand Befindliches tragen); Früchte, Blüten tragen; Schmerz etc. ertragen. *To bear* wird gelegentlich auch als gewählterer Ausdruck für *to carry* gebraucht, z. B. *to bear responsibility* gegenüber *to carry responsibility*. Darüber hinaus wird *bear* in einer Reihe fester Wendungen verwendet (siehe obige Kollokationen).

To support the weight of a thing which is at rest; to suffer, to tolerate, to endure. *To bear* can be used as a formal or poetic term for *to carry*.

to wear: She wore a pair of white gloves.

Hair is worn longer these days.

Collocations: to wear a hat / shoes / spectacles; to wear one's hair short / long, etc.; to wear a beard; to wear a smile / sour look, etc.

(Am Körper) tragen mit Bezug auf Kleidung, Schmuck, Brille, Frisur etc.; (einen bestimmten Gesichtsausdruck etc.) zur Schau tragen.

To have on the body (with reference to clothing, adornment, etc.); to show on the face, in one's manners, to exhibit.

Exercise 117 (A) Insert a suitable term of the above group.

1. I can't . . . to look at harrowing scenes on TV.
2. You . . . an honoured name. Don't besmirch it.
3. He ran as fast as his legs would . . . him.
4. Can you . . . all those figures in your head?
5. Mini skirts are being . . . less these days.
6. It . . . an inscription of great historical significance.
7. Mummy, I'm tired. Can you . . . me?
8. Don't . . . *that* hat with *that* coat, please.
9. I'll . . . the cost if you'll do the work.
10. To . . . coals to Newcastle is an old saying.
11. We . . . less in summer than in winter.
12. My wife is always complaining that she has nothing to . . .
13. Don't! It's more than I can . . .
14. His voice . . . right across the valley.
15. You will . . . witness that I resisted temptation.
16. Atlas was a mythological figure, . . . the world on his shoulders.
17. Burn that handkerchief, it . . . germs.
18. It is no longer Paris that dictates what women will . . .
19. He . . . great responsibility.
20. Her face . . . an expression of rapture.

118
Ufer
shore, bank, beach

shore: The waves were quietly lapping the shore.

Das Ufer eines großen Sees oder der Küstenstreifen eines Meeres.

The land adjacent to a large lake or the sea.

bank: Many holiday makers had pitched their tents on the banks of the river.

Das Ufer eines Wasserlaufes (Flusses, Baches etc.).

The strip of land on the margin of a river.

beach: We sunbathed on the beach all day.

Brighton's beach has pebbles; Bournemouth's is sandy.

Der Strand am Meer.

That part of the shore of the sea which is washed by the waves, usually sandy or pebbly.

Exercise 118 (A) Insert a suitable term of the above group.

1. We undressed on the . . . and went for a swim.
2. After the great rains, the river overflowed its . . .
3. The . . . was so crowded we could hardly find a place for our deck-chair.
4. I walked along the silent . . ., meditating.
5. The . . . of the river were lined with onlookers.
6. Weeping willows grew on the . . .
7. The ship drew up on the . . .
8. They stepped on . . . for the first time in many months.
9. It's amazing what can be found on the . . . at the end of the season.
10. We must build up the . . . of the river to prevent flooding.
11. The . . . of the lake were distant now.
12. We sailed to distant . . .
13. . . . combers sometimes make valuable finds.
14. Oil is ruining Britain's . . .
15. Some water birds nest on river . . .
16. Canvas wind-breaks are sometimes used on the . . .

119

unterdrücken

to oppress, to suppress, to repress

to oppress: The native population was ruthlessly oppressed by the colonial government.

Collocations: to be (mercilessly/ruthlessly) oppressed; an oppressive atmosphere; to be oppressed by sorrow; oppressive taxation.

Durch politische Gewalt Unterdrückung ausüben; durch persönliches Verhalten die Freiheit anderer rücksichtslos einengen.

To oppress is used in the sense of keeping people down by overwhelming (political or personal) violence; to ill-treat, make unhappy. (N.: *oppression*; Adj.: *oppressive*)

to suppress: The troops were not able to suppress the rebellion.
I could not suppress a sneeze.

Collocations: to suppress a revolt/an organization/the publication of some book/article/news; to suppress resistance/one's anger/one's laughter, etc.; to suppress the flow of blood.

Einen Aufstand u. ä. unterdrücken, niederwerfen; Gefühlsäußerungen unterdrücken; die Veröffentlichung oder Bekanntgabe von etwas verhindern.

To put down (a rebellion, etc.); to put an end to an activity by force;

to prevent from appearing, being printed or made public. *Suppress* usually implies the use of great power. (N.: *suppression*)

to repress: The police repressed any attempts at plundering.
I had repressed my feelings long enough; now they burst out.

Collocations: to repress instincts / one's feelings / some desire / one's curiosity.

Unterdrücken im Sinne von zurückdrängen, im Zaume halten, hemmen.

To hold back, to check or restrain; to prevent from finding an outlet. (N.: *repression*)

Exercise 119 (A) Insert a suitable term of the above group.

1. The news of the disaster was . . .
2. The peasants of the Middle Ages were . . . by their lords.
3. The school bully . . . the smaller boys.
4. You must . . . his tendency to talk too much.
5. Teach them to . . . their greed.
6. The teacher favoured the girls and . . . the boys.
7. My article was . . .
8. The slave revolt was . . . after three days.
9. Her father is a tyrant. The atmosphere there is . . .
10. The nurse could not . . . the flow of blood.
11. . . . of natural instincts is the cause of unhappiness.
12. Only his firm hold . . . the dog's savage attack.
13. They tried to . . . revolutionary groups.
14. The war lords . . . the people in the areas they conquered.
15. It is your duty to . . . the planned revolt.
16. The strong often . . . the weak.
17. Newspapers . . . far more news than they print.
18. Captain Bligh failed to . . . the mutiny on the "Bounty".
19. Rise up and rid yourselves of this . . .!
20. You could easily . . . your desire to smoke.
21. The state . . . and punishes criminals.
22. Try to . . . your delight or you might give the game away.
23. Taxes were heavy, punishment severe and unfair, there was no justice–in a word, the people were . . .
24. If you . . . their wishes now, you will not need to . . . their actions later.
25. Hitler . . . occupied Europe.
26. I deliberately . . . the evidence of his guilt.

120
Urteil
judgement, sentence, verdict

judgement: In my judgement a lastingly happy life is impossible without a great deal of self-discipline.
One should not rely on other people's judgement.
Collocations: to show good / poor judgement; a man of sound judgement; to give one's judgement on something; to form one's judgement on something; in my / his, etc. judgement; to pass judgement.
Der allgemeine Ausdruck für Urteil; Urteilskraft; auch das gerichtliche Urteil. Judgement bezieht sich i. allg. auf eine ausführlichere Stellungnahme der ein Urteil abgebenden Person.
The act of judging; the ability to judge, the faculty enabling one to distinguish right from wrong; also the judicial decision in court. *Judgement* usually implies a longer explanation of why some opinion has been formed. (V.: *to judge*)

sentence: The shop-lifter is serving a sentence of two years imprisonment.
Collocations: to pass / serve a sentence; to pronounce sentence; a sentence of death; a life sentence; a severe / light sentence.
Das gerichtliche Urteil, der Rechtsspruch.
The punishment meted out to a guilty party by a court of justice. (V.: *to sentence*)

verdict: The election results are a clear verdict of the public against anti-strike legislation.
The verdict of the jury was "Not guilty".
Der Urteilsspruch der Geschworenen; das besonders nach einem speziellen Test, einer Probe von etwas abgegebene knappe Urteil, z. B. „Gut!" oder „Schlecht!"; „Schuldig!" oder „Nicht schuldig!" etc.
The finding of the jury in court; the decision or opinion given after a test or trial. *A verdict* is usually shorter than a judgement, i.e. either "Guilty!" or "Not guilty!"

Exercise 120 (A) Insert a suitable term of the above group.
1. "Should I risk it?"–"Use your own . . ."
2. The judge is bound to accept the jury's . . .
3. Well, my dear, you've had a look at it. What is your . . .?
4. In passing . . . the judge took his extreme youth into account.
5. I'm afraid my . . . was sadly at fault on that occasion.
6. The judge paused before pronouncing . . .
7. Public opinion often passes . . . without trial.
8. In my . . . he has absolutely no chance.
9. In summing up, the judge showed wise . . .
10. "What do you think of him?"–"I don't feel qualified to sit in . . ."
11. The jury brought in a . . . of "not proven".

12. The . . . of death was commuted to life imprisonment.
13. Marriage is a life . . .
14. He was released on probation before he had served his . . .
15. Only the well-informed can form independent . . .
16. He waited anxiously. Would the . . . go against him, or in his favour?
17. It was a very severe . . . for so slight a misdemeanour.
18. Tell me 'yes' or 'no'. I shall be content with your . . .
19. (Judge:) "Gentlemen of the jury, what is your . . .?"
20. "O . . . thou art fled to brutish beasts." (Mark Antony in "Julius Caesar")
21. The . . . on Charles I was executed–and so was the king!
22. Every week the paper's theatre critic passes his . . . on the play at the local theatre.
23. "We are all under . . . of death." (Daniel Defoe)
24. Each man determines what is good, right or wrong according to his own . . .
25. He seems to be bereft of all . . .
26. (Hostess to guest after the meal:) "Well, what's the . . .?"

121
veraltet
old-fashioned, out-of-date, outmoded, obsolete, antiquated, archaic

old-fashioned: My father wears old-fashioned clothes.

Collocations: an old-fashioned dress/hat, etc.; a good, old-fashioned house; a good, old-fashioned girl (not having "modern" ideas); I may be old-fashioned, but . . .

Altmodisch mit Bezug auf Personen und Dinge. *Old-fashioned* hat nicht notwendigerweise negativen Sinn (siehe obige Kollokationen). *Old-fashioned* bezieht sich oft auf Gestalt und Form.

Not up to date in shape, form or character; not in accordance with modern tastes. *Old-fashioned* is not necessarily pejorative. "Buy our good old-fashioned bread" might be an advertising slogan. (Certain foods, e.g. bread, are thought to have deteriorated in modern times.) *Old-fashioned* can also be used for other things thought to have been better in the "good old days".

out-of-date: His advice is out-of-date.

Collocations: facts/statistics/information, etc. may be out-of-date (i.e. it *was* accurate *once*, but is no longer).

Veraltet mit Bezug auf Ansichten, Theorien etc.; nicht mehr gültig wegen Überschreitung einer zeitlichen Grenze.

Out of season; what has surpassed its proper date or time.
Out-of-date may have the direct meaning of "not of the right date", e.g. last year's calendar/catalogue, etc.

outmoded: These methods are outmoded.

Collocations: outmoded ideas.

Aus der Mode gekommen; von der Entwicklung überholt und deshalb nicht länger akzeptabel. Leicht gehobene Stilebene.

To be out of style; left behind by development and thus no longer meeting with approval. Somewhat literary or oratorical in style.

obsolete: We don't produce that model any more. It is obsolete.

Collocations: an obsolete model / pattern, etc.; obsolete ideas; built-in obsolescence.

Obsolete bezieht sich häufig auf Erzeugnisse, Verfahren, technische Entwicklungen u. ä. Von der Entwicklung überholt und deshalb außer Gebrauch gekommen.

No longer of standard production; gone out of use. *Obsolete* has a certain historical connotation. (N.: *obsolescence*)

antiquated: Those antiquated curtain rings will ruin the curtain.

Collocations: antiquated equipment / tools / methods.

Antiquated enthält oft einen Anflug von Spott, verächtlicher Einstellung oder auch leicht humorvoller Kritik; rückständig.

Quite often *antiquated* implies a slight touch of (good-natured or not so good-natured) contempt or humour. Ill-adapted to present use.

archaic: That word is no longer in normal use, it's archaic.

Collocations: an archaic expression / form / language / dialect.

Altertümlich, vor allem mit Bezug auf die Sprache, Wortwahl.

Usually with reference to words belonging to ancient times and no longer in use.

Exercise 121 (A) Insert a suitable term of the above group.

1. This vacuum cleaner belonged to my grandmother. It's . . . now.
2. My army boots look very . . . today.
3. That word's . . .; it's seldom used now.
4. My diary is . . .
5. Cars begin to look . . . long before they wear out.
6. The railway time-table is . . .
7. My grandmother is an . . . woman.
8. I've had this lighter for 30 years but I can't get another one of these. The man told me they've been . . . for 10 years.
9. This poem is too difficult; it contains so many . . . words.
10. She's an . . . girl; she wears no make-up.
11. "Venerable Sir" is an . . . form of address.
12. The origin of our own language is to be found in . . . languages.
13. This aircraft is . . . They haven't been making them for years.
14. I have an . . . hat that I like to wear when I go fishing.
15. You are . . . with ideas like that.
16. Only Classicists should use . . . expressions.

Exercise 121 (B)

1. That blue-print is . . .; designs are more advanced today.
2. They shouldn't revive . . . laws.
3. Whist is an . . . pastime.
4. Croquet is . . ., too.
5. Schopenhauer's philosophy is . . .
6. That machine will be . . . by next spring. We're going to market with a completely new model then.
7. Wearing full evening dress, old chap? Rather . . ., isn't it?
8. Those in the primitive interior used expressions that were already . . . in the more sophisticated areas of the country.
9. That idea is . . .
10. Corporal punishment is a rather . . . form of discipline.
11. That . . . hammer will hardly do the job.
12. He was using . . . garden shears that were no longer effective.

122
verdienen
to earn, to deserve, to merit

to earn: They earn very little money.

Collocations: to earn one's living / livelihood / daily bread; to earn an honest living; to earn respect / admiration / hatred / a rebuke, etc.; well-earned rest.

Lebensunterhalt, Geld, Lob, Anerkennung verdienen.

To acquire an adequate reward (money, praise, etc.) for one's labour, service, or performance. (N.: *earnings*)

to deserve: Such a selfish man does not deserve such a good-natured wife. The problem deserves your attention.

Collocations: to deserve well of; to deserve the credit for something; according to one's deserts.

Mit Recht eine Belohnung oder Strafe bekommen; einer Belohnung, Anerkennung etc. würdig sein.

Rightfully to get some reward or punishment for one's actions or behaviour; to be entitled to such reward; to merit punishment, esteem, etc. (N.: *deserts*)

to merit: Your essay merits all the praise it was given.

To merit wird im gleichen Sinne gebraucht wie *to deserve*, ist aber ein gewählterer Ausdruck und wird überwiegend im lobenden Sinne verwendet. Beachte, daß unmittelbar auf *merit* kein Verb folgen darf.

To merit means the same as *to deserve*, but it is a more formal term than the latter. Besides, it is more often used to express praise than criticism. Note that merit cannot immediately be followed by a verb. (N.: *merit*)

Exercise 122 (A) Insert a suitable term of the above group.

1. You . . . a medal for such an act of bravery.
2. You can . . . a lot of money during the season.
3. They . . . to be treated better than that.
4. I shall . . . their admiration, but you–only their hatred.
5. Dickens more than . . . his reputation as one of the great novelists.
6. She . . . her keep by running errands and helping around the house.
7. Nelson . . . well of his country.
8. One good turn . . . another. (saying)
9. They . . . all the praise that was lavished on them.
10. We . . . our daily bread by the sweat of our brow.
11. His insolence . . . him an instant rebuke.
12. It is difficult to . . . a good living these days.

Exercise 122 (B)

1. We must treat every case on its . . .
2. Average . . . for all adult males were over £ 20 per week.
3. I admit that he . . . all the credit for our achievement.
4. They . . . the best we can do for them.
5. Something attempted, something done, has . . . a night's repose.
6. He . . . a mention in "Who's Who".
7. He was given a well-. . . rise.
8. She . . . all that life can give her.
9. What . . . is there in conduct of that kind?
10. He received a well-. . . snub.
11. It was only his sustained effort that . . . him a respite.
12. Some believe that one acquires . . . in this life, which stands one in good stead in the next.

123
verfolgen
to pursue, to persecute, to prosecute

to pursue: The police constable pursued the thief.

I fully approve of the policy pursued by the government.

Collocations: to pursue an enemy; to be pursued by bad luck / illness, etc.; to pursue an aim / an end / a plan / a purpose / a certain course of action; to pursue one's way; to pursue one's studies / a trade; in pursuit of happiness, etc.; in pursuance of a policy.

Jemanden verfolgen, um ihn einzuholen oder zu fangen. Darüber hinaus in übertragener Bedeutung.

To follow in order to reach or catch, to chase. It is also used in a figurative sense. (N.: *pursuance; pursuit; pursuer*)

to persecute: There have always been people persecuted for their religious or political beliefs.

Jemanden wegen seiner politischen oder religiösen Überzeugungen verfolgen.

To harass and oppress people with unjust or cruel treatment, esp. on account of religious or political opinions. (N.: *persecution*)

to prosecute: Trespassers will be prosecuted.

Collocations: prosecuting counsel; witness for the prosecution.

Strafrechtlich, gerichtlich verfolgen. Im Sinne von (Studien) betreiben, (einen Plan) verfolgen gehört *prosecute* gehobener Stilebene an.

To institute legal proceedings against somebody. In the sense of *prosecute* studies or a plan it is a formal, rather high-flown term. (*Prosecute* does not always take an object.) (N.: *prosecution*)

Exercise 123 (A) Insert a suitable term of the above group.

1. The counsel questioned the witness for the ...
2. This is the plan we should ...
3. I belong to a ...ed minority.
4. Ill luck ... him to the grave.
5. Insult me again, and I shall ... you.
6. She ... her studies with steady determination.
7. He looked back. His ... were gaining on him.
8. The hounds ... the fox to its lair.
9. When my indebtedness reached £ 100, the firm decided to ... me.
10. The judge called the counsel for the ...
11. The enemy were in headlong flight, but we did not ... them.
12. Wherever he went, he was ... by autograph-hunters.
13. They threatened to ... him, but he refused to be intimidated.
14. Not all those arrested were ...
15. The Quakers were relentlessly ... during the Restoration Period.

Exercise 123 (B)

1. The slightest criticism, and she puts on that ... look.
2. Dissent invites ...
3. The star dashed off, hotly ... by her admirers.
4. He warned me I should be ... if I did not obey the instructions.
5. The other boys ... him because they were jealous of his success.
6. There was no need to ... them, they settled out of court.
7. When I asked him for my money back, he accused me of ... him.
8. They ... their way undeterred.
9. They only ... when no other course is open.
10. They ... her, constantly subjecting her to taunts and blows.

124
verlassen
to leave, to quit, to abandon, to forsake, to desert

to leave: He left the country for good.
My son has left home. (i.e. permanently)
Collocations: to leave school / work / the house / the neighbourhood, etc.
Allgemeiner, neutraler Ausdruck für verlassen.
To go away from a place or person. To leave is the general term.

to quit: The population wanted the occupying forces to quit the country.
The house owner gave the tenants notice to quit.
Plötzlich oder für immer verlassen. *To quit* klingt dramatischer als *to leave.* Es hat einen leichten amerikanischen Einschlag und ist gewöhnlich der umgangssprachlichen Stilebene zuzurechnen.
To leave suddenly or to leave for good. *To quit* has a dramatic ring and always sounds slightly American. *To quit* usually indicates informal English, e.g. "*I had had enough, so I quit.*"

to abandon: He abandoned all hope.
Rats always abandon a sinking ship.
Collocations: to abandon s.o. to his fate; to abandon one's prejudices/ plans, etc.; to abandon a hopeless task.
Im Stich lassen; aufgeben; preisgeben.
To desert, leave behind; give up completely, to withdraw from persons or things.

to forsake: A doctor may not forsake his patients when they need treatment.
Collocations: to forsake the world, to forsake one's friends.
Einer Bindung an Menschen oder Dinge untreu werden; entsagen. *Forsake* hat emotionale Färbung und gehört der gehobenen Stilebene an.
Forsake suggests a violation of obligations, the withdrawing of one's help, affection, or association. It has emotional connotations and indicates literary style.

to desert: A man who deserts his wife has to pay her an allowance.
Collocations: to desert the army / one's post.
To desert ist der stärkste Ausdruck dieser Gruppe. Aus Pflichtvergessenheit, böser Absicht, ganz bewußt, in einer schwierigen Situation im Stich lassen. Auch im bildlichen Sinn.
To desert is the strongest term of this group. To leave intentionally in violation of duty, at a difficult time and in a difficult position. Also in the sense of to fail with regard to courage, hope, etc.

Exercise 124 (A) Insert a suitable term of the above group.
1. My husband . . . home early this morning. (i.e. to go to work)
2. You can't sack me. I . . .!

3. Have you . . . your intention of going on the stage?
4. He . . . the army after one day.
5. A captain must never . . . his ship.
6. What sort of impression do you think I . . . on them?
7. I advise you to . . . before it is too late.
8. "I'm . . . school next summer."—"What's the school-. . .ing age now?"
9. As soon as she . . . one idea, she started snatching at another.
10. When the bomb exploded, the whole audience rose and . . . the theatre!
11. Not one soldier . . . throughout the whole campaign.
12. The crew . . . the captain, and left him to his fate.
13. I'm glad that family has . . . this neighbourhood.
14. Only politeness prevented me from . . . the room earlier.
15. He . . . the room in anger.
16. She . . . the firm under a cloud. (i.e. under suspicion of some misdemeanour)
17. "Friends may . . . me,
    Let 'em all . . . me,
    I still have you,
    Sonny Boy." (from pop song "Sonny Boy")
18. You must . . . all thoughts of escape.
19. They . . . the hotel without paying the bill.
20. I'm . . .; I've had enough.

Exercise 124 (B)

1. Courage . . . them when they saw that the odds were against them.
2. Never . . . a friend in need.
3. Wretched parents sometimes . . . their babies in church doorways.
4. The beach was . . . as it was lunch-time.
5. He . . . the army as he disliked the discipline.
6. A monk . . . all wordly pleasures.
7. . . . my sight—and never return.
8. I cannot and will not . . . those who have placed their trust in me.
9. An . . . wife is to be pitied.
10. She felt so . . . and alone.

125
verletzen
to hurt, to injure

to hurt: He felt hurt by your remark.

Did you hurt yourself? (=Haben Sie sich weh getan?)

Collocations: to hurt oneself; to hurt s.o.'s feelings; hurt pride; to feel hurt; to suffer a bad hurt (from a fall, etc.); to be slightly/badly/seriously hurt (when bodily damage is meant); to be very (much) hurt at s.th. (when unhappiness caused by a person is meant).

Im körperlichen und übertragenen Sinne verletzen oder schmerzen. Mit *hurt* in der Bedeutung von 'verletzen' verbindet sich stets zugleich die Vorstellung von körperlichem Schmerz. Auch intransitiv verwendet.

To cause pain (bodily or mental); to inflict a wound (the idea of the pain caused thereby is always implied). *To hurt* can be used intransitively. (N.: *hurt*; Adj.: *hurtful*)

to injure: Seven people were injured in the road accident.
The injured (people) were taken to hospital.

Collocations: to sustain an injury; to suffer serious injuries (to the legs, arms, etc.); severe injuries; to injure one's spine/shoulder, etc.; to injure s.o.'s reputation/prospects; to add insult to injury.

To injure ist ein stärkerer Ausdruck als *to hurt*. Es bezeichnet jede Art von körperlichem Schaden, den jemand erleidet oder verursacht. Darüber hinaus wird *injure* auch im Sinne von 'Unrecht tun' verwendet.

To injure is a stronger term than *to hurt*, and it is more generalised and broader than the latter. It is also used in the sense of to do wrong to someone. (Note that one may be injured without being hurt, i.e. it may be a painless injury. And, of course, one may also be hurt without being injured.) Contrary *to hurt*, *injure* is always used transitively. (N.: *injury;* Adj.: *injurious*)

Exercise 125 (A) Insert a suitable term of the above group.

1. "I've been to the dentist." – "Did it . . .?"
2. They can say what they like, but they cannot . . . my reputation.
3. The . . . passengers were taken to hospital.
4. That shoe is too tight over the instep. It . . .
5. She squeezed me so hard, it . . .
6. He dressed carefully for the interview so as not to . . . his prospects.
7. Smoking is . . . to health.
8. He is now fully recovered from his . . .
9. Unkindness . . . more than blows.
10. He punched me but didn't . . . me.

Exercise 125 (B)

1. Stop making such . . . remarks.
2. "When have I . . . thee? When done thee wrong?" (Shakespeare)
3. They succeeded by sticking to their motto: "An . . . to one is an . . . to all."
4. Keep out of this quarrel or you may get . . .
5. She looked . . . but said nothing.
6. (Father, about to chastise son:) "This is going to . . . me, more than it . . . you."–(Son:) "Don't be too hard on yourself, Dad."
7. . . . pride is often due to over-sensitivity.
8. The sword-thrust missed the mark, but . . . his left hand.
9. He . . . his knee when he fell off the ladder.
10. (Appeal for funds:) "Give–until it . . ."

126
vorsichtig
careful, cautious, wary, prudent

careful: Be careful with that vase. It is a very expensive one.
Be careful (about) what you say.
Collocations: a careful housewife / worker / driver; to drive carefully; to examine s.th. carefully; be careful not to drop that cup / to dirty your new dress, etc.
Vorsichtig im Sinne von sorgfältig, achtsam oder gründlich sein.
Paying close attention to what one is doing so as to avoid danger or mistakes. (N.: *care; carefulness*)

cautious: He was very cautious, and pondered long before taking action.
He looked round cautiously before he climbed through the window.
Vorsichtig im Sinne von auf der Hut sein, um von etwas Unerwünschtem nicht überrascht zu werden. Dabei schwingt nicht selten der Gedanke an übergroße Vorsicht, ja Ängstlichkeit mit.
Cautious means being on one's guard for fear of failure, injury and the like. It frequently even suggests the idea of being too careful. (N.: *caution; cautiousness*)

wary: You'd better be wary in your business transactions with them. The fox is a wary animal, difficult to catch.
Collocations: to keep a wary eye on s.o. or s.th.; to be wary of doing s.th. (=sich hüten, etwas zu tun).
Vorsichtig, argwöhnisch und schlau zugleich sein. *Wary* kann auch ein Element der Furcht enthalten.
To be watchful with a special connotation of suspiciousness and cunning. It may also imply a suggestion of fear. (N.: *wariness*)

prudent: Our government pursues a prudent policy.
Collocations: a prudent housewife / housekeeper.
Auf Grund reicher praktischer Erfahrung umsichtig und besonnen sein, also mit einem Blick auf die zu erwartenden Folgen.
Prudent suggests being wise on the basis of rich practical experience and with an eye to the possible consequences. *Prudent* can be praise or indicate merit. (N.: *prudence*)

Exercise 126 (A) Insert a suitable term of the above group.
1. She laid the Dresden china . . . on the table.
2. He had been . . . in his youth, and was now the master of a small fortune.
3. Extreme . . . can be as dangerous as extreme rashness.
4. The . . . man thinks . . ., and then plans ahead.
5. After years of . . . research, he published his findings.
6. They approached the town at night with great . . .
7. He kept a . . . eye on his wife's expenditure.

8. We decided it would be more . . . to retreat, than to fight on.
9. A . . . gambler is a contradiction in terms.
10. It was his . . . policy to examine all angles, before passing an opinion.
11. We opened the door . . ., suspecting a booby-trap.
12. Be . . . not to offend her – she's very rich.
13. He is a very . . . worker and seldom produces faulty products.
14. The guard-dog eyed us . . .
15. He had invested . . . for years, and now had no financial problems.
16. Be . . . with new acquaintances.
17. I noticed the . . . way in which the surgeon used his scalpel.
18. (Notice, at town border:) Newton welcomes . . . drivers.
19. He was quick in his thinking but . . . in his movements.
20. The hunters approached the cave . . .

Exercise 126 (B)

1. Alas, our . . . tactics only served to delay the inevitable.
2. Fortune favours the . . .; but pleasure often evades them.
3. Goodbye–and be . . . how you go.
4. She looked at us with . . ., hooded eyes.
5. The Scots have a name for being mean–or . . ., as they like to put it.
6. He was too . . . a player to be drawn into the trap.
7. If you can't be good, be . . . (saying)
8. . . . now! Easy does it!
9. Our losses made us . . .
10. They were . . . of all new ventures.

127
werden
to become, to get, to grow, to turn, to go

to become: At an advanced stage English becomes more and more difficult.
When he heard that, he became angry.
He has become a lawyer.
It has become much colder.

Collocations: to become a habit / a nuisance / a laughing stock; to become clear, etc.

To become steht im Sinne von werden vor allem bei Substantiven, Adjektiven im Komparativ und als Adjektiv gebrauchten Partizipien. Im Zusammenhang mit Adjektiven und Partizipien können jedoch auch andere Verben dieser Synonymgruppe gebraucht werden; mit Substantiven aber nicht, außer *to turn* z. B.: *He turned Buddhist. To become* ist gegenüber *to get* etwas weniger umgangssprachlich.

To become, denoting a gradual development or its result, is usually used with nouns, adjectives in the comparative degree and participles. Also other terms of this group of synonyms can be employed with adjectives and participles; with nouns, however, only *become* is possible, apart from a few special cases where *to turn* applies, e.g. *to turn Buddhist.*

to get: We'd better take our umbrellas, otherwise we may get wet.
It is getting dark / late / cold, etc.

Collocations: to get rich / late / old / weak / tired, etc.

To get wird umgangssprachlich sehr häufig im Sinne von werden verwendet, vor allem in Verbindungen mit Adjektiven (besonders wenn diese nicht im Komparativ gebraucht werden) und Partizipien. *To get* wird oft in der Verlaufsform verwendet.

To get is more colloquial than *to become.* It is used in connection with adjectives (especially if they are not used in the comparative degree) and with participles, and frequently in the progressive form at that.

to grow: He is growing old. It is growing dark. "Absence makes the heart grow fonder."

Collocations: to grow dark and stormy; to grow fond of s.th. or s.o.; to grow tedious; to be growing fat.

To grow im Sinne von 'werden' hebt den Prozeß der Entwicklung oder Wandlung aus einer Qualität in eine andere hervor. Dabei handelt es sich gewöhnlich um einen allmählich verlaufenden Vorgang. Es gibt jedoch Ausnahmen, z. B.: *After the sunset it suddenly grew cold.*

To grow stresses the process from one quality into another one and frequently implies a gradual change. It is, however, also applicable to a rapid process, e.g. *After sunset it suddenly grew cold.*

to turn: He turned traitor. (=Er wurde zum Verräter)
At the age of thirty he turned Roman Catholic.
When she read the telegram she turned pale.

Collocations: to turn sour; on the turn (i.e. about to become).

To turn bezeichnet ein (meist plötzliches) Umschlagen aus einer Qualität in eine andere. In der Verbindung *turn* + Substantiv steht letzteres ohne Artikel.

To turn denotes a sudden change from one quality or state into another one. If *turn* is followed by a noun, the latter is used without an article.

to go: He went green with envy. The milk went sour.

Collocations: to go mad; to go blind; to go off (i.e. sour), etc.

To go im Sinne von 'werden' bezeichnet häufig etwas Negatives.

In some collocations *to go* is also used in the sense of *become.* It often suggests a development which is thought of as something negative or bad.

Exercise 127 (A) Insert a suitable term of the above group.

1. It has . . . my habit to take a walk after dinner.
2. The problem is . . . more acute.
3. You must be frozen! You've . . . blue.

4. People tend to . . . more mellow as they age.
5. Throw it away–it's . . . sour.
6. We are bound to . . . older, but we are not bound to . . . wiser.
7. She . . . red with shame.
8. It was . . . late, as we started for home.
9. What will . . . of me, if you leave me?
10. The madman . . . berserk.
11. The cheese has . . . off.
12. I poured the chemical into the tube and the contents . . . mauve.
13. After our quarrel he . . . my best friend.
14. After their marriage they . . . more alike than ever.
15. I think it's going to snow, it's . . . terribly cold.
16. The gnome . . . smaller and smaller until he finally vanished away.
17. They . . . terribly excited at the news.
18. They . . . green with envy when they saw our new house.
19. As he . . . older he turned into an interesting companion.
20. I have . . . a great believer in early rising.

Exercise 127 (B)

1. When he saw he could not persuade us, he . . . nasty.
2. I'm . . . stark, raving mad with worry.
3. He . . . pale under his tan.
4. After a little experience he . . . into an excellent worker.
5. I could feel myself . . . red all over.
6. He . . . handsomer with the years.
7. The night . . . dark and stormy.
8. She is . . . to be a problem.
9. He liked her at first, but his sentiments . . . into love.
10. In autumn the leaves . . . yellow, red and brown.

128
Wunder
wonder, marvel, prodigy, miracle

wonder: Space travels to the moon are one of the wonders of modern science and technology.

Collocations: the seven wonders of the world; to work (or do) wonders (=Wunder wirken); childish/open-mouthed wonder; a nine days' wonder; the wonder of the century/of the age; to be filled with wonder; to wonder/marvel at s.th.; I wonder! (indicates doubt or even disbelief).

Wonder bezieht sich auf Erscheinungen, die sich verstandesmäßiger Erklärung zu entziehen scheinen und uns deshalb mit Staunen oder Bewunderung erfüllen. Zumindest unterschwellig verbindet sich mit *wonder* häufig das Bedürfnis nach Erkenntnis der Zusammenhänge.

Wonder refers to something which surprises or fills with admiration due to its seeming inexplicableness. This sensation is often associated with the wish to find out about what gives rise to it. (V.: *to wonder*)

marvel: He is a marvel of energy. The new spaceship is a marvel.
The sculpture was a marvel of artistic skill.

Collocations: the marvels (or wonders) of modern engineering; a scientific marvel; the marvels of nature.

Bei *marvel* steht vor allem das zuweilen fast an Ehrfurcht grenzende Erstaunen an sich im Vordergrund. *Marvel* kann häufig in den gleichen Situationen verwendet werden wie *wonder*, ist jedoch ein etwas gewählterer Ausdruck.

Marvel suggests the ideas of pleased astonishment and almost awe-inspiring surprise. This term is somewhat more dignified than *wonder*. (V.: *to marvel*)

prodigy: He is a mathematical prodigy.
This pear is a prodigy; it's several times the usual size!

Collocations: a prodigy of learning (=ein Wunder an Gelehrsamkeit); a child prodigy (=ein Wunderkind); prodigies of strength; prodigies of sacrifice; prodigious feats.

Prodigy bezeichnet etwas in erstaunlichem Maße von den Normen des Natürlichen Abweichendes, also ein überragendes Beispiel für menschliche Leistungsfähigkeit, eine erstaunliche Leistung der Natur, ein Wunderwerk, Wunderding.

Something that arouses our astonishment because it seems to be out of the course of nature. (Adj.: *prodigious*)

miracle: If he recovers from that illness, it will be a miracle.

Collocations: to believe in miracles; to expect miracles; to work miracles.

Ein scheinbar übernatürliches Wunder. Hier steht der Gedanke an das unerklärbar Erscheinende im Vordergrund.

A wonderful event that is seemingly due to some supernatural power. (Adj.: *miraculous*)

Exercise 128 (A) Insert a suitable term of the above group.

1. Do you believe in . . .?
2. (Advertising slogan:) Our beer works . . .
3. Einstein was a . . . of learning.
4. They examined the bright object in childish . . .
5. He had a . . . escape when his car crashed.
6. They performed . . . feats of strength and skill.
7. My wife works . . . on five-pounds a week.
8. H. G. Wells wrote a book called, "The man who could work . . ."
9. The Spinning Jenny was a . . . of ingenuity.
10. Mozart was a child . . .
11. He was a . . . of strength and determination.
12. His life can only be saved by a . . . now.

13. The Forth Bridge is a . . . of engineering.
14. A horseless carriage would have seemed a . . . to our forefathers.
15. It's no good waiting for a . . . We'll have to do something ourselves.
16. I must say, I . . . at your temerity.
17. The . . . of nature outdo the . . . of science.
18. It's a . . . he's lived this long.
19. The roast turkey was a . . . of culinary perfection.
20. . . . never happen. (saying)

Exercise 128 (B)

1. The old wizard could no longer perform his . . .
2. Gargantua had a . . . appetite.
3. I don't believe the stories about the . . . of bravery they were supposed to have performed.
4. His hair-do was a . . . of the hairdresser's art.
5. Turner's sunsets are . . . of colour.
6. Shakespeare was a . . . of the theatre.
7. ". . . will never cease!" (an exclamation when something surprising happens)
8. Travel abroad reveals the . . . of other lands.
9. She stared in open-mouthed . . .
10. The war gave rise to . . . of sacrifice.

129
Zahl
number, figure

number: Children learn whole numbers at an early age.
There are a number of foreigners among the students.

Collocations: a phone number; a car number; an even (or odd) number; fractional/decimal/whole numbers; cardinal/ordinal numbers; numbers of (i.e. many); in great/small numbers; the total number; to be the number one (i.e. be the best in some sphere or the first to be picked for s.th.)

Das Zahlzeichen; die Nummer; Anzahl.

A numeral; the particular numeral indicating the place of something in a series; a (small or large) quantity of persons or things. (*Decimals* is often preferred to *decimal numbers* and *fractions* to *fractional numbers.*) (V.: *to number*)

figure: The offers run into three figures. (=Die Angebote gehen in die Hunderte/sind dreistellig)
You must write the sum in figures and in words.
The figures in the table are incorrect.

Collocations: a four-figure (five-figure, etc.) income; to run into double figures; to add up some figures; the figure 4, the figure 25, etc.

Die Zahl beim Rechnen; die Ziffer.

A value expressed in numbers; a numerical symbol, esp. one of the ten Arabic numerals.

Exercise 129 (A) Insert a suitable term of the above group.

1. Cheques are made out in both words and . . .
2. If . . . fall much lower, we shall have to cancel the course.
3. Would you leave your phone. . ., please?
4. One million contains seven . . .
5. He has a five-. . . income.
6. We were besieged by great . . . of autograph-hunters.
7. He is . . . among the finest musicians in the country.
8. Has our . . . come up in the lottery?
9. She told them they could name their own . . . for the painting.
10. My overdraft runs into three . . .
11. Teenagers are . . . one target today for the advertisers.
12. What a match! Our score reached double . . .
13. Some books have their chapters . . . in Roman . . .
14. . . . less millions will thank us for this discovery.
15. What are the . . . for full-time students? (i.e. statistics)
16. Can you add up these . . . for me?
17. Please write your . . . more clearly.
18. After four hours solid checking of the . . . they began to dance before my eyes.

130
Ziel
aim, target, goal, mark, destination, objective

aim: Heaping up money was his only aim in life.

Collocations: to take aim; a straight aim; an aim in life; to miss one's aim; to be aimless; the aims of education, etc.

Aim impliziert vor allem den Gedanken der Zielgerichtetheit des Bemühens; die Schußrichtung. Im übertragenen Sinne auch in der Bedeutung von Zweck, Vorhaben oder Absicht verwendet.

Aim suggests the direction of one's efforts. It can also denote an intention or purpose. (V.: *to aim*)

target: Not all production targets could be reached.
He aimed carefully but missed the target.

Collocations: a target figure; to hit/miss/set up a target; to identify one's target.

Der Zielgegenstand, die Zielscheibe; das Produktionsziel; das Ziel des Spottes etc.

An object to be shot at; figuratively, an object of derision, scorn, abuse, etc.; a level of production to be reached.

goal: "Look not backwards, but ever forwards to our glorious goal." (Conan Doyle, "The lost world")

Collocations: our glorious goal; to reach one's goal; a goal in sight.

Goal impliziert ehrgeiziges Bemühen, Überwindung von Schwierigkeiten in der Realisierung des Zieles. Es ist ein emotional, zuweilen sogar poetisch gefärbter Ausdruck, der sich oft mit der Empfindung einer gewissen Dramatik verbindet. Auch im Sinne von Ziel eines Wettrennens verwendet.

Goal implies ambitious endeavour or struggle, the overcoming of difficulty in achieving some result. It is an emotional, dramatic, sometimes even poetic term. Goal can also denote the terminal point of a race.

mark: What you said was wide of the mark. (=Deine Bemerkung ging weit am Ziel vorbei.)

Collocations: to hit / miss / find one's mark; wide of the mark (also: beside the mark).

Das Ziel, auf das geschossen wird (wie *target*, aber ohne dessen zusätzliche Anwendungsmöglichkeiten). Im übertragenen Sinne wird es in der Bedeutung von 'ins Schwarze treffen', sein Ziel (oder seinen Zweck) verfehlen, 'danebenhauen' verwendet.

An object aimed at, as *target*. Used figuratively, it suggests the idea of 'imprecise, irrelevant, far from correct' (wide of / beside the mark) or to succeed / fail in an attempt (to hit / miss the mark). *Mark* is a colloquial term.

destination: The letter has not reached its destination.

Collocations: to state one's destination; to arrive at one's destination.

Der Bestimmungsort; das Ziel einer Warensendung, eines Schiffes, einer Reise.

A place to which somebody or something is sent; the predetermined end of a journey or voyage.

objective: I always set myself limited objectives, objectives within my powers.

Collocations: ultimate objective (or aim); short-term / long-term objectives; limited objective; immediate objective.

Objective verbindet sich mit dem Gedanken an die Erreichbarkeit eines konkreten Zieles; ein Ziel, das in gewisser automatischer Abfolge erreicht wird, ähnlich wie bei *destination*.

Objective implies the attainability of some concrete end and is, in this way, similar to destination. It is more formal than the other terms.

Exercise 130 (A) Insert a suitable term of the above group.

1. The bomber crews were given their . . . for the night.
2. My . . . is the same as yours; but my route is different.
3. Bravo! You've hit the . . . right in the middle.
4. You want to become a millionaire? Is that an attainable . . .?

5. Their . . . was a profit of £ 100 per week.
6. Columbus's . . . was India—but he sailed westwards!
7. I became the . . . of much ill-informed abuse.
8. Our . . . are similar, we should unite to achieve them.
9. A man should have a . . . towards which he strives.
10. They reached their . . . figures with ease.
11. The . . . is to achieve higher standards all round.
12. Our final . . . was Samarkand; but could we reach it?
13. She missed her . . . , but damaged my shoulder.
14. (Sergeant:) "At your . . . in front, five rounds—Fire!"
15. She thinks early marriage a desirable . . .
16. The trainer's . . . was to produce all-round fitness.
17. I shall have a hot bath, when we reach our . . .
18. In game-shooting each hunter has his own . . .
19. My . . . was clearly visible on the brow of the hill.
20. His results always fell short of his . . .

Exercise 130 (B)

1. What possible . . . could you have in blackening my name so?
2. The knight's lance found its . . .
3. Such high-flown . . . were in conflict with his actions.
4. We sent up a shout of triumph. Our . . . was in sight.
5. The . . . are still the old ones; it is the methods that are new.
6. My . . . was to win his confidence.
7. She was bitterly disappointed. She had failed in her . . .
8. A comfortable retirement was his only . . .
9. That's right. You've hit the . . . straight away.
10. Don't set up a . . . you know you can't achieve.

KEY TO THE EXERCISES

(If reference is made to the "introduction", this term refers to the introductory comments preceding the exercises.)

1 (A)

1. resembling (=looking like; *like* my . . ., not necessarily in appearance, it could be in other ways; *who was similar to*, usually needs indication of *in which ways* she was similar. So all three are possible and the explanations should be noted for those that follow.). 2. similar. 3. alike. 4. similar. 5. similar. 6. resembling. 7. similar (similar is the "correctest"; *like subjects* and *the like* sound a bit mannered.) 8. similar (*anything similar* or *of a similar nature* is the normal; *anything like it* is a little vaguer; *of a like nature* is somewhat more mannered). 9. alike. 10. similar. 11. alike. 12. resembling (means the same as *who looked like*). 13. similar. 14. alike. 15. resembling. 16. alike. 17. resembling (or *two similar personalities*, i.e. comparable on several levels). 18. like. 19. similar. 20. similar. 21. alike. 22. likeness.

2 (A)

1. elderly. 2. ancient. 3. ancient. 4. old (*ancient* would imply much older than 200 years, perhaps 2000 years). 5. aged. 6. old. 7. antique. 8. antique; antique. 9. ancient. 10. elderly. 11. aged. 12. elderly. 13. old. 14. antique. 15. old. 16. aged. 17. elderly. 18. aged. 19. ancient (*old* not impossible, but it would not suggest something dating back to some remote period, and then "*love* to examine" suggests something more out of the ordinary than just e.g. an old pair of tongs). 20. antique.

3 (A)

1. alter. 2. vary. 3. change. 4. alter. 5. alter (*change the design* suggests something more thorough, e.g. a completely *new* plan). 6. modify (it suggests that the original expression was too extreme). 7. change. 8. change (or alter). 9. changes. 10. vary. 11. alterations. 12. change. 13. modified. 14. change. 15. vary. 16. altered (*changed* would suggest a greater difference than alter). 17. vary. 18. altered (*altered* here suggests appearance, whereas *changed* would have wider implications).

3 (B)

1. alter. 2. modified (*modify* is not a fundamental change, whereas *change* would be; *alter* is somewhere between). 3. varies. 4. modified ("a little" suggests modify). 5. modifies. 6. alter (*change* could almost mean hanging up a *different* portrait). 7. change. 8. modify (*modify* =alter details and leave basic framework; *change* could mean: write a new syllabus, perhaps on a different period). 9. alter (or change). 10. modified (*modify behaviour* or *attitude* suggests a calculated change of *some aspects* to gain advantage or avoid disadvantage. It can suggest slyness or cunning.)

4 (A)

1. job. 2. task (*job* is possible but it is more neutral). 3. work (*job* is more colloquial). 4. labour. 5. jobs. 6. work. 7. job. 8. task. 9. grind. 10. drudgery. 11. labour

(or work). 12. job. 13. drudgery. 14. tasks. 15. toil. 16. working. 17. work. 18. work.

4 (B)

1. grind (or: is *(sheer) drudgery. Grind* suggests the repetitive, whilst *drudgery* stresses the *continued unpleasantness*). 2. work. 3. toil (*grind* is possible; *drudgery* also possible, but without "a"). 4. grind. 5. drudgery. 6. toil (*drudgery* and *grind* don't seem quite to arise from the causes given). 7. labour. 8. toil. 9. drudgery. 10. grind. 11. grind (again it is the repetitive idea which is uppermost). 12. drudgery (*a grind* is possible; *just* =only, it stresses the pejorative and so *drudgery* or *grind* tally with the context).

5 (A)

1. ended. 2. stop. 3. finish. 4. finished (or concluded). 5. stop. 6. finishes (or ends or stops; *finishes* is probably the commonest usage; *stops* could imply that the interruption of work is only temporary). 7. stop. 8. finished. 9. discontinue. 10. finished. 11. stop (*cease* is possible, it is more emotional than *stop*, so usage depends on one's mood; *end* would be wrong because it suggests ending only *one* war). 12. conclude. 13. ended. 14. stop. 15. stopped (or discontinued). 16. ended.

5 (B)

1. discontinued. 2. ceased. 3. conclude. 4. discontinued (or ceased; *discontinued* is common usage when something has been going on at regular intervals for some time; *ceased* suggests abrupt, almost *emotional* ending). 5. ceased. 6. ceased (or *was stopped*, which would imply perhaps an order or an unspoken command, whereas *ceased* implies that his personality, popularity, or force of argument led people to stop of their own accord. 7. stopped (or ceased; *ceased* suggests the welcome peace and quiet that ensues, whilst *stopped* almost suggests that the noise is still going on in one's mind). 8. stopped (or ceased). 9. concluding. 10. ceased (or *has been ended*; *ceased* is more poetic and fits the mood better; so usage is a question of style).

6 (A)

1. postponed (*put off* would be more colloquial and not "official" enough and it could mean *indefinitely* and, if that *were* the case, it would have to be specifically stated with *postponed*). 2. delayed. 3. put off (*put off* gives the necessary degree of a) offhandedness and b) uncertainty of final intentions; *postponed* too official; *defer* also more official and elegant; it is seldom in ordinary speech; *delay* implies no decision to cancel *yet* made; even suggests that I may do it at a later date). 4. delayed 5. put off (*postponed* likely if e.g. on an official notice at the dance hall; *deferred* would be unlikely, wrong register). 6. delay. 7. postponed. 8. put off (see No. 5). 9. defer. 10. postponement. 11. put off (*put off* because this is meant as a colloquial remark between friends, i.e. *intimate*, so *postpone* would be false). 12. postponed. 13. delay 14. put off. 15. postponed.

6 (B)

1. procrastination. 2. put off (or *procrastinate*, but *without* object! and a more literary speaker would be suggested and it could be a little facetious). 3. delay. 4. procrastinate (***see*** No. 2; sometimes, in moments of irritation, people wax a little "poetic", *procrastinate* is not *exclusively* literary, one sometimes feels one doesn't wish to search for an object; *delay* would be the only other possible intransitive verb, but even this is happier with an object). 5. delayed. 6. procrastination. 7. delays. 8. defer (*defer* tallies better with *assessment*; *postpone* is too much like *official information*). 9. procrastinator. 10. postponed. 11. defer (*defer*

somehow tallies with *important*, but this is not an "iron rule", just a nuance; *put off* is possible, but it alters the *tone*). 12. procrastination.

7 (A)

1. stand up (*rise* possible, but less colloquial). 2. got up. 3. rose. 4. stand up (*rise* would be too formal in this situation, it is not usual in spoken English). 5. rose. 6. stand up. 7. get up. 8. get up. 9. rise. 10. rose. 11. get up (*rise* not impossible, but not very likely in speech). 12. stood up (or: *they all rose and . . .*; somehow *everybody* seems less stylish, so *stood up* is used; a nuance only). 13. get up. 14. rose (*rose* matches *orator*; also, *got up*, which could suggest that he was about to leave the hall; *rose* suggests smooth mobility). 15. stand up. 16. got up (*get up and go* is a standard colloq. phrase, so get up seems better when you are about to go; *rose* is likelier in lit. style). 17. stand up or rise (*rise* has an emotional content which a writer might use deliberately). 18. get up (*off the floor* is the clue here; the other two verbs could not precede that phrase though *rise from the floor* would be just possible). 19. stand up (*stand up* suggests straight-backed manliness, so it fits the context better than *get up*). 20. got up (*stood up* or *rose* also possible; for differences see introduction). 21. rose. 22. get up. 23. rise. 24. rose.

8 (A)

1. executed (*carried out* would be more colloq.). 2. carried out (*performed* is more formal, it implies a slight hint of artistic, technical excellence or elan; *accomplished* suggests a sense of achievement; *executed* would NOT be normal usage with *task*). 3. effected. 4. perform (it suggests the skill involved; *carried out* would be colloq.). 5. carry out (*execute instructions* would NOT be acceptable usage). 6. execute (the orde r is for *goods*, i.e. the firm delivers the goods). 7. effected. 8. executed. 9. effect. 10. accomplish. 11. carry out. 12. executed (*executed* suggests precision; *performed* suggests artistry). 13. effected. 14. accomplish. 15. carry out. 16. performed. 17. accomplished. 18. perform.

8 (B)

1. executed (*performed* possible; *execute* suggests precision and so sounds sharper, more like a criticism voiced). 2. performed. 3. accomplished (or *performed*; the latter is the most usual, but note different nuances; *effected* would be unusual). 4. accomplished. 5. performed (*executed* also possible, esp. in a really serious journal or critique; *carried out* would be colloq.). 6. executed (*carried out*: colloq.). 7. accomplishment. 8. performed (*carried out*: colloq.). 9. performed (*accomplished*; *carried out*: **see** introduction for nuances). 10. performance.

9 (A)

1. bathed. 2. bath. 3. swam. 4. swimming. 5. bath. 6. bath. 7. bathe. 8. bathing. 9. bath. 10. sunbathing. 11. bathing. 12. bath. 13. swimming. 14. bathing. 15. bath; bath. 16. swim. 17. bath. 18. bathed. 19. bathed. 20. bath. 21. bathing. 22. bath. 23. swimming. 24. bathed.

10 (A)

1. pretended. 2. maintain (*till you burst* tallies with maintain; *assert* is possible, it would then be *stressed* in speech to indicate the gap between the *assertion* and the "true facts" (as seen by the other speaker); *allege* not really possible unless used by first speaker in the first place). 3. assert. 4. allegation. 5. pretended. 6. asserted. 7. maintain. 8. alleged. 9. pretended. 10. maintain. 11. claim. 12. contended. 13. contended. 14. assert (use of *force* suggests *assert*; *maintain* would apply after alteration of context, e.g. you must *continue* to maintain it or you will

not be believed; "with all your force' would have to be omitted). 15. alleged. 16. contended (*assert* does not match the uncertainty in *may*; *maintain* suggests that this follows a lengthy argument). 17. maintain (*still* suggests *maintain*). 18. pretend. 19. claimed. 20. assert (*assert* matches *conviction* better than the others).

10 (B)

1. claim (fits the "moral right" idea; others possible with different nuances as explained in introduction). 2. alleged (*alleged* is best when reporting an accusation, suggesting suspicion of judgement till evidence is available). 3. maintain (*maintain* suggests that the belief has been held and argued over for a long period and is continuous and persistent; to *assert* may be to do so for the first time and is also more *aggressive* and *dogmatic* in feeling; *contend* suggests the to and fro of argument). 4. contend (*assert* would suggest aggressiveness). 5. pretence. 6. claimed (the intention is clear: to state a *right* to s.th., namely, her recognition as their daughter; none of the others contain this element of "wanting others to recognise the truth"; ***see*** introduction). 7. contend. 8. claim. 9. alleged. 10. asserted ("You can take it from me . . ." is the clue for *assert*; *maintained* would suggest that he had been saying it for a long time).

11 (A)

1. receive. 2. get (*obtain* would spoil the slightly derisory effect; *receive* would need *when* rather than *where* and would alter the context considerably). 3. got. 4. obtain. 5. obtain (*obtain* suggests buying; *get* would imply wider possibility, e.g. borrow or steal). 6. received (*got* could indicate a different method; *obtained* would suggest activity on the part of the speaker, e.g. collecting it from somewhere). 7. obtained (*got*: much more colloquial). 8. got. 9. obtained. 10. received. 11. got. 12. received. 13. received (here the use of *got* in the Perfect would be impossible as it would imply possession! It would have to be: "I have had hundreds of . . ."). 14. obtain (*got*: much more colloq.; *obtain* sounds a little mannered in ordinary speech and somehow "official"). 15. get. 16. obtained. 17. got (*received* suggests that the wages were sent or transferred; *obtained* is unnecessarily vague). 18. received (*got*: much more colloq.). 19. obtain. 20. get. 21. receiving. 22. obtain.

12 (A)

1. affront. 2. offend. 3. abusing. 4. outraged. 5. abused (*abuse* =personal, verbal attack, so suitable here; *offend*: too weak for the context; *insult* need not be in words; *affront*: *rarer* as higher register; *outrage* indicates far greater offence). 6. offended. 7. offence. 8. insults (or *abuse*, but different meaning). 9. offended (*insulted* suggests *intention*; *outraged* simply multiplies offence, but could suggest extreme anger). 10. offence. 11. abuse. 12. affronted. 13. offended. 14. insults or abuse (in that context both mean the same, i.e. *personal* comments; *abuse* always means this, whereas *insult* has a wider range of application, e.g. it could refer to not inviting a person to one's birthday party despite long friendship). 15. offend. 16. abuse. 17. affronting. 18. insult (*outrage* and *affront* would be wrong register, i.e. unsuitable style for the particular situation; *offend* is an obvious contradiction in this context; *abuse* not quite impossible but not very likely, ***see*** introduction); offence.

12 (B)

1. outraged (*outrage* denotes the degree here). 2. abuse. 3. insulted. 4. abuse. 5. outraged (degree indicated). 6. insult. 7. affronts or insults (*offence* and *outrage* syntactically impossible; *imaginary* abuse is difficult to—imagine!). 8. insulted

(*abused* possible; *offended* not possible; "right and left" too colloq. to be coupled with *affront* or *outrage*). 9. insult (*offence* could be confusing because of legal implications; *abuse*: syntactically wrong; *affront* possible, but rarer; *outrage*: too strong). 10. affront. 11. affront. 12. insulted (*insult* is what the perpetrator does i.e. it is usually Active Voice; *offend* is more about the feelings of the receiver i.e. often in Passive Voice; *affront* is too strong here).

13 (A)

1. observe. 2. noticed. 3. perceive (*observe* would imply *see*). 4. perception. 5. noticeable. 6. perception. 7. noticed. 8. observe (*notice* would not be strong enough). 9. notice (*observe* would imply active interest). 10. perceive. 11. perception. 12. observed. 13. observe (*notice* is casual). 14. notice.

13 (B)

1. perceive. 2. perceived. 3. observant. 4. noticed (*perceived* also possible, it flatters, implies intelligence and ability to read between the lines, etc.). 5. notice (*observe* would be more active). 6. observation or perception (*perception* is vaguer, abstract). 7. perceive (*notice* is slighter; *observe* =see). 8. perceived (this is a deduction, not to be *noticed* or *observed* concretely). 9. observe (*notice* would be more casual). 10. notice (*observe* would be ironical). 11. observed (sterner than *noticed*). 12. observe. 13. notice (*observe* might be ironical). 14. perceive.

14 (A)

1. profession. 2. occupation. 3. trade. 4. occupation. 5. profession. 6. trade. 7. occupation. 8. professional. 9. trade. 10. profession.

14 (B)

1. vocation. 2. calling. 3. trade. 4. occupation. 5. vocation. 6. calling. 7. trade. 8. vocation (all others possible). 9. profession. 10. occupational.

15 (A)

1. make up my mind. 2. resolved. 3. decision. 4. settled. 5. make up her mind. 6. decide or settle (*decide* is rather neutral; *settle* suggests previously *un*settled [wavering]). 7. decided. 8. resolved (*decided* not strong enough; *made up my mind*: colloq.). 9. make up your mind. 10. resolution (suits the context). 11. settle (suggests preceding uncertainty / argument). 12. resolved. 13. decisive. 14. decided. 15. make up your mind.

15 (B)

1. resolved. 2. settled (for or on). 3. settle. 4. make up my mind (or decide). 5. resolved (none of the others suggest resolution of conflict). 6. settled (*decide* would call for: . . . has been decided upon). 7. made up his mind. 8. resolved. 9. resolved (*decided* poss., but more neutral and colloq.; words like *resolve* often involve *artistic choice*, i.e. they are more literary). 10. settled (*decided / resolved* poss. with differences as explained). 11. settled. 12. resolved (*made up their minds / decided* poss. with nuances as explained). 13. decide (*make up my mind*: slightly more colloq.). 14. decided (*settled*: after a fairly neutral to and fro; *resolved* suggests it had caused a knotty problem apart from the stylistic difference).

16 (A)

1. permanent. 2. constant. 3. permanent. 4. perpetual. 5. constantly. 6. continuous (or constant). 7. permanent. 8. perpetuity. 9. continuous. 10. constant. 11. constant. 12. perpetual. 13. permanently. 14. continual (*perpetual* gives strongest emphasis, suggests *endless, never interrupted*, also often *irritation*, e.g. *perpetual*

nagging; *constant* suggests determination and reliability, i.e. he never gave up this "warfare", but also irritation if the action is unpleasant). 15. continuous. 16. perpetual or constant (*perpetual* much stronger than constant, therefore to be preferred here). 17. continually (*constantly* normally means: unchanging over a very long period and this nuance makes it slightly less suitable here). 18. continually (*constantly, perpetually* with differences as explained). 19. constant. 20. permanent.

16 (B)

1. continual, constant, or perpetual. 2. constant, continuous, or perpetual. 3. continually, perpetually, or constantly. 4. perpetual; constant (*permanent* instead of perpetual would not be in accordance with the poetic mood of the sentence and therefore *not suitable*; *permanent* is more scientific: *perma*frost). 5. continuous (*constant* would stress the length of time it continued; strictly, a *constant* stream is one that does not markedly vary in its composition.). 6. continual (i.e. there *are* lulls in it although it recurs again and again; *constant*: **see** No. 5; *continuous* =without any lulls; *perpetual*: far greater stress on its continuity and so greater *irritation*; *permanent* stresses the *sameness* and that it is or will be long lasting). 7. perpetual or constant. 8. continuously or constantly. 9. continually, constantly, or perpetually (with differences as explained). 10. continually, constantly, or perpetually.

17 (A)

1. visited. 2. attend. 3. calls on (*visit* would suggest longer duration). 4. attendance. 5. attended. 6. call. 7. visiting. 8. attend. 9. visitor. 10. attendance. 11. visitors. 12. frequent. 13. called on. 14. pay; call. 15. frequents. 16. visitors. 17. frequented (*paid a visit to* or *paid some visits to* =not so regularly or frequently; incidentally, "to pay a visit" is a slang expression for "to go to the lavatory" e.g. "I've been dying to pay a visit ever since we left home!"). 18. went; a visit. 19. attend. 20. attendance.

17 (B)

1. call. 2. frequent (*visit* poss.). 3. frequent. 4. visiting (*calling* would suggest shorter duration). 5. frequenter (here frequenter suggests somehow an unusual passion). 6. visit. 7. visited. 8. caller (*visitor* would indicate a visit of possibly longer duration). 9. visit. 10. call.

18 (A)

1. keep. 2. preserved. 3. maintains. 4. keep. 5. preserved. 6. retain (*keep:* less formal). 7. preserve. 8. maintain. 9. keep (*for keeps*: sl.). 10. preserve. 11. keep. 12. preservation. 13. keep. 14. keep; keep. 15. retained. 16. maintains (*keeps* would be too "homely" for such a national force). 17. preserve. 18. preserve. 19. keep. 20. keep.

18 (B)

1. maintained (*kept*: less formal). 2. preserved. 3. maintenance; keeps. 4. preserved. 5. retained. 6. kept (*maintained*: formal). 7. retained (officialese for *kept*). 8. maintain (or keep). 9. retentive. 10. preserve.

19 (A)

1. remained. 2. remained. 3. stay. 4. remained. 5. stopped. 6. remained (*stayed*: less likely). 7. stopped. 8. remained. 9. remained. 10. stopped. 11. stay (*stop* would suggest that he had another visit). 12. remained. 13. remain. 14. stayed (*remain*: formal; *stop* less likely but not imposs.)

19 (B)

1. stay (*remain* poss.). 2. stay (*remain*: not so usual in this colloq. context; *stop* would sound more *sudden* and *temporary*; *stay* has a longer "feel" about it and so it is the most natural term here). 3. remained. 4. stayed (*stopped* would suggest that there is a further journey ahead; *remained*: formal, less "holidayish"). 5. remained. 6. remain; remain. 7. stay. 8. stop (*stay* would suggest that movement is possible; *remain*: formal). 9. remains (*stays*; *stops* would suggest visit). 10. stayed (or *remained* with difference as explained). 11. stop. 12. remained.

20 (A)

1. glimpse. 2. look. 3. gaze. 4. gazed. 5. glimpse. 6. look. 7. stared (*gaze* would be too weak for "in open astonishment", *stare* suggests a rude even *crude, uncontrolled* look). 8. glance. 9. stare. 10. glimpse. 11. look. 12. glimpse. 13. look or glance or glimpse. 14. glance. 15. gaze. 16. glance. 17. looked. 18. glance (*look* poss. but *glance* matches *arrow*). 19. gaze. 20. gazing.

20 (B)

1. staring. 2. glimpse. 3. glance (*glance* carries an *unspoken message*, here. It goes like this: "I don't really need to consult my notes as I'm on top of the subject" or "I know what I'm going to say, by heart".—*look* could suggest too great dependence on the notes.). 4. stare. 5. glanced. 6. look. 7. looked or stared or gazed. 8. glanced. 9. glances. 10. glimpsed.

21 (A)

1. blooming. 2. prosper. 3. flourished. 4. flourished (*prospered* poss., but *flourished* avoids financial implication and includes *health, increased population*, etc.). 5. prosperity. 6. prosper. 7. bloom. 8. flourished (*bloomed* poss.) 9. prosperity. 10. blooming. 11. flourishing. 12. flourished. 13. bloom (here, *bloom* is used both literally and figuratively). 14. flourished.

21 (B)

1. bloom. 2. blossom. 3. flourishing. 4. blossoms (*blossoms* matches *first* . . . were *out*, i.e. suggestion of an early stage). 5. prosper. 6. blossoms (*blooms* would be a bit grand for a dog-rose). 7. bloom (figurative usage as e.g. in: The bloom had gone off their marriage.). 8. flourishing. 9. blossom (only poss. prefix for-time). 10. blossom (*blossom* just right for the start of s.th.; *bloom* poss. but different stage).

22 (A)

1. soil. 2. bottom. 3. ground. 4. ground. 5. soil. 6. ground. 7. bottom. 8. bottom. 9. soil. 10. ground. 11. ground. 12. soil. 13. ground. 14. soil. 15. bottom. 16. soil. 17. soil. 18. bottom. 19. ground. 20. bottom.

22 (B)

1. bottom. 2. bottom. 3. ground. 4. ground. 5. bottom. 6. soil. 7. soil. 8. ground. 9. soil. 10. soil.

23 (A)

1. brings. 2. brought. 3. take. 4. bring. 5. take. 6. brought. 7. bring. 8. took. 9. take. 10. brings. 11. take or bring (choice depends on where the speaker is). 12. bring. 13. take. 14. took. 15. take. 16. brought. 17. bring. 18. take. 19. brought. 20. take.

24 (A)

1. chest. 2. chest; chest. 3. breasts. 4. bosom. 5. bosom (*breast* would be lewder). 6. chest. 7. chest. 8. breasted. 9. bosom. 10. bosom. 11. breasts. 12. chests. 13. breast. 14. chest. 15. bosom. 16. chested. 17. bosom. 18. breasts. 19. chest. 20. chest. 21. breast. 22. bosom (*breast* poss.).

25 (A)

1. married. 2. wedding. 3. marriage. 4. wedding. 5. matrimony (*matrimony* is used rather than *marriage* to indicate formal, or mannered, speech). 6. wedlock. 7. wedding. 8. matrimony. 9. marriage. 10. wedding. 11. wedlock (*marriage* and *matrimony* poss., *wedlock* usually confined to literary or legal use or its—facetious—imitation). 12. wedding. 13. married. 14. wedding. 15. marriage. 16. wedding. 17. marriage. 18. matrimony. 19. wedding. 20. marriages.

25 (B)

1. matrimonial. 2. wedlock. 3. matrimony (*marriage* would be less formal). 4. wedlock. 5. marriage. 6. matrimonial. 7. wedlock. 8. matrimonial. 9. wedlock. 10. wedding.

26 (A)

1. property. 2. quality. 3. qualities. 4. properties. 5. quality. 6. qualities. 7. property. 8. properties. 9. qualities. 10. quality. 11. properties. 12. quality. 13. quality. 14. quality. 15. quality. 16. properties. 17. properties. 18. qualities. 19. properties. 20. quality.

27 (A)

1. simple (or plain). 2. simply (*plainly* =straightforward). 3. plain. 4. plain. 5. simple (or plain). 6. plain. 7. plain. 8. simple. 9. Plain. 10. plainly. 11. simply. 12. plain. 13. plainly. 14. simple (or plainly furnished). 15. plain. 16. plain; plain. 17. simple. 18. simply.

28 (A)

1. entrance. 2. admission. 3. entrance. 4. access. 5. admission. 6. entrance. 7. admission. 8. entrance. 9. access. 10. admissions. 11. access (*entry* poss., suggesting an illegal act, here). 12. entry. 13. admission. 14. entrance. 15. entrance or admission. 16. access. 17. admission. 18. entry. 19. entrance. 20. entry.

28 (B)

1. admission. 2. entry. 3. entrance. 4. admission. 5. admittance (*admission* less likely). 6. access (all others also possible, with different nuances). 7. entry (*entry into a profession* is official usage, the same way as *entrance to university* [**see** A 19] or *university entrance* is). 8. admittance (*admission* poss.). 9. access. 10. entry.

29 (A)

1. reception. 2. reception. 3. receipt. 4. receipt. 5. reception. 6. receipt. 7. reception. 8. reception. 9. receipt. 10. reception. 11. receptions. 12. receipt. 13. reception. 14. reception. 15. receipt. 16. receipt. 17. receipt. 18. reception. 19. reception. 20. receipt.

30 (A)

1. discovered; discovered; discovered. 2. discovered. 3. detect (or discover). 4. discovery. 5. detected. 6. detect. 7. discovered. 8. detected. 9. detect. 10. discovery. 11. detected. 12. detected. 13. discovered. 14. discovered. 15. discovered. 16. discover. 17. detect. 18. detected. 19. discovered. 20. detected (or discovered).

31 (A)

1. discharged. 2. dismiss. 3. give you the sack. 4. discharged. 5. dismissals. 6. got the sack. 7. discharged. 8. discharge. 9. dismissed. 10. released. 11. dismiss, 12. release. 13. getting the sack. 14. discharge. 15. released. 16. discharge. 17. release. 18. dismissed. 19. sack. 20. dismiss.

31 (B)

1. released (*dismissed* would suggest quite a different feeling; *dismissed* stresses the *school's* action, *released* suggests *his* feeling of release). 2. discharged (*discharged* indicates *emphasis* here). 3. dismissal (discharge poss.). 4. release. 5. sacked. 6. release. 7. discharging (dismissing is possible, but *discharging* is to be preferred in this context because it could be *from hospital* and it would suggest regular "getting rid of", perhaps according to plan). 8. dismissed. 9. dismissed. 10. discharged (or dismissed; *discharged* is a trifle more formal than *dismissed*; on the other hand, the boss would be most unlikely to say: "You're discharged!").

32 (A)

1. remind. 2. remember. 3. remember. 4. remind. 5. remember. 6. recollections. 7. reminds. 8. remember. 9. recollection. 10. remind. 11. remind. 12. recollection. 13. reminder. 14. remind.

32 (B)

1. Remembrance. 2. recall. 3. remember; recall (*recollect* could be used instead of recall). 4. remember (*remember* is preferable with *do*, *recall* and *recollect* with *can:* Do you remember . . .?—Can you recollect / recall . . .?). 5. recollect (*remember* poss.). 6. recollect (*remember* poss.). 7. recall. 8. recall. 9. recollect (*recall / remember* poss. but different stylistic levels: *remember* lowest, *recall* highest). 10. remember (recollect / recall). 11. reminding. 12. recall (the activity inherent in *recall* tallies with 'was able to' do it 'many years later'). 13. remember. 14. recall (*recollect* and *remember* poss., but *recall* fits best the *style* of the sentence because *occasion* and *widespread* agreement suggest slightly higher level).

33 (A)

1. explained. 2. accounts for. 3. explanation. 4. interpretation. 5. account for (*explain* poss.). 6. interpretation. 7. accounting for. 8. account for (*explain* poss., but it would not really indicate the reason WHY). 9. explained. 10. interpret. 11. accounting for. 12. explained. 13. interpretation. 14. elucidation.

33 (B)

1. expound (*expound* tallies with *loved* suggesting commitment, the object *doctrines* and with doing it *at great length.*, **see** Introduction.). 2. elucidation (explanation poss.). 3. expounding. 4. elucidate (*explain* poss., but stylistic level is different because *elucidate* is lit., even a bit "high-flown".). 5. account for. 6. expounding. 7. elucidate (*explain* poss.). 8. accounts for (*explain* poss. but more general and diffuse). 9. expounded. 10. account for. 11. elucidate. 12. elucidate (*elucidate* = make clearer, shed light on). 13. account for. 14. expound. 15. elucidation.

34 (A)

1. statement. 2. declaration. 3. declared. 4. proclaimed. 5. stated. 6. statement. 7. declare. 8. stated. 9. proclaimed. 10. state. 11. state. 12. declared. 13. statement. 14. proclamation. 15. declared. 16. proclaimed. 17. declared. 18. state. 19. proclaimed. 20. declared.

34 (B)

1. pronounced. 2. stated (*stated* is quite neutral; *declared* suggests that people or the police didn't believe him and so he had to be emphatic). 3. pronounce. 4. proclaimed. 5. proclaim. 6. declare. 7. declaration. 8. pronouncement. 9. state. 10. declaration.

35 (A)

1. allow. 2. permitted. 3. permission. 4. admits of. 5. allow. 6. permission. 7. permitted. 8. admits of 9. admits of. 10. allow. 11. permission. 12. permit; allowed. 13. admits of. 14. allowed.

35 (B)

1. allowed. 2. permission. 3. admits of. 4. allowed. 5. permit (*permit* is more formal—distanzierend—than *allow*). 6. admits of. 7. admits of. 8. allowed (*allow* is somehow softer than *permit*; mother *allows*, authority *permits*). 9. allowed. 10. permitted. 11. admits of. 12. permit (*permit* is a little more formal and decisive than *allow*). 13. admit of. 14. admit of.

36 (A)

1. relief. 2. lighten. 3. facilitated. 4. eased (*relieved* and *alleviated* poss.; *eased* = made it easier, *relieved* suggests up to then you were under constraint, *alleviated* is a higher level of style for both). 5. lightened. 6. facilitated. 7. lightened. 8. relieve (*ease* = slowly, perhaps slightly lessen, *relieve* = more complete removal of pain [although not permanent]). 9. easing. 10. relief. 11. lighten (ease). 12. ease. 13. relieved. 14. relieve (ease). 15. facilitates. 16. lightened. 17. facilitated. 18. relieved. 19. alleviated (*relieved* = she so to speak removed it; *mitigated* not impossible, but it sounds a bit awkward). 20. alleviate (*ease* less formal; *relieve*: see No. 8; *alleviate*: higher level of style).

36 (B)

1. relieved (*alleviated* not imposs.). 2. relieve (*ease* suggests temporary, slower and less effective betterment; *alleviate* poss.). 3. allay. 4. alleviation. 5. mitigate. 6. alleviate (*ease* would be a bit weak for *torture; relieve* would need a person here as an object; *facilitate* would have the *opposite* meaning!). 7. mitigated. 8. alleviate. 9. allay. 10. ease (or *relieve* you of / from your pain). 11. lighten. 12. facilitated.

37 (A)

1. crops. 2. crop. 3. harvest; crop. 4. harvesting. 5. crop. 6. crop. 7. harvest. 8. crop. 9. harvest. 10. crop. 11. harvest. 12. cropped. 13. crop. 14. harvesting. 15. crop. 16. harvest. 17. crop. 18. harvest. 19. harvest (*crop* might mean that it looked marvellous whilst still in the ground).

38 (A)

1. smothered. 2. choked. 3. stifle. 4. stifle. 5. smother (one usually *smothers the fire* but *stifles the flames; smother* suggests putting, say, a blanket over it, *stifle* could also mean this, but it is not quite so definite. It is only a nuance.). 6. choke. 7. smother. 8. choke. 9. stifling (*suffocating* poss.). 10. suffocated. 11. stifling. 12. choke. 13. suffocated. 14. stifle. 15. choked. 16. stifle. 17. smother. 18. choked.

38 (B)

1. smothered. 2. stifled. 3. suffocating (here *discipline* calls for *suffocating* because discipline suggests a more general kind of repression than e.g. active re-

pression on the part of some person; for active repression *stifle* would be preferable; and then a *stifling* atmosphere would suggest complete prevention of action which *suffocating* atmosphere does not). 4. choked. 5. smothered (or *stifled; smother* would suggest covering a wider area). 6. suffocation. 7. stifle. 8. choking. 9. stifle. 10. choked. 11. stifled. 12. suffocating. (*stifling* atmosphere would suggest *dryness*; in a figurative sense stifling atmosphere would be possible).

39 (A)

1. looking forward to. 2. expect. 3. looking forward to. 4. awaited. 5. looking forward to. 6. expectations. 7. expect. 8. awaited. 9. look forward to. 10. anticipated. 11. awaited. 12. expecting. 13. awaiting. 14. looking forward to. 15. anticipation. 16. expecting. 17. looking forward to. 18. anticipation. 19. expect. 20. looking forward to.

39 (B)

1. anticipation. 2. expecting. 3. awaited; anticipation. 4. expecting. 5. awaits. 6. await. 7. anticipation. 8. anticipate (or expect). 9. expected. 10. anticipation.

40 (A)

1. brought up. 2. educated. 3. bred. 4. rearing. 5. rearing. 6. breeds. 7. education. 8. breeding. 9. brought up. 10. educated. 11. training. 12. educate. 13. breed. 14. brought up. 15. train. 16. rears. 17. education. 18. train. 19. breeding; breed. 20. brought up.

40 (B)

1. bringing up. 2. reared. 3. breeds. 4. breeders. 5. rearing. 6. training. 7. breed. 8. brought up. (*reared* poss. but less colloquial). 9. trained; training. 10. brought up. (*reared* poss. but less colloq.).

41 (A)

1. apt. 2. capable. 3. able. 4. capable. 5. able. 6. capable. 7. apt. 8. capable. 9. able. 10. capable. 11. ability. 12. ability; ability. 13. able. 14. able. 15. capable. 16. ability. 17. apt. 18. capable of. 19. able. 20. capable of.

41 (B)

1. aptitudes (aptitude is normal usage, especially as object of *testing*, as it suggests something *narrow*, of lower intellectual requirement). 2. ability. 3. apt. 4. apt (*able* and *capable* would not apply here because this would mean taking a *punster too seriously*; *apt*, on the other hand, plays down the importance of whatever it is). 5. aptness (*ability* poss.; raises it to a higher level). 6. able. 7. apt at (or: apt to pick up . . .). 8. aptitude. 9. capable. 10. apt at (or: apt to . . .).

42 (A)

1. rode. 2. go. 3. travelling. 4. drive. 5. driver. 6. travelling. 7. ride. 8. went. 9. drivers. 10. ride. 11. go. 12. went. 13. drive. 14. drove. 15. rode. 16. drive; ride (or drive). 17. go. 18. travel. 19. drive. 20. ride. 21. driving. 22. travelling. 23. driving. 24. ride. 25. drove.

43 (A)

1. lacks. 2. missing. 3. absent. 4. absence. 5. missing. 6. lack. 7. lack. 8. missing. 9. absent. 10. missing. 11. lacks. 12. absent. 13. missing. 14. absence (or lack; but note difference of nuance; *lack* could mean that more inhibitions would be desirable; so *absence* is a kindlier, less aggressive "accusation"). 15. absent. 16. lack. 17. absent. 18. wanting (lacking). 19. lack. 20. want.

43 (B)

1. wanting. 2. absence. 3. wanted. 4. wanting (lacking). 5. missing. 6. lacked. 7. wanting. 8. lacking (*missing*, i.e. all things needed are still there, nothing has been taken away). 9. want. 10. want.

44 (A)

1. failings (or faults). 2. flaw. 3. fault. 4. fault. 5. slip. 6. blunder. 7. mistakes. 8. failing (*fault* not poss. here because it could lead to confusion of meaning, i.e. I am *not to blame* for laziness (my own or other people's). 9. errors (*mistakes* or *blunders* poss. with differences as explained). 10. faultless. 11. faults (or failings). 12. err. 13. faults (*mistakes* poss., but different meaning; mistakes are seen as one's own responsibility, whereas *faults* may not be). 14. mistake. 15. failings. 16. mistakes. 17. blundering. 18. flaw. 19. slip (*mistake*, *error*, *blunder* poss.). 20. flaw.

44 (B)

1. error. 2. fault. 3. fault. 4. flaw. 5. mistaken. 6. failings. 7. error (mistake). 8. fault. 9. flaw. 10. blunders (*mistakes* would possibly not cost lives, *blunders*, however, usually do).

45 (A)

1. festival. 2. fete. 3. festival. 4. feast. 5. fete. 6. festivity. 7. festival. 8. feast. 9. festival. 10. feast. 11. fete. 12. festive. 13. festivity. 14. festival. 15. feast. 16. Festival. 17. festivities. 18. festivities. 19. festival. 20. festive.

45 (B)

1. feasted. 2. fete. 3. feast. 4. festivity. 5. festival. 6. feasted. 7. feted (*feasted* would simply mean wine and dine him, *feted* suggests more than that). 8. fete (*festival* poss., but it would mean something a little grander, possibly lasting several days; *festivity* also poss., but it is vaguer). 9. festivities. 10. fete (*feast* poss. but different meaning; *festival* not imposs. but not very likely; *festivity* poss., but vaguer).

46 (A)

1. fast. 2. firmly. 3. steady. 4. fast. 5. fast. 6. firm. 7. fast. 8. fixed. 9. firm. 10. steady. 11. fast. 12. firm. 13. steady. 14. fixed. 15. fast. 16. fast. 17. firm. 18. solid. 19. firm. 20. solid.

46 (B)

1. solids. 2. fixed. 3. firm. 4. steady. 5. solid. 6. firm. 7. solid. 8. fast. 9. fixed. 10. firm (*fixed* intention could be slightly pejorative =*obstinacy* in the sense of the French *idee fix*, so its use would be unwise here).

47 (A)

1. spot. 2. stain. 3. patches. 4. blot. 5. stain. 6. patch. 7. speck. 8. spot. 9. blot. 10. speck (*speck* suggests a slight *splashing*, whereas *spot* would sound more fixed, less spreading). 11. stains. 12. speck. 13. stains. 14. blot. 15. stain. 16. spots. 17. spot. 18. speckled. 19. spots (*stain* poss. but a little more *serious*, i.e. it might be more difficult to remove a *stain*; *spot* is more neutral; *speck* also poss. with a slight suggestion of *splash* which produced it). 20. speck.

47 (B)

1. stained. 2. spotty. 3. speckled. 4. spotted. 5. patched. 6. stain (*blot* poss., but *stain* has a more specific pejorative nuance). 7. speck. 8. patches. 9. blots. 10. stain.

48 (A)

1. flesh. 2. flesh. 3. meat; meat. 4. meat. 5. flesh. 6. meat. 7. flesh. 8. meat. 9. meat. 10. meat. 11. flesh. 12. flesh. 13. meat. 14. meat. 15. flesh. 16. flesh. 17. flesh. 18. horseflesh.

49 (A)

1. madam. 2. lady. 3. women. 4. wife. 5. Madam. 6. madam. 7. women. 8. women. 9. lady. 10. madam. 11. wife. 12. woman. 13. wife. 14. women. 15. ladies (*women* would be unpardonable, here). 16. wife. 17. woman. 18. madam. 19. lady. 20. lady. 21. woman. 22. wife. 23. lady. 24. madam. 25. lady. 26. wife. 27. Madam. 28. wife.

50 (A)

1. vacant. 2. free. 3. free. 4. vacant. 5. spare. 6. liberal. 7. disengaged. 8. vacant. 9. liberal. 10. free (or spare). 11. free. 12. liberal. 13. vacant. 14. free. 15. spare. 16. liberal. 17. spare. 18. free. 19. spare; spare. 20. disengaged.

50 (B)

1. vacancies. 2. disengaged (or free). 3. free. 4. liberal. 5. vacancy. 6. disengaged. 7. vacant. 8. free. 9. vacant. 10. free.

51 (A)

1. strange. 2. Foreign. 3. strange. 4. aliens. 5. foreigners. 6. strange. 7. stranger. 8. aliens. 9. foreign (*strange* poss. but different meaning). 10. strange. 11. alien (*alien* would be tantamount to repugnant here; *strange* would mean *unusual* but not necessarily repugnant). 12. strangely. 13. foreign. 14. foreign.

51 (B)

1. Aliens. 2. foreign (*alien* poss.). 3. estranged. 4. strange; foreigner. 5. alienated. 6. foreign. 7. foreigners. 8. alien (or foreign). 9. stranger. 10. foreign. 11. alien (*alien* carries with it an implication of *unpleasantness*. Sentence No. 11 could mean both: being abroad and–figuratively–moving in a field of knowledge one is not well acquainted with). 12. stranger; strange (*foreigner* and *foreign* not impossible, but the sense of mystery, fear of the unknown would be lost. One can be quite at home in a foreign country. And *strange* is more literary, poetic, and emotional). 13. alien (*alien* means unpleasant, strange; *foreign* would mean that I could not *understand* it). 14. alien.

52 (A)

1. guide. 2. lead. 3. lead. 4. conducted. 5. guide. 6. directing. 7. lead. 8. guide. 9. conducted. 10. lead. 11. guide. 12. directed (*conducted* poss., but *directed* is more forceful, virile, commanding). 13. conductor. 14. guide. 15. guided. 16. conduct. (*conduct* =go with me and show me the way; *direct* =tell me [but not necessarily accompany me]; *guide* would be a little "precious" and suggest that the route is complicated; *lead* would almost suggest that he is blind). 17. guide. 18. conductor. 19. conduct. 20. guide.

52 (B)

1. director. 2. guide. 3. led. 4. guide. 5. lead. 6. conducted. 7. conduct. 8. direct. 9. direction. 10. led.

53 (A)

1. all. 2. whole. 3. total. 4. whole. 5. all. 6. entirely. 7. total. 8. all; all. 9. whole (*entire* would give more emphasis). 10. whole (*all* the time poss., but it would be

less pejorative; the *entire time* would be bad style because it is uneuphonious). 11. entire (*whole* would be less emphatic). 12. all; all. 13. total. 14. entire (*whole* is less emphatic). 15. all. 16. totally (*entirely* poss., but *totally false* is more usual). 17. entirely. 18. whole. 19. whole. 20. whole.

53 (B)

1. whole. 2. totality. 3. entire (*entire* more emphatic than *whole*). 4. total. 5. entirely. 6. whole. 7. total. 8. entirely. 9. all. 10. entire (*whole* less emphatic).

54 (A)

1. senses, 1 a. sense. 2. feelings. 3. sensations. 4. emotional. 5. feeling (*sensation* poss. but higher stylistic level, and *had* would be preferable to *felt* with sensation). 6. sensation. 7. sentimental (*sentimental mood* is associated with *mawkish* tenderness). 8. feelings. 9. emotions. 10. sensation. 11. sense. 12. feelings. 13. sentiments. 14. sensations. 15. feelings (or emotions). 16. sense. 17. emotion. 18. feelng. 19. sensation. 20. emotion.

54 (B)

1. sentiment. 2. sense. 3. emotions. 4. sensed. 5. emotional. 6. sensation. 7. sentiments. 8. feelings. 9. sensation. 10. sentiments.

55 (A)

1. theme (*subject* for/of a treatise poss.). 2. object. 3. theme. 4. matter (*subject* poss.). 5. object. 6. topic (*subject* poss.). 7. topics (*subjects, themes* poss.). 8. subject. 9. object. 10. topic (*subject* poss. but *topic* better in this context). 11. matter (*matter* traditional in this context). 12. theme. 13. subject-matter. 14. topic (*subject* poss.). 15. subject. 16. theme (*topic, subject* poss.). 17. subject (*object* poss.). 18. matter. 19. theme. 20. topic.

55 (B)

1. subject. 2. matter (*subject, topic, theme* poss.). 3. subject (*theme* for her novel poss. and also *topic*). 4. topic (*subject* poss.). 5. matter. 6. theme. 7. object. 8. subject (*theme* possible in: ... the theme of women's rights was one she returned to again and again; *matter* could be used in: "Now, Miss Brown, to return to this matter of women's rights–and of yours in particular!" i.e. she and her boss are going to discuss complaints she has made about her conditions, etc.). 9. topic (*subject* would sound more weighty). 10. topics.

56 (A)

1. go. 2. walking. 3. strides. 4. walk. 5. stepped. 6. going. 7. walked. 8. go. 9. walk. 10. step. 11. walking. 12. step. 13. going. 14. stride (*walk* poss., but it would not suggest a special gait as stride does; *stride* suggests: with *energy* and *determination*, and *vigour*, so suitable in this context). 15. go. 16. step; step. 17. strides. 18. steps. 19. strode (*walked* **see** No. 14). 20. walking.

56 (B)

1. stalked. 2. go. 3. stride. 4. strides. 5. stalked. 6. step. 7. strode (*stepped* would have a similar meaning but it is less forceful; *walked* and *went* would be too weak; *stalked* would give a special flavour, see definition). 8. steps. 9. stalked (*all* other synonyms poss. but different nuances as explained). 10. strides.

57 (A)

1. mind's. 2. spirits. 3. spirited. 4. mind. 5. ghost. 6. geniuses. 7. mind. 8. spirit. 9. mind. 10. spirit. 11. geniuses. 12. ghost. 13. minds. 14. ghost. 15. mind. 16. spirit. 17. mind. 18. spirits. 19. genius. 20. spirits.

57 (B)

1. genius. 2. minds. 3. spirits. 4. mind. 5. genius. 6. mind. 7. mind. 8. mind. 9. spirited. 10. genius.

58 (A)

1. intellect. 2. intellectuals. 3. mental. 4. mental. 5. mentality. 6. intellect. 7. mental. 8. intellectual. 9. intellectual. 10. mental. 11. intellectuals. 12. mental. 13. mental. 14. intellectual. 15. intellectualise. 16. mental. 17. intellectual. 18. intellectual. 19. mental. 20. intellectual.

59 (A)

1. chance. 2. occasion. 3. facilities. 4. chance. 5. opportunity (*chance* poss.). 6. chance; chance. 7. facilities. 8. occasion. 9. opportunity (*chance* poss.). 10. chance. 11. facilities. 12. opportunities (*chances* poss.). 13. opportunities. 14. facilities. 15. occasion. 16. facilities. 17. occasion. 18. chance. 19. occasions. 20. facilities.

59 (B)

1. chance. 2. opportunity. 3. opportunity. 4. occasion. 5. facilities. 6. chances. 7. occasion. 8. opportunities. 9. occasion. 10. chance.

60 (A)

1. business; business. 2. bargain. 3. transaction. 4. concern (*business* poss.). 5. business. 6. bargain. 7. transactions. 8. transaction. 9. business. 10. business. 11. concerns. 12. business. 13. bargains. 14. bargain. 15. business. 16. transactions. 17. business. 18. concern. 19. business. 20. bargain.

60 (B)

1. business; concern. 2. transactions. 3. bargain. 4. bargain. 5. concern (*business* could be *any* size; *concern* usually suggests *large*). 6. transactions. 7. bargain; bargain. 8. business. 9. bargained. 10. bargain.

61 (A)

1. historic. 2. historic. 3. historical. 4. historical. 5. historic. 6. historical. 7. historical. 8. historic. 9. historical. 10. historical. 11. historic. 12. historic. 13. historic. 14. historical. 15. historic. 16. historical. 17. historic. 18. historical.

62 (A)

1. company. 2. society. 3. society. 4. party. 5. company. 6. company. 7. party. 8. party. 9. society. 10. party. 11. society. 12. company. 13. company. 14. society. 15. party. 16. society. 17. company. 18. parties. 19. party. 20. company. 21. party. 22. company. 23. Society; Society. 24. party.

63 (A)

1. legal. 2. lawful. 3. legitimate. 4. lawful. 5. legal. 6. lawful (or legitimate). 7. legal. 8. legitimate. 9. legitimate. 10. lawful. 11. legal (*lawful* less likely as it introduces an emotional slant). 12. rightful (*lawful* poss.; *rightful* suggests that someone has challenged their right). 13. legitimate. 14. rightful (all others poss.). 15. legally. 16. legitimate. 17. lawful. 18. rightful (*lawful* and *legal* poss.). 19. lawful. 20. legal; lawfully.

63 (B)

1. legitimately. 2. legal (*lawful* and *legitimate* poss.). 3. legalise. 4. legitimate. 5. lawful. 6. rightful (e.g. with reference to a son-in-law in his parents-in-law's

home; *legal* e.g. *she* was not given her legal due. Perhaps because her divorced husband had not paid her alimony.). 7. legitimate. 8. rightful. 9. legality. 10. legitimate.

64 (A)

1. healthy. 2. wholesome. 3. healthier. 4. wholesome. 5. sound. 6. sane. 7. healthy. 8. wholesome. 9. healthy. 10. sane. 11. healthy. 12. sound. 13. sane. 14. sound. 15. healthy. 16. sound. 17. health. 18. sound (*sane* suggests that her views are *not wild* or *extravagant*; *sound* means *well-reasoned*, i.e. that the speaker *agrees with them*.). 19. healthy; healthy. 20. wholesome; wholesome.

64 (B)

1. sound; sane. 2. sane. 3. sanity. 4. wholesome. 5. sound (*healthy* poss., but much less likely). 6. sane. 7. sound. 8. soundness (or *sanity*). 9. wholesomely. 10. sound.

65 (A)

1. gained. 2. won. 3. win. 4. gaining. 5. won. 6. win. 7. gaining. 8. gained. 9. win. 10. won. 11. won. 12. gain. 13. won. 14. gain. 15. won. 16. won. 17. gained. 18. winning.

66 (A)

1. happiness. 2. luck. 3. luck. 4. fortune. 5. luck. 6. lucky. 7. happiness. 8. happiness. 9. luck. 10. happily. 11. fortune. 12. happy. 13. Luck. 14. happiness; happiness. 15. luck. 16. fortune. 17. happiness. 18. fortune.

66 (B)

1. fortune. 2. fortune. 3. happiness. 4. luck. 5. luck. 6. happy. 7. fortune. 8. luck. 9. happiness. 10. fortune.

67 (A)

1. border. 2. limit. 3. boundary. 4. limit. 5. frontiers. 6. border. 7. frontiers. 8. borders. 9. border. 10. limited. 11. bounds. 12. boundaries. 13. frontier or border (*frontier* is suitable because of the somewhat literary context; frontier is grander and more emotional sometimes even poetic than *border*). 14. border (*frontier* poss. but sounds more literary). 15. boundary. 16. bounds. 17. limit. 18. boundary. 19. border (*frontier* poss. but more literary). 20. bordered.

67 (B)

1. bounds. 2. frontiers. 3. boundary. 4. bounds. 5. frontier (or border). 6. frontiersman. 7. boundary. 8. limits. 9. frontier; boundaries. 10. border (or frontier).

68 (A)

1. tallest. 2. large. 3. big. 4. large. 5. great; great; 6. grand. 7. tall. 8. great. 9. great; great. 10. big. 11. tall. 12. large. 13. great. 14. great. 15. tall. 16. large. 17. big. 18. great. 19. grand. 20. large.

68 (B)

1. grand. 2. big. 3. grand. 4. large. 5. grand. 6. big. 7. great. 8. tallness. 9. large. 10. big.

69 (A)

1. reason or cause. 2. ground. 3. reason. 4. cause. 5. grounds. 6. reasons. 7. grounds. 8. reason (or: give me any good *grounds*). 9. cause. 10. reason (*cause of* poss., but different meaning, see introductions). 11. grounds. 12. occasion.

13. grounds. 14. reasons. 15. grounds. 16. occasion. 17. cause; cause. 18. reason. 19. grounds. 20. cause.

69 (B)

1. occasion. 2. reason. 3. occasion; reason. 4. grounds (reasons or causes). 5. causal. 6. occasion. 7. reasons (or: the *grounds* you give). 8. grounds (or reasons; *occasion* is not impossible, but it sounds a bit artificial). 9. cause. 10. occasioned.

70 (A)

1. port; ports. 2. port. 3. haven. 4. harbour (*port* would mean the whole apparatus for export and import and possibly the town as well; *harbour* simply means the place where the ships go out from and come back to, to tie up for the night, i.e. the actual water and possibly the surrounding installations, pier, wall, etc.; one can *swim* in the *harbour*, one cannot swim in the port!). 5. Harbour (the *Port* of Portsmouth poss., but the *vessels* anchor or tie up in the *harbour*). 6. port. 7. port. 8. harbour. 9. port. 10. haven, 11. Harbour (same as No. 4). 12. haven. 13. harbour. 14. port. 15. haven. 16. haven. 17. port. 18. harbour. 19. haven. 20. port. 21. harbour (*in port* poss. although this would imply looking at the situation in a somewhat different way; what the ships are actually *in*, is the *water* and thus *harbour* is quite natural). 22. haven.

71 (A)

1. held. 2. keep. 3. keep. 4. held. 5. holding. 6. keep. 7. keep. 8. keep. 9. holding. 10. keep. 11. holder. 12. hold. 13. keep. 14. held. 15. hold. 16. keep; keeping. 17. keep. 18. hold. 19. keep. 20. hold. 21. hold. 22. kept. 23. held. 24. keep. 25. kept.

72 (A)

1. cure. 2. cure. 3. heal. 4. healing. 5. cured. 6. healing. 7. heal (suffering cannot be *cured*; it is as much a spiritual as a physical thing and has a more emotional / poetic connotation than just illness). 8. cure. 9. cured. 10. cure. 11. healing. 12. curative. 13. heal. 14. healing. 15. cure. 16. heal. 17. Healer. 18. cure. 19. healer. 20. cure.

73 (A)

1. herd. 2. flocks. 3. flock. 4. herd. 5. herd. 6. flocks. 7. herd. 8. herd. 9. flock. 10. herd.

74 (A)

1. reigned. 2. govern. 3. reigning. 4. rule. 5. govern. 6. rule. 7. reign. 8. government. 9. reign. 10. rule. 11. governing. 12. governed. 13. ruled. 14. reign.

74 (B)

1. ruled. 2. reigned. 3. ruled. 4. reigned. 5. reigned. 6. reigned. 7. ruled. 8. governed. 9. rule. 10. reigns (i.e. where a usurper is on the throne).

75 (A)

1. each; each. 2. any (*every* =all; *each* suggests the individual). 3. every. 4. every. 5. each (*every* poss. but *each* stresses individuality). 6. any. 7. either (*any one* possible). 8. any. 9. each. 10. every. 11. any. 12. any. 13. every. 14. each (*every* possible but *each* stresses the whole idea). 15. each. 16. every. 17. each (*either* not possible because it would suggest that he took *one* hand but the writer does not know which!). 18. every. 19. each. 20. any.

75 (B)

1. either. 2. every. 3. any. 4. either. 5. every. 6. every. 7. each. 8. either (*any* poss. only if more than two; it suggests that I am even less choosey). 9. each. 10. either.

76 (A)

1. canal. 2. canals. 3. channel. 4. Channel. 5. Canal. 6. canals. 7. Channel. 8. Channel. 9. canals. 10. Channel. 11. canals. 12. channels. 13. Channel. 14. channel. 15. Canal. 16. channels. 17. canals. 18. canals. 19. channels. 20. canal.

77 (A)

1. little (*small* poss.). 2. small; small. 3. small. 4. little. 5. small. 6. small. 7. short. 8. little. 9. small. 10. small. 11. short. 12. little. 13. little. 14. short. 15. little. 16. small. 17. small. 18. little.

78 (A)

1. intelligence (or: It wasn't very *sensible*, was it?). 2. clever. 3. sensible. 4. wisdom. 5. intelligent. 6. clever. 7. intelligence. 8. wisdom. 9. wise. 10. sensible. 11. wise. 12. intelligent. 13. wise. 14. sensible. 15. clever. 16. wise. 17. Intelligence; intelligence. 18. sensible. 19. wise. 20. sensible.

78 (B)

1. clever. 2. intelligent. 3. clever. 4. sensible. 5. sensible. 6. clever. 7. intelligent. 8. sensible. 9. clever. 10. clever.

79 (A)

1. boil. 2. boil. 3. cooks. 4. boiled. 5. cook. 6. cooking. 7. cooking. 8. boiling. 9. cook. 10. boiled. 11. boiled. 12. cook. 13. boiling; boiling. 14. boiling. 15. cook. 16. cooking. 17. boiled. 18. cooked.

80 (A)

1. come. 2. come. 3. come. 4. got. 5. came. 6. get. 7. come. 8. came. 9. got. 10. come; came. 11. got. 12. come. 13. get. 14. get. 15. come. 16. come. 17. get. 18. got. 19. come. 20. get; get (Cos = because).

81 (A)

1. power. 2. strength. 3. forces. 4. strength. 5. power. 6. strength. 7. power. 8. powered. 9. strength. 10. strength. 11. power. 12. power. 13. vigour. 14. forces. 15. forces. 16. force. 17. powerful. 18. power. 19. powerful. 20. strong.

81 (B)

1. forced. 2. vigorously. 3. force. 4. vigour. 5. power. 6. force. 7. vigour. 8. force. 9. strength. 10. vigorously.

82 (A)

1. ill. 2. illness. 3. sick. 4. ill. 5. ill. 6. sick. 7. sick. 8. ill. 9. sick. 10. sick. 11. ill. 12. sick. 13. sick. 14. sick. 15. ill. 16. illness. 17. sick. 18. ill.

83 (A)

1. reviews. 2. criticism. 3. reviewing. 4. critique. 5. critique. 6. review. 7. criticism. 8. reviews. 9. critique. 10. reviews. 11. criticism. 12. critique; criticism. 13. criticism. 14. review. 15. criticising. 16. critic.

84 (A)

1. land. 2. land. 3. country. 4. land. 5. country. 6. country. 7. country. 8. land.

9. country. 10. country. 11. land. 12. land. 13. land. 14. country. 15. land. 16. country. 17. country. 18. Land's.

85 (A)

1. landscapes. 2. scenery (*landscape* poss. but different nuance. ***see*** introductions). 3. scenery. 4. landscapes. 5. scenery. 6. landscape. 7. landscapes. 8. scenery. 9. scenery. 10. landscapes (*scenery* poss.). 11. landscape (*scenery* poss.). 12. landscape. 13. scenery (*study* suggests details and so *scenery*). 14. scenery. 15. landscape (the *overall* picture is indicated and so *landscape*, but *scenery* not impossible.). 16. scenery. 17. scenery. 18. landscape.

86 (A)

1. placed. 2. put; put. 3. put. 4. placed. 5. laying. 6. place (*put* poss. but a bit more careless than *place*, place indicates care and exactness; *lay* would be odd, because it would mean almost comparing a hand with cutlery or a table-cloth). 7. put. 8. laid. 9. put; put. 10. placed (*laid* would suggest neatness, order, and care, *put* less so; *placed* is somewhere in between). 11. putting. 12. put; put. 13. put. 14. laid. 15. lays. 16. placed. 17. put; put. 18. laid. 19. put. 20. placed (*placed* suggests more *care* than *put*). 21. placed (*put* would suggest putting it almost anywhere, *placed* suggests a more precise action, on a *small* area.) 22. put. 23. put. 24. laid. 25. place.

87 (A)

1. borrow. 2. lend. 3. lend. 4. loan. 5. loaned. 6. borrow. 7. borrow. 8. lending. 9. loan. 10. lending. 11. borrowed. 12. loan. 13. borrowed. 14. lend. 15. borrowed. 16. loaned. 17. loaned. 18. borrow. 19. lend. 20. lends. 21. borrowed. 22. loaned. 23. lend. 24. borrow.

88 (A)

1. made. 2. do. 3. do. 4. makes. 5. made. 6. make. 7. do. 8. doing. 9. made. 10. doing. 11. made. 12. make. 13. doing. 14. made. 15. do.

89 (A)

1. man. 2. husband. 3. man; husband. 4. male. 5. husband. 6. man. 7. man. 8. male. 9. males. 10. husband. 11. man. 12. husband. 13. male. 14. husbands. 15. man. 16. man. 17. husband. 18. man. 19. man. 20. males. 21. husband. 22. husbands. 23. men. 24. males; males.

90 (A)

1. engine. 2. engine. 3. machine. 4. machine. 5. engine. 6. machines. 7. machines. 8. engines. 9. machines. 10. machine. 11. engine. 12. machine. 13. machine. 14. engine.

91 (A)

1. remedy. 2. means. 3. medium. 4. medium. 5. means. 6. means. 7. remedy. 8. medium. 9. remedy. 10. means. 11. medium. 12. means. 13. remedy. 14. means. 15. medium. 16. medium. 17. means. 18. remedy. 19. means. 20. means.

91 (B)

1. medium. 2. remedy. 3. means. 4. medium. 5. remedial. 6. Means. 7. medium. 8. medium. 9. means. 10. remedied.

92 (A)

1. zero. 2. nought (of course, *nothing*, could be used here). 3. zero. 4. nil; nil (or nought, nought). 5. zero. 6. noughts. 7. nil. 8. nil. 9. zero. 10. zero. 11. nil.

12. nought. 13. nil. 14. nought. 15. nought; nought. 16. nil (or: but our efforts came to *nought*).

93 (A)

1. politics. 2. politics. 3. policy. 4. policy. 5. politics. 6. policy. 7. policy. 8. politics; politics. 9. policy. 10. policy; policy. 11. politics. 12. politics. 13. policy. 14. politics. 15. policy. 16. policy. 17. policies. 18. policy.

94 (A)

1. rim. 2. brim. 3. margin. 4. margins. 5. rim. 6. edge. 7. verge; verge. 8. brink. 9. edges. 10. verge. 11. rim. 12. brink. 13. edge. 14. rimmed. 15. rim. 16. margin. 17. brim. 18. margin. 19. verge. 20. brink.

94 (B)

1. verging. 2. margin (or around its *edges.*). 3. brink. 4. verges. 5. brink. 6. rimmed. 7. edge. 8. brink (or *edge.* 'Hanging on a cliff edge' is a popular metaphor. *Brink* is more literary or even poetic.). 9. rim. 10. brim.

95 (A)

1. ripe. 2. ripe. 3. mature. 4. ripen. 5. mature. 6. ripe. 7. ripe. 8. mature. 9. ripe. 10. ripe. 11. mature. 12. ripe. 13. matured; ripe. 14. mature. 15. ripe. 16. mature. 17. maturity. 18. matured.

96 (A)

1. voyage. 2. journey. 3. tour. 4. trip. 5. travelling. 6. trip. 7. journey. 8. traveller; travel. 9. tour. 10. travels. 11. tours. 12. voyage. 13. journey. 14. voyage. 15. trip. 16. journey. 17. trip. 18. voyage. 19. journey. 20. travel.

96 (B)

1. tours. 2. voyages. 3. trippers. 4. travellers. 5. trips (all other terms also possible). 6. journeys. 7. travel. 8. journeying. 9. Tour. 10. trip.

97 (A)

1. remainder. 2. rest. 3. remnant. 4. rest. 5. remains. 6. rest (or remainder). 7. rest (*remainder* would not fit in with the everyday situation). 8. remainder (*rest* impossible because it cannot take the indefinite article, except in the meaning of "Ruhe"). 9. remains. 10. rest. 11. remainder (*remainder* suggests a certain formality as against *rest*). 12. relic. 13. rest (*remainder* would not really go with *family*). 14. remains. 15. relics. 16. remainder (or rest). 17. rest. 18. remnants. 19. remains. 20. rest.

97 (B)

1. remnant. 2. remains. 3. rest. 4. relic. 5. remnants. 6. relic. 7. remains (others poss. according to different nuances and meanings). 8. relic. 9. remnants. 10. rest (or remainder).

98 (A)

1. say. 2. say; tell. 3. said. 4. tell; tell. 5. say. 6. say. 7. tell. 8. telling. 9. says. 10. say.

98 (B)

1. tell. 2. tell. 3. say; said. 4. telling. 5. say. 6. tell. 7. say. 8. telling. 9. tell. 10. says; say.

99 (A)

1. damage. 2. harm. 3. injuries. 4. harm. 5. damaged. 6. damages. 7. harm (or damage). 8. damage. 9. injury. 10. harmful.

99 (B)

1. injury. 2. injury. 3. damaged. 4. injury; injury. 5. harm. 6. harm. 7. harm. 8. harm. 9. injury; injury. 10. harm's.

100 (A)

1. paring. 2. peels. 3. peel. 4. skinned. 5. peeled. 6. skin. 7. pare (of course, *cut* poss.). 8. peeling. 9. skin (or peel). 10. peeling. 11. paring. 12. skin. 13. peeling. 14. pare. 15. skin. 16. peeling. 17. peeled. 18. skin.

101 (A)

1. estimate. 2. appraise (*estimate* would be odd unless we mean how much *money* he is worth! *Appraise,* being a more formal term than estimate, fits in with the context, i.e. finding out about a person's qualities and thus his true worth). 3. appreciate. 4. estimate. 5. esteemed. 6. appraised. (or estimated). 7. appreciate. 8. estimate. 9. valued (*estimate* would necessitate a modification of the words used in the sentence, e.g.: Jewellery whose value was estimated to be ...; one *estimates* the value / weight / cost, etc. of s.th.; *appraised* would be quite wrong because it is normally only used when speaking of the official valuer, so here it would introduce an incongruous note.) 10. estimate (*appraise* would not apply to indebtedness; *appreciate* would alter the meaning and the sentence would have to be changed, e.g. I could appreciate the full extent . . .). 11. estimate. 12. appreciate. 13. estimate. 14. valued (or esteemed, or appreciated). 15. estimate. 16. esteem. 17. valued. 18. value. 19. appreciate. 20. estimate.

101 (B)

1. appraising (*appreciating,* but different nuance of meaning). 2. esteemed. 3. value (*or appreciate* =I am grateful for). 4. invaluable. 5. appraise. 6. estimate. 7. appreciate. 8. valued. 9. appraising. 10. appraisal (*appraisal* has the right touch of elegance, here. *Estimate* would introduce quite a different level of style and register viz. business. So it is a question of just *what* is being submitted.).

102 (A)

1. fortune. 2. fate (*fate* used semi-facetiously, here). 3. fortune. 4. fate. 5. fortune. 6. destiny. 7. fortune. 8. lot. 9. fate. 10. fate. 11. destiny. 12. fortune. 13. fate. 14. destiny. 15. fortune. 16. fate. 17. lot. 18. Fate. 19. lot. 20. destiny (fate or lot poss.).

102 (B)

1. fate. 2. destinies. 3. fated. 4. Fate. 5. fortune. 6. lot. 7. lot. 8. fate. 9. fate. 10. fortune.

103 (A)

1. beat. 2. stroke. 3. hit. 4. beating. 5. strike. 6. hit. 7. struck. 8. beating. 9. beat. 10. hit. 11. strike. 12. beaten. 13. struck. 14. hit (*strike* would be more dramatic or even melodramatic, so it is sometimes used facetiously, or in mock indignation, like in B.5). 15. strike. 16. beats. 17. hit. 18. beaten. 19. hits. 20. beats; beater.

103 (B)

1. hit. 2. struck. 3. hit. 4. striking. 5. struck. 6. strike. 7. hitting (or beating). 8. struck. 9. hit. 10. struck (*hit* would be lower style than struck, but poss).

104 (A)

1. lock. 2. closed. 3. shut (or closed). 4. shut. 5. lock (*shut* or *close* poss., but they would suggest something less effective). 6. closed (or shut). 7. close (or shut). 8. locked. 9. shut. 10. lock (or shut). 11. locked. 12. locked (*shut* poss., but with a different meaning). 13. closed. 14. shutting. 15. shut. 16. locked. 17. closed. 18. lock. 19. closing. 20. shutting. 21. close. 22. closing.

105 (A)

1. fast. 2. rapid. 3. faster. 4. quick (*rapid* would be more official and elegant). 5. fast. 6. quick. 7. rapidly (or quickly). 8. fast (*rapidly* would make sense if the context and suggested situation implied e.g. growing danger; *quickly* would suggest *human* rather than mineral action, which could also make sense). 9. rapid (or quick). 10. swift (all other terms poss.; *swift* is more poetic, *quick* suggests simply short duration; *rapid* would be stronger than swift and quick; so the choice of synonym is a matter of "feel", here). 11. quick. 12. fast. 13. fast. 14. swift *a*) *swift blow* is the usual collocation). 15. quick. 16. faster. 17. rapid (*rapid* and river go together; *swift* would introduce a poetic element; the other terms imposs. here). 18. rapidly. 19. quicken. 20. rapidity.

105 (B)

1. quick, 2. swiftly. 3. quick. 4. rapidly (or quickly). 5. quick (quick as lightning is a common collocation). 6. swift. 7. rapidly (*rapidly* and *spread* go together). 8. rapidly. 9. rapid (*rapid* is the usual adjective with *calculation*, but *quick* would be possible). 10. swiftly (*swiftly* is just the right poetic style here.)

106 (A)

1. beautiful. 2. beautiful. 3. handsome. 4. pretty (or beautiful). 5. good-looking. 6. beautiful (*beautiful* is in accordance with *near perfect*). 7. pretty. 8. beautiful (*pretty* poss. with differences as explained; *handsome* would normally refer to a man; *good-looking* is less likely as it would be a bit awkward with *face*). 9. good-looks (or *beauty*, which, however, would flatter). 10. good-looking. 11. good-looking. 12. handsome (or good-looking). 13. handsome. 14. handsome (or good-looking). 15. handsome. 16. good-looks (or beauty). 17. good-looking (beautiful or pretty). 18. beauty. 19. good-looking (*good-looking* is best as it is not gender orientated, so it can apply to both sexes; *pretty* would mean either a pejorative sarcastic statement or indicate a certain femininity of the man). 20. pretty (*beautiful* and *little* ribbons would not go together; *pretty* suggests quickly attractive in a simple way and not necessarily long-lasting or deep, so just the right term here. The same applies to sentence No. 7.).

106 (B)

1. beauty. 2. handsomest. 3. good-looking. 4. pretty (pejorative use of pretty here). 5. pretty (sarcastic use of pretty). 6. handsome. 7. handsome. 8. beautiful. 9. pretty. 10. handsome.

107 (A)

1. see. 2. look. 3. glanced (or *looked*, even *gazed* makes sense). 4. gazing (or looking). 5. see. 6. see. 7. look. 8. gazed (or looked). 9. look. 10. see. 11. see. 12. looked (or glanced; in both cases). 13. look. 14. gazing. 15. looking. 16. gazed (or looked). 17. see. 18. seen. 19. look. 20. gazed (or looked).

107 (B)

1. look; see. 2. see. 3. glance. 4. gaze (*look* would not match *marvels*). 5. gazing. 6. glanced. 7. gazed (*looked* and *glanced* possible, although *gazed* matches the

situation better). 8. looked; looked ('until our eyes ached' suggests *looked* rather than *gazed*). 9. gazed. 10. glanced (*glanced* matches *winked*).

108 (A)

1. sure; sure. 2. certain. 3. sure (certain). 4. sure. 5. certain. 6. sure. 7. certain. 8. sure. 9. certainly. 10. sure. 11. sure. 12. sure. 13. certain (sure). 14. certain (sure).

109 (A)

1. securely (safely). 2. safe. 3. safe. 4. secure (safe). 5. safe. 6. safe. 7. secure. 8. safely. 9. safely. 10. safe. 11. secure (safe). 12. secure (safe). 13. safe (secure). 14. safe. 15. secure.

110 (A)

1. game. 2. match (game). 3. game. 4. play. 5. play. 6. game. 7. game. 8. match (game). 9. play. 10. play. 11. games. 12. match. 13. match. 14. play. 15. play. 16. games. 17. playful. 18. match (game). 19. match (game). 20. play. 21. game. 22. game. 23. match (game). 24. play. 25. match.

111 (A)

1. summit (or peak). 2. top. 3. head (or top or: she headed the list). 4. peak. 5. top. 6. head. 7. top. 8. peak (or top). 9. summit. 10. head. 11 summit (or peak). 12. top. 13. summit. 14. head. 15. peak. 16. head. 17. top. 18. top (*summit* or *peak* with differences as explained). 19. top. 20. head.

111 (B)

1. peak. 2. summit. 3. top. 4. peak. 5. summit; summit. 6. peak. 7. head. 8. peak. 9. summit. 10. peak.

112 (A)

1. trace. 2. tracks. 3. traces. 4. trace. 5. trace (or vestige). 6. trail. 7. tracks. 8. vestige (or trace). 9. traces. 10. track (or trail). 11. trail. 12. vestiges (or vestige). 13. trace. 14. trail. 15. tracks. 16. trail. 17. trace. 18. vestige (*not a/no vestige of proof* is a well worn collocation, almost a cliché, similarly: *a trace of evidence*). 19. track. 20. trace.

112 (B)

1. tracks. 2. tracks. 3. trail. 4. track. 5. vestige. 6. track. 7. trail (or track). 8. vestiges. 9. track. 10. trace.

113 (A)

1. jobs (or situations). 2. Situations. 3. position. 4. jobs (or places). 5. positions (or posts). 6. job. 7. place (here *place* is almost physical, like sitting in someone's seat when they have left it; also the context suggests *place*: to *take* someone's place; however, to *fill* a post; but *job* or *post* are not wrong). 8. job. 9. place (*situation, job, post.* Actually a housekeeper is or was just the sort of job to which even *position* might apply; it has or had a certain social status which is higher than e.g. a maid or cleaner.). 10. posts (positions or jobs). 11. job (or situation). 12. post. 13. situation (*position, place, job, post* poss.) 14. posts. 15. job (*post* is poss.) Actually, with 'took' job is preferable. But even *position* might be possible. The "importance" of a job is often differently assessed by the employer, the outside observer, and the employee, especially when the latter is boasting to his friends!). 16. position (*post* is possible; but *position* and 'manager' fit better). 17. Situations. 18. post. 19. situation (or job). 20. job.

113 (B)
1. job. 2. situation (*situation* in the given context suggests a subordinate job). 3. place. 4. post. 5. job. 6. position. 7. post (or position). 8. post; post. 9. job (*situation* would sound a bit old-fashioned). 10. job.

114 (A)
1. strict. 2. severe. 3. strict. 4. strict. 5. severe. 6. severe. 7. strict. 8. strict. 9. severe. 10. severe (or strict). 11. severe. 12. stern (or severe). 13. strict. 14. severe; severe. 15. strictly. 16. severe. 17. strictly. 18. strict. 19. stern. 20. stern.

114 (B)
1. severe. 2. stern (*stern* is in line with *look*; of course, a judge who passes severe *sentences* will be considered to be *severe*). 3. sternly. 4. severe (*stern* poss.; it would suggest that she will stand no nonsense, but *severe* adds a harsh note). 5. stern. 6. severe. 7. stern. 8. stern. 9. stern. 10. stern.

115 (A)
1. looking for (or searching for). 2. looking for. 3. looking for. 4. search. 5. seeking. 6. searched. 7. look for. 8. searched. 9. looking for. 10. searched. 11. search. 12. looking for. 13. sought. 14. looking for. 15. searched. 16. search.

115 (B)
1. sought. 2. search. 3. sought. 4. seeking. 5. looking for. 6. seek. 7. looked. 8. looking for. 9. seeking. 10. seek.

116 (A)
1. deeds. 2. action. 3. act. 4. action. 5. feat (*exploit* is poss., but it would suggest a more *lightweight* accomplishment). 6. action. 7. act. 8. feat (*act* and *action* would be too "ordinary" for the context; *deed* somehow suggests a more moral or practical purpose and therefore it would not really fit in; *feat* refers to the *difficulty* of doing it; *exploit* refers to the *daring* and perhaps even *flamboyance* of the undertaking and so it would not be impossible in the given context). 9. actions (or deeds). 10. exploits. 11. deed. 12. act (or *action*, if used without "vengeance"). 13. feats. 14. exploits. 15. deed (*feat* poss.; one does not, however, *perform* an exploit). 16. action. 17. action. 18. act. 19. act. 20. action; action.

116 (B)
1. feat. 2. exploits (*exploits* suggests irony, here). 3. feats. 4. act. 5. exploits (similar to No. 2). 6. act (or action). 7. feat. 8. deed. 9. feat. 10. feat.

117 (A)
1. bear. 2. bear. 3. carry. 4. carry. 5. worn. 6. bears. 7. carry. 8. wear. 9. bear. 10. carry. 11. wear. 12. wear. 13. bear. 14. carried. 15. bear. 16. bearing. 17. carries. 18. wear. 19. carries (or bears). 20. wore.

118 (A)
1. beach. 2. banks. 3. beach. 4. shore (*beach* poss., but 'along' suggests shore rather than beach). 5. banks. 6. shore (or banks). 7. shore (or beach). 8. shore. 9. beach. 10. banks. 11. shores. 12. shores. 13. beach. 14. beaches (or *shores*; the latter would suggest the whole shoreline, whilst beaches means the sand (or pebbles) on which people sit, sunbathe, etc.). 15. banks. 16. beach.

119 (A)
1. suppressed. 2. oppressed. 3. oppressed. 4. repress. 5. repress. 6. oppressed. 7. suppressed. 8. suppressed. 9. oppressive. 10. suppress. 11. repression. 12.

repressed. 13. suppress. 14. oppressed. 15. repress, 16. oppress. 17. suppress. 18. suppress. 19. oppression. 20. repress (or suppress). 21. represses. 22. suppress. 23. oppressed. 24. repress; suppress. 25. oppressed. 26. suppressed.

Note on No. 15: Compare the different context in sentence No. 8. where a revolt had already broken out and consequently had to be defeated. In No. 15, however, it is a case of preventing the outbreak of a revolt and so of "holding it back".

120 (A)

1. judgement. 2. verdict. 3. verdict. 4. sentence. 5. judgement. 6. sentence. 7. verdicts. 8. judgement. 9. judgement. 10. judgement. 11. verdict. 12. sentence. 13. sentence. 14. sentence. 15. judgements. 16. verdict. 17. sentence. 18. verdict. 19. verdict. 20. judgement. 21. sentence. 22. judgement. 23. sentence. 24. judgement. 25. judgement. 26. verdict.

121 (A)

1. obsolete. 2. old-fashioned. 3. archaic. 4. out-of-date. 5. old-fashioned. 6. out-of-date. 7. old-fashioned. 8. obsolete. 9. archaic. 10. old-fashioned. 11. outmoded (i.e. an address which is no longer acceptable; the question behind it could be: who would use such an address nowadays?). 12. archaic. 13. obsolete. 14. old-fashioned. 15. out-of-date. 16. archaic.

121 (B)

1. obsolete. 2. antiquated (the context suggests a slight touch of contempt or deprecation; the statement implies a critical attitude). 3. outmoded (who plays whist these days?) 4. outmoded (*old-fashioned* also poss.; this is also true of No. 3). 5. out-of-date (*old-fashioned* would not be quite right; a philosophy is not usually *outmoded*; *obsolete* is possible). 6. obsolete. 7. outmoded (or *old-fashioned*; *outmoded* suggests a somewhat higher register). 8. archaic. 9. out-of-date (*outmoded* and *antiquated* are possible; *old-fashioned* less so, it would be more vague). 10. outmoded (literally, no longer "in fashion"; it should be noted that educational and disciplinary ideas are often matters of fashion: "fashionable ideas"; and furthermore the context suggests the idea of "no longer meeting with approval"). 11. antiquated. 12. antiquated (the suggestion is that the shears were almost antiques; it's a bit of an exaggeration; the same applies to No. 11).

122 (A)

1. deserve. 2. earn. 3. deserve. 4. earn. 5. merits (or deserves). 6. earned. 7. deserved. 8. deserves. 9. merited (or deserved). 10. earned. 11. earned. 12. earn.

122 (B)

1. merits. 2. earnings. 3. deserves. 4. merit (or deserve). 5. earned. 6. merits (or *deserves*, which would, however, mean that he doesn't necessarily *get* one; *earns* would be rather odd with "mention", though not impossible). 7. deserved (*earned* or *merited*). 8. deserves. 9. merit. 10. deserved (*merited* or *earned*). 11. earned. 12. merit.

123 (A)

1. prosecution. 2. pursue. 3. persecuted. 4. pursued. 5. prosecute. 6. pursued. 7. pursuers. 8. pursued. 9. prosecute. 10. prosecution. 11. pursue. 12. pursued. 13. prosecute. 14. prosecuted. 15. persecuted.

123 (B)

1. persecuted. 2. persecution. 3. pursued. 4. prosecuted. 5. persecuted. 6. prosecute. 7. persecuting. 8. pursued. 9. prosecute. 10. persecuted.

124 (A)

1. left. 2. quit. 3. abandoned. 4. deserted. 5. desert (or abandon). 6. left. 7. quit. 8. leaving; leaving. 9. abandoned. 10. left. 11. deserted. 12. abandoned. 13. left (or quit or quitted). 14. leaving. 15. quit (or left). 16. left. 17. forsake; forsake. 18. abandon. 19. left. 20. quitting.

124 (B)

1. deserted. 2. forsake (or desert). 3. abandon. 4. deserted. 5. quit (or quitted; *deserted* would suggest leaving the army permanently *without permission*). 6. forsakes (or abandons). 7. quit. 8. forsake (*abandon* or *desert*, but with different nuances as explained). 9. abandoned (or deserted). 10. deserted (or abandoned).

125 (A)

1. hurt. 2. injure. 3. injured. 4. hurts. 5. hurt. 6. injure. 7. injurious. 8. injuries. 9. hurts. 10. hurt.

125 (B)

1. hurtful. 2. injured. 3. injury. 4. hurt. 5. hurt. 6. hurt; hurts. 7. hurt. 8. injured. 9. hurt (or injured). 10. hurts.

126 (A)

1. carefully. 2. prudent. 3. caution. 4. prudent; carefully. 5. careful. 6. caution. 7. wary. 8. prudent. 9. cautious. 10. prudent. 11. cautiously (or warily). 12. prudent (or careful or wary). 13. careful. 14. warily. 15. prudently. 16. cautious (or careful). 17. careful. 18. careful. 19. cautious (or careful). 20. warily (or cautiously).

126 (B)

1. wary (or cautious). 2. wary. 3. careful. 4. cautious. 5. careful. 6. prudent (or wary). 7. careful. 8. careful. 9. cautions. 10. wary.

127 (A)

1. become. 2. getting (becoming or growing). 3. turned (or gone). 4. grow (become or get). 5. turned. 6. grow; grow (*grow* and *old* are obvious companions but *become* is also possible for the second one). 7. went (or turned). 8. getting. 9. become. 10. went. 11. gone. 12. turned. 13. became. 14. grew (or became). 15. getting. 16. became (*grew* not quite imposs., but it would be a little incongruous in connection with *smaller and smaller*). 17. got (became or grew). 18. turned (became or went). 19. became (got or grew). 20. become.

127 (B)

1. turned. 2. going. 3. went (or turned). 4. turned (or *became* an excellent worker). 5. going (growing, turning, or getting). 6. became (grew or got). 7. grew (all other synonyms of this group poss., but *grew* fits the dramatic mood best). 8. getting (or *becoming* a problem). 9. grew. 10. turn (*turn* is the normal one here).

128 (A)

1. miracles. 2. wonders. 3. prodigy. 4. wonder. 5. miraculous. 6. prodigious. 7. wonders. 8. miracles (in principle, with "work" *wonders* would also be possible; *miracle*, however, stresses slightly the idea of the inexplicable, or, at least, of what *seems* to be inexplicable). 9. marvel. 10. prodigy. 11. prodigy. 12. miracle. 13. marvel (or wonder). 14. miracle (the idea of a horseless carriage being, at the

time, something completely inexplicable is prominent). 15. miracle. 16. wonder. 17. marvels (or wonders; hardly *miracles*, except in a figurative sense, since it would presuppose the existence of supernatural powers; *miracle* and *science* would be even more incompatible). 18. wonder (or miracle; but the two terms would suggest different attitudes viz: *wonder* indicates *surprise*; *miracle*, however, would mean believing in supernatural aid). 19. marvel (or wonder; *marvel* would be preferable to *wonder* since the main idea is one of *amazement* and *surprise*; *miracle* would be too exaggerated). 20. miracles.

128 (B)

1. marvels (*marvel* does seem to go with *wizard*; *miracle* suggests divine [Judeo-Christian] interference; *wizardry* is pagan). 2. prodigious. 3. prodigies. 4. marvel. 5. marvels (*miracle* would be too exaggerated like a divine "trick"; the other synonyms would not be possible, either). 6. prodigy (although *prodigy* usually suggests *youth*, it can refer to any exceptional talent). 7. wonders. 8. marvels (or wonders). 9. wonder. 10. prodigies.

129 (A)

1. figures. 2. numbers. 3. number. 4. figures. 5. figure. 6. numbers. 7. numbered. 8. number. 9. figure. 10. figures. 11. number. 12. figures. 13. numbered; numbers (or numerals). 14. number. 15. figures. 16. figures (or numbers). 17. figures (or numbers). 18. figures.

130 (A)

1. targets. 2. destination. 3. target. 4. goal (the collocation "an aim in life" might suggest *aim* in this context; however, together with *attainable* it would be a bit awkward and so not recommendable). 5. target (or aim, or objective; *goal* would not match the context since "reaching one's goal" suggests finality, the context, however, does not). 6. destination. 7. target. 8. aims (or objectives; "our goals", i.e. goal in plural, would not be recommendable since goal suggests something more or less outstanding and so the plural would strike one as somewhat unnatural whereas "we have a common goal . . ." would not contain such a contradictory element). 9. goal (*goal* suits "strive towards"; *aim*, for example, would not). 10. target. 11. aim (*objective* not impossible, but less likely; *target* would be too narrow; *aim* seems to pinpoint it). 12. destination (*goal* would be more poetic; *destination* is more factual, 'pedestrian'). 13. mark (*target* would not apply here, since it suggests one whole thing; *mark*, however, suggests one point on a target, perhaps she *aimed at* his heart, but *hit* his shoulder, *he* being the *target*). 14. target. 15. goal (*desirable* plus *aim* would hardly make for a satisfactory collocation; but "she *aims* to marry early" would be poss.). 16. objective (or aim). 17. destination. 18. mark (***see*** No. 13). 19. target. 20. aims.

130 (B)

1. objective (or aim). 2. mark. 3. aims. 4. goal. 5. objectives. 6. objective. 7. objective (*fail/succeed in* call for *objective*; *aim* would have been poss. with *reach*). 8. goal (*goal* implies strong desire and longing for it). 9. mark (*hit* and *miss* the *mark* are wellworn collocations; also in figurative use). 10. target.

German index of the synonyms dealt with

(This index also contains the most important synonyms of the head-words mentioned in the instructions. The numbers refer to the various groups.)

English index of the synonyms dealt with